RENEWALS 458-4574
DATE DUE

Cultural Heritage Management in China

Cultural Heritage Management in China presents a thematic examination of the development of cultural heritage management (CHM), using a Western-derived analytical framework within an Asian context. Based on three years of fieldwork, collation and interpretation, the book details how cultural, political, historical and economic factors have shaped the development of CHM in the Pearl River Delta's key cities of Hong Kong, Macau and Guangzhou (Canton). A multidisciplinary team of international contributors analyse these key cities by examining their administrative characteristics, economic growth attributes and linkages with cultural identity and human relationships.

Providing an innovative study of CHM, this book highlights the complexity of interactions between global and local factors in influencing the context and contour of CHM within China's leading transitional cities. As such, *Cultural Heritage Management in China* will be of interest to students of Asian and cultural studies, as well as those studying urban planning, geography and sociology.

Hilary du Cros is an Invited Professor at the Institute For Tourism Studies in Macao, People's Republic of China.

Yok-shiu F. Lee is an Associate Professor in Geography at the University of Hong Kong, People's Republic of China.

Routledge Contemporary China Series

1 **Nationalism, Democracy and National Integration in China**
   Leong Liew and Wang Shaoguang

2 **Hong Kong's Tortuous Democratization**
   A comparative analysis
   Ming Sing

3 **China's Business Reforms**
   Institutional challenges in a globalised economy
   Edited by Russell Smyth and Cherrie Zhu

4 **Challenges for China's Development**
   An enterprise perspective
   Edited by David H. Brown and Alasdair MacBean

5 **New Crime in China**
   Public order and human rights
   Ron Keith and Zhiqiu Lin

6 **Non-Governmental Organizations in Contemporary China**
   Paving the way to civil society?
   Qiusha Ma

7 **Globalization and the Chinese City**
   Fulong Wu

8 **The Politics of China's Accession to the World Trade Organization**
   The dragon goes global
   Hui Feng

9 **Narrating China**
   Jia Pingwa and his fictional world
   Yiyan Wang

10 Sex, Science and Morality in China
   Joanne McMillan

11 Politics in China Since 1949
   Legitimizing authoritarian rule
   Robert Weatherley

12 International Human Resource Management in Chinese Multinationals
   Jie Shen and Vincent Edwards

13 Unemployment in China
   Economy, human resources and labour markets
   Edited by Grace Lee and Malcolm Warner

14 China and Africa
   Engagement and compromise
   Ian Taylor

15 Gender and Education in China
   Gender discourses and women's schooling in the early twentieth century
   Paul J. Bailey

16 SARS
   Reception and interpretation in three Chinese cities
   Edited by Deborah Davis and Helen Siu

17 Human Security and the Chinese State
   Historical transformations and the modern quest for sovereignty
   Robert E. Bedeski

18 Gender and Work in Urban China
   Women workers of the unlucky generation
   Liu Jieyu

19 China's State Enterprise Reform
   From Marx to the market
   John Hassard, Jackie Sheehan, Meixiang Zhou, Jane Terpstra-Tong and Jonathan Morris

20 Cultural Heritage Management in China
   Preserving the cities of the Pearl River Delta
   Edited by Hilary du Cros and Yok-shiu F. Lee

Cultural Heritage Management in China
Preserving the cities of the
Pearl River Delta

Edited by Hilary du Cros and
Yok-shiu F. Lee

LONDON AND NEW YORK

First published 2007 by Routledge
2 Park Square, Milton Park, Abingdon, Oxon OX14 4RN

Simultaneously published in the USA and Canada
by Routledge
270 Madison Avenue, New York, NY 10016

*Routledge is an imprint of the Taylor & Francis Group,
an informa business*

© 2007 Hilary du Cros and Yok-shiu F. Lee

Typeset in 10/12pt Sabon by Graphicraft Limited, Hong Kong
Printed and bound in Great Britain by MPG Books Ltd, Bodmin

All rights reserved. No part of this book may be reprinted or
reproduced or utilised in any form or by any electronic, mechanical,
or other means, now known or hereafter invented, including
photocopying and recording, or in any information storage or
retrieval system, without permission in writing from the publishers.

British Library Cataloguing in Publication Data
A catalogue record for this book is available from the
British Library

Library of Congress Cataloging in Publication Data

Cultural heritage management in China : preserving the cities of the Pearl River
Delta / edited by Hilary du Cros and Yok-shiu F. Lee. – 1st ed.
    p. cm. – (Routledge contemporary China series ; 20)

Includes bibliographical references.

ISBN-13: 978-0-415-39719-3 (hardback : alk. paper) 1. Cultural property–
China–Hong Kong–Protection. 2. Hong Kong (China)–Cultural policy.
3. Cultural property–China–Macau (Special Administrative Region)–Protection.
4. Macau (China : Special Administrative Region)–Cultural policy. 5. Cultural
property–China–Guangzhou Shi–Protection. 6. Guangzhou Shi (China)–Cultural
policy. I. Du Cros, Hilary. II. Lee, Yok-shiu F. III. Title: Preserving the cities
of the Pearl River Delta.
DS796.H75C85 2007
363.6′909512–dc22
2006033157

ISBN 10: 0-415-39719-7 (hbk)
ISBN 10: 0-203-96359-8 (ebk)

ISBN 13: 978-0-415-39719-3 (hbk)
ISBN 13: 978-0-203-96359-3 (ebk)

Contents

List of plates	ix
List of figures	xi
List of tables	xiii
Acknowledgements	xv
List of abbreviations	xvii
List of contributors	xix
Preface	xxi

1 Introduction   1
Y.S.F. LEE, H. DU CROS, L. DISTEFANO AND W. LOGAN

Why reflect on cultural heritage management? 1
The Western-derived notional CHM framework and its rationale 6
The influence of global and local factors 14
The Pearl River Delta 17

2 The Pearl River Delta: one region, three systems   23
H. DU CROS, Y.S.F. LEE, A. SAUVIGRAIN-MCCLELLAND,
E. CHOW AND D. LUNG

Key administrative characteristics of the case study cities 23
Establishing inventories 26
Initial legislation 36
Implications for the preservation of cultural heritage assets 42

3 The rise of professionalism   49
H. DU CROS, Y.S.F. LEE, A. SAUVIGRAIN-MCCLELLAND,
E. CHOW AND W. LOGAN

Key economic, political and social characteristics 49
Increased professionalism 52

viii Contents

Implications for understanding the impact of global and local factors 78

4 Economic growth and cultural identity   85
H. DU CROS, Y.S.F. LEE, D. LUNG AND L. DISTEFANO

Emergence of a wide array of stakeholders 85
Stakeholder consultation: local conventions versus international best practices 87
The review phase: PRD cities and mature practice 105
Implications for the preservation and conservation of cultural heritage assets 111

5 The human factor and cultural affinity   117
Y.S.F. LEE AND H. DU CROS

Cross-cultural influences on CHM: Britain, Portugal and China 117
Inter-ethnic and intra-regional influences in cultural identity 122
Bridging the gaps and creating new relationships 127

6 Conclusion   139
Y.S.F. LEE AND H. DU CROS

Key global and local factors revealed 139
The future of CHM in the Pearl River Delta 141
Further research agenda for CHM in the other parts of China 143
Implications and lessons for Western-derived frameworks 145

Glossary of common heritage terms   147
References   151
Index   163

Plates

2.1 Guangzhou Museum (Hilary du Cros) — 33
2.2 Guangdong Museum of Folk Arts and Handicrafts (Yok-shiu F. Lee) — 40
3.1 'Shamian the Romantic European Culture Island' billboard on the northern side of Shamian Island in Guangzhou. The Shamian Island Street Management Office hopes that it can attract tourists of all kinds and related businesses to the location with various promotions (Hilary du Cros) — 52
3.2 The Nanyue Palace Site excavation in Guangzhou was still in progress when the authors visited it in early 2005. The site is massive and also includes a Qing dynasty shipyard (Hilary du Cros) — 72
4.1 Macau's Tak Seng On Pawn Shop interior in 2003, after restoration (Hilary du Cros) — 104
4.2 This fake paper bun tower was part of a display for the 'Culture and Heritage Celebration' put on by the Hong Kong Tourism Board between 20 April and 7 May 2006 to promote the Cheung Chau Bun Festival – and a mishmash of other forms of intangible heritage in Hong Kong (Hilary du Cros) — 111

Figures

1.1 The theoretical framework of cultural heritage management   12
2.1 The location of the Pearl River Delta   24
2.2 The location of places mentioned for Hong Kong   28
2.3 The location of places mentioned for Macau   29
3.1 The location of places mentioned for Guangzhou   75
4.1 The location of places mentioned for urban Hong Kong   100

Tables

1.1	Western frameworks and the historical development of cultural heritage management, tourism, planning and other considerations	9
1.2	Cultural heritage management's evolving framework	13
1.3	The evolving framework for cultural heritage management: indicating how a regional tradition might develop its perspective and refine its practice over time	15
1.4	Characteristics of case study cities	18
5.1	Summary of CHM phases for the colonial, transition and postcolonial phases for Hong Kong and Macau, and for the historical events affecting Guangzhou	119
5.2	Comparing cultural orientations for mapping exercises (based on DiStefano and Maznevski, 2003)	129
5.3	Likely CHM orientations for Hong Kong, Macau, and Guangzhou	135

Acknowledgements

A number of heritage professionals and others contributed to this book by talking to us about their situations or by giving advice generally. In particular, the authors would like to thank, first of all from Macau: Paulo Cheang, Jose Luis de Sales Marques, Leonardo Dioko, Carla Figueiredo, Long Lao, Carlos Marreiros, Eurico Teng, Cecilia Tse and Fanny Vong.

From Hong Kong we would like to express thanks to David Au, Ian Brownlee, Ellen Cameron, Peter Cookson Smith, Wai Kwan Chan, Winnifred Chung, Happy Harun, Trevor Holmes, Andrew Lam, Hoyin Lee, Tracey Lu, Bob McKercher, William Meacham, Louis Ng, Roger Nissim, Duncan Pescod, Susanna Siu, Joseph Ting, Caitlin Wong, Sylvia Shih-Chin Wong, Ada Wong and Ada Yau.

Last, but far from least, we were assisted by our valuable colleagues in Guangzhou: Chen, Yue Kai; Chen, Wei Han; Ding, Shao Jun; Feng, Yong Qu; Lang, Guan Lin; Le, Wen Jing; Li, Ji Guang; Li, Lan; Li, Lin Na; Li, Ming Yong; Li, Sui Mei; Mai, Ying Hao; Wu, Ling Yun; Zhang, Jia Ji; Tracey Zhu and Zhu, Zhong Ping.

A special thank you is required for Stephan Chan, Pamela Rumball-Rogers and Jian Jun Cheng for their contributions and the benefit of their vast experience of cultural heritage management in the region.

We would like to thank the Institute For Tourism Studies and the University of Hong Kong for the institutional support we received in the course of preparing this manuscript. Y.S.F. Lee would like to thank the Faculty of Arts at the University of Hong Kong for awarding a Research Support Scheme Grant to enable him to concentrate on this work. Lastly, we would like to thank Joe DiStefano for allowing us to use some of his research data and giving us useful advice.

The work described in this book was fully supported by a grant from the Research Grants Council of the Hong Kong Special Administrative Region, China (Project No. HKU 7310/03H).

Abbreviations

AAB	Antiquities Advisory Board
AMO	Antiquities and Monuments Office
CAB	Cultural Affairs Bureau
CBD	Central Business District
CH	Cultural Heritage
CHIA	Cultural Heritage Impact Assessment
CHM	Cultural Heritage Management
CUHK	Chinese University of Hong Kong
CUPEM	Centre of Urban Planning and Environmental Management
EIA	Environmental Impact Assessment
EIS	Environmental Impact Studies
FIT	Free Independent Travellers
GIS	Geographic Information System
GONGOs	Government organised non-governmental organizations
GST	Goods and services tax
HAB	Home Affairs Bureau
HKTB	Hong Kong Tourism Board
HKU	University of Hong Kong
ICAC	Independent Commission Against Corruption
ICCROM	International Centre for the Study of the Preservation and Restoration of Cultural Property
ICOM	International Council of Museums
ICOMOS	International Council on Monuments and Sites
IFC	International Finance Centre
IFT	Institute For Tourism Studies
IGOs	Inter-governmental organizations
LDC	Land Development Corporation
LCSD	Leisure and Cultural Services Department
LWHT	Lord Wilson Heritage Trust
$MOP	Macau Patacas
NGOs	Non-governmental organizations
NPS	National Park Service

PRD	Pearl River Delta
RTHK	Radio Television Hong Kong
SACH	State Administration for Cultural Heritage
SAR	Special Administrative Region
SCMP	South China Morning Post
TPB	Town Planning Board
UNESCO	United Nations Educational Scientific and Cultural Organization
UEA	University of East Asia
URA	Urban Renewal Authority
WTO	World Trade Organization

Contributors

Euphemia Chow, Research Affiliate, Architectural Conservation Programme Coordinator, Department of Architecture, The University of Hong Kong

Lynne DiStefano, Associate Professor, Architectural Conservation Programme Director, Department of Architecture, University of Hong Kong

William Logan, UNESCO Chair Professor of Heritage and Urbanism in the School of Social and International Studies, Deakin University, Melbourne

David P.Y. Lung, Professor of the Department of Architecture, The University of Hong Kong

Alexandra Sauvegrain-McClelland, Research Affiliate, Architectural Conservation Programme Coordinator, Department of Architecture, The University of Hong Kong

Preface

The idea for this book came as a logical extension of work that was already being done to enhance teaching and research programs on cultural heritage management, architectural conservation, urban studies and cultural tourism in Hong Kong. The authors wanted to go beyond the single city/disciplinary approach evident in some of this work to produce a book that can be used as a reference for those within and without the Pearl River Delta. The work has been the result of efforts over the last three years (possibly more) to collect data, and analyse and interpret it in terms of the local and global factors affecting cultural heritage management (CHM) in Southern China.

The book gives a structure to the analysis of these factors by applying a notional model for a CHM framework, complemented by details on the cultural, political, historical and economic aspects that have shaped the development of CHM at the local level. While it was relatively easy to collect information on all this in Hong Kong and Macau, mainland China (as it is known for most of the book) is another story, even for researchers who are nominally part of the 'Motherland'. Even so, positive relationships were extended and built with our counterparts across the border as part of this work, and useful information collected. However, information on basic elements of the system was sometimes difficult to access or decipher. We have done the best we can within the scope of the study and hope that future researchers will refine and improve on our work.

1 Introduction

*Yok-shiu F. Lee, Hilary du Cros,
Lynne DiStefano and William Logan*

Why reflect on cultural heritage management?

Cultural heritage management (CHM)[1] is a term used most commonly amongst heritage professionals who are responsible for the care of such assets as heritage places, sites, artefacts, cultural property, and other tangible heritage items in a society. For the purposes of this book, the *process* of undertaking activities to care for such heritage items will be termed 'cultural heritage management' and the word 'resource' will pertain to cultural heritage assets in general. Caring for cultural heritage assets is important, because our society has a responsibility towards present and future generations to manage such heritage assets to the best of our ability. CHM has also become increasingly intertwined with other principal objectives of sustainable development, an ecological framework that considers such precious resources as important cultural capital.

CHM is now a global phenomenon. A series of internationally recognized charters and conventions, such as the Venice Charter (ICOMOS, 2006) and the UNESCO World Heritage Convention (UNESCO, 2006a), dictate its core principles. These principles are embodied in formal heritage protection legislation or accepted heritage management policies for most localities. The best evidence for claims of maturity in heritage conservation in any country is when cultural heritage management has acquired its own past. In some countries, formalized management started with such overarching themes as: 'cultural resources' and their management (in the 1970s in America and Europe); the 'historic environment' with its emphasis on human interaction with the surroundings (in the 1980s internationally) and, more recently, 'sustainability' with its explicit acknowledgement of the need for grassroots support from local and indigenous communities (in the 1990s) (Baker, 1999).

It could be argued here that, while CHM is a global phenomenon, its practitioners have no real sense of being a part of it. When reviewing the professional literature and related internet sites, it is evident that there are many practitioners who concentrate on regional or local-level disciplinary

2   *Introduction*

and thematic issues. However, this level of work rarely addresses CHM as a multidisciplinary, multicultural activity that transcends borders. If those who work for international heritage bodies, such as ICCROM, ICOMOS and UNESCO, had more time and resources they would no doubt be able to generate a series of relevant publications. However, it has been left to academics, who are mainly geographers by training, to come closest to this objective in recent years (Askew and Logan, 1994; Tunbridge and Ashworth, 1996; Hall and McArthur, 1998; Logan, 2002).

However, despite some fuzzy notions of CHM as part of the globalization of professional management practice, concerns at the local level are being raised every day about other aspects of globalization. The preservation of heritage assets in relation to threats (real or imaginary) brought by the globalization of culture and transnational investment is becoming increasingly a concern of many CH stakeholders and CH agencies at all levels, particularly at the local level where day-to-day CH actions play out. As such, we need to ask the following questions: To what extent, and why, should heritage managers and related stakeholders be interested in how local CHM relates to practices elsewhere? Is it good to have purely international or locally adapted 'best practices' evident in CHM? Will reflecting on this issue actually assist in the better management of heritage assets for present and future generations? The authors of this book believe that such a reflection is crucial to the resolution of tensions being experienced by CHM practitioners in many localities. These tensions frequently reduce the effectiveness of even the most passionately caring cultural heritage managers and stakeholders. The major issues currently facing CHM in many countries are those relating to understanding heritage and how best to protect the heritage values embedded in specific assets. More specifically, how can one create a shared understanding of local history and local heritage? Who should be responsible for defining heritage? How can dissonant views be addressed and resolved? What are the issues revolving around private versus public heritage? What is meant by 'authenticity' and how can the authenticity of heritage assets be retained? How can heritage values be protected in an environment under pressure from economic rationalist imperatives?

CHM literature reviewed over the past two decades indicates that many analysts tend to view cultural heritage assets as: power; an integral element to a good quality of life; a resource that requires specialist and community care; and a commodity and educational resource.

Power

Tensions in cultural heritage management are known to arise in regard to issues of control over heritage activities. Although heritage cannot be easily accorded a set of economic values, it is part of everyone's life in some way and a part that people increasingly have an opinion about. Depending on local circumstances, changing the definition of what constitutes heritage can be fraught with power struggles. Some governments prefer to keep definitions tightly in line with existing heritage protection legislation and heritage experts' opinions. Others may encourage debate in order to ensure that site inventories, collections and archives reflect public opinion more fully by including heritage assets such as historic places that have high current social value.

Conflict over cultural heritage assets can trigger a power struggle between stakeholder groups that can go beyond the initial heritage issues. For instance, the controversy over the creation of the Southwest Tasmanian World Heritage Area in order to save ancient archaeological sites assisted the Australian Labor Party to power in the 1983 federal election (du Cros, 2002b). Issues of authority over heritage assets can flow on into other realms of politics, e.g. colonialism and repatriation of cultural property (Hillier, 1981; Wilson, 1985; Lowenthal, 1988; Hitchens, 1988; Palmer, 1989; AusAnthrop, 2006) and human remains (Fforde, 1992; Mulvaney 1991; Pardoe, 1991) as well as indigenous autonomy and land rights (Lilley, 2000). Some of the earliest explorations of such power issues were examined by heritage analysts in the New World, particularly Canada and Australia, with archaeologists and anthropologists taking on some of the most challenging issues in this area (Langford, 1983; McBryde, 1985; Layton, 1989; Marrie, 1989; Trigger, 1989; du Cros, 1996).

Quality of life

Heritage has been viewed in both negative and positive lights throughout human history. There is concern in CHM circles that 'heritage assets' can be seen as a burden, the 'dead hand of the past' in the eyes of some members of society. Certain government officials, architects and developers still find that the sheer mass of the past's tangible remains can limit the opportunity for modern creative enterprise and is overly expensive to conserve (Clark, 1982:7; Tunbridge and Ashworth, 1996). On the other hand, its proponents assert that 'loving the ancient' is essential for validity and reaffirmation of individuals, groups and nations (Wang, 1985; Lowenthal, 1985; Koshar, 1998). For instance, land use planning conflicts over development schemes, which could start by conservationists citing heritage concerns as the rationale for stopping or modifying the projects, can have detrimental economic effects for the project proponents in the short term. However, in the longer-term perspective, conserving heritage assets can contribute to a higher degree of creativity and economic development as well as a better quality of life for society as a whole (Ashworth and

Tunbridge, 2002; Hall, 2002; Throsby, 2000). In other words, as American conservation architect Arthur Cotton Moore (1998) puts it, problems of quality of life associated with the community's use of heritage assets could arise if the economic rights of a few should predominate over the social benefits accrued to the many (Moore, 1998). David Lowenthal (2003:43), for instance, notes that the United States has accepted 'free enterprise and private property rights as American articles of faith, [and] conservation leaders have habitually forsworn general programs of land reform as unworkable'. Hence, only selected key areas of public land have become 'special places worth conserving' and, as a consequence, making 'the rest of the country undeserving of attention'. Most Western countries are, to varying degrees, guilty of this.

Many authorities see cultural heritage assets as ensuring a higher level of quality of life through the broadening of heritage-significance assessment criteria to include assets of social value. This means that the incorporation of some items representative of everyday life, not just monuments and ancient relics in public parks, is becoming more important to many societies. For instance, concerns about the impacts of growing globalization on heritage assets have been raised recently (Logan, 2002). In particular, an increasing number of researchers have focused on the question of how CHM could be fully integrated within the general framework of sustainable development, particularly in relation to that most global of all industries – tourism (Boniface and Fowler, 1993; Bramwell and Lane, 1993; Mowforth and Munt, 1998; UNESCO and the Nordic World Heritage Office, 2000; Page and Hall, 2003). Debates about tourism impacts within cultural heritage management discourse have been going on since the 1970s at the international level.[2] However, a similar debate has taken place only fairly recently in some regions, such as Asia, particularly in countries that urgently require the economic benefits that tourism can sometimes bring (Harris, 2003; Spearritt, 1991; Johnston, 1994; Mason and Avrami, 2000; Klosek-Kowzlowska, 2002; Taylor, 2004).

Specialist and community care

Specialist knowledge and community involvement are both important for the comprehensive care of heritage assets. However, conflict can sometimes arise between and among stakeholder groups about who knows best regarding what criteria and principles should be followed (Fowler, 1981; Mallam, 1989; Stone, 1992; du Cros, 1996; Cotter *et al.*, 2001). As with town and urban planning (Hall, 2002), cultural heritage professionals may be more capable and more experienced than the average person at conducting this kind of work, but they are not necessarily uniquely expert. For instance, what if heritage managers do not have the support from the community or sufficient resources to manage heritage assets properly? Very often, the best examples of heritage management are recorded when a community group engages heritage professionals to advise on or facilitate its work (Pearson and Sullivan, 1999; Lowenthal, 2003; Council for British Archaeology, 2004). To this end, a number of publications have been and are being developed by cultural heritage managers and non-governmental organizations to help facilitate the public's participation in the process (see Australian Heritage Commission, 1998; Ancient Monuments Society, 2005; National Trust for Historic Preservation, 2005). Moreover, leading onfrom this development, archaeology and history in some countries have generated new sub-disciplines of community-focused areas of expertise. Examples of this phenomenon are known as 'public archaeology' and 'public history' respectively, and often occur complete with their own professional organizations and degree programmes (Davison, 1991; Kass and Liston, 1991; Binghamton University, 2004; New Mexico State University, 2004).

Commodity and educational resource

In the past ten years or so, many analysts have written on the impact of commodification on cultural heritage assets and have examined the questions of how, and to what extent, heritage assets, through commercial use, have been transmuted to feed the consumption needs of specific audiences (Lowenthal, 1992; Jokilehto, 1995; Jafari, 1996; Hall and McArthur, 1998; McKercher and du Cros, 2002; Page and Hall, 2003). Cultural heritage managers aim to encourage these publics or audiences, to 'need' heritage as an important aspect of their lives. Towards this end, the presentation of heritage assets has to include a pluralistic narrative approach, a wide array of activities and a special sensitivity to broader issues (Tunbridge and Ashworth, 1996; Ballantyne, 1998; Baker, 1999).

Viewing cultural heritage management as a system and framework

The debate outlined above has tried to cover many aspects of how we think, feel, care for and consume the past. What still needs to be explored is how a group of related disciplines (such as those that refer to heritage assets as a common resource) might develop an all-embracing management system or framework that includes research, planning, care and interpretation for heritage assets. It should be applicable to different places in order to distinguish global and local factors about how a culture or tradition of CHM has eventuated in that place. To be useful and relevant, such a framework should help us recognize the factors influencing change over time as well as the dynamics of processes relating to the adoption, rejection and accumulation of ideas and practices. Of course, during such changes, there are those concepts and tools that have not been totally transformed but have been merely refined in a series of shifts in the general approach to CHM. Change in any disciplinary culture, even a multidisciplinary one like CHM, will witness some ideas being carried forward and others falling by the wayside.

Understanding the history and development of cultural heritage management as a series of shifts of this nature is crucial to heritage professionals who have come from a wide variety of disciplines. Such an understanding could assist them in devising ways to move towards an integrative and strategic system for managing cultural heritage assets that suits local conditions, while taking into consideration lessons drawn from praxis external to their individual heritage professions. Self-reflexivity of this kind is not just useful for heritage professionals in order to hone their effectiveness, but it also helps ensure that the care of heritage assets could become a constant, conscious and central concern in the utilization of heritage assets by society.

The essential elements of the current Western-based international framework of CHM (and its historical antecedents) are identified and discussed in the following section as a first step in comparing a Western-derived notional model with Eastern CHM approaches in three major cities within the Pearl River Delta. It has also been applied to assist in the understanding of the operation of local and global factors and the similarities and differences that they generate amongst the three cities in how CHM is practised.

The Western-derived notional CHM framework and its rationale

Cultural heritage management can be understood as a multidisciplinary practice- and policy-generating system that can help us achieve the larger societal goals of sustainable development by caring appropriately for heritage assets. The past 200 years have witnessed a continuous evolution of terminology, ideas and strategies that guide individual and group actions to manage cultural heritage items as important cultural capital assets. However, only a small number of academics, and a still far smaller number of practitioners, have had the opportunity to review the historical development and effectiveness of such a system with attention to the differential influences of global and local factors. When it does happen, sorting one's way through the confusions (and sometimes even conflicts) pertaining to terminology used on this topic is often the first barrier that needs to be overcome in the pathway towards analysis. Without reviewing every single definition offered for words such as 'preservation' and 'conservation', it should be noted that the lack of consistency over the meaning of these terms appears to be both geographically based and disciplinarily driven. In North America, for instance, 'preservation' is associated with the notion of basic retention of heritage assets that may be under threat and of their continuing care. As such, this concept evokes a broader meaning than in many other countries.

The application of the term 'management' to 'cultural resources' or 'cultural heritage' has a history of its own that should be briefly visited in this context. 'Cultural resources management' was a term originally used by the United States National Park Service (NPS), archaeologists undertaking Environmental Impact Studies (EIS) and some universities. It first appeared in the NPS organizational structure in May 1976, when the Cultural Resources Management Division was set up under an Associate Director for Management and Operations, after a restructuring introduced by the NPS Director, Gary Everhardt (Olsen, 1985). Around the same time, Michael Schiffer, a professor of archaeology at the University of Arizona, edited a book with George Gumerman on its relevance to archaeological conservation and contract archaeology (Schiffer and Gumerman, 1977). Soon the term had spread to Australia and New Zealand as a result of exchange visits and conferences in the late 1970s (McKinlay and Jones, 1979). It gained a foothold in similar contexts there and in Asia, before being reinterpreted as 'cultural heritage management' in an effort to be more inclusive of wider community concerns about heritage (or heritage assets). Even so, the National Park Service and many American heritage professionals still use 'cultural resource management' to represent the same concept, although it now encompasses a different range of responsibilities than it did in 1976 (Macintosh, 1999; National Park Service, 2005).

Whether a heritage professional is called a 'preservationist', 'cultural heritage manager' or 'historic buildings conservationist' has as much to do with his/her cultural and disciplinary background as it does with cross-regional influences in the field. It is not unusual to find that different countries have used different terms, both specialised and generalist, to describe essentially similar activities. Accordingly, some universities offer specialist heritage-oriented degree programmes and more generalist ones that attempt to break down some of the barriers between disciplines for more integrated heritage management.

Historical antecedents

Historically, much of the expertise in heritage management has been acquired in developed Western countries (Byrne, 1991). However, the Asia–Pacific region is beginning to break this mould by offering courses, such as those offered by the University of Hong Kong, on heritage management and architectural conservation. Some mainland Chinese universities[3] are now offering specific programmes in the field as well.

8 *Introduction*

Global and local factors influencing most Western developed countries' CHM frameworks are closely linked to such intellectual concepts as nineteenth-century notions of scientific discovery, classification and preservation, as well as the twentieth century's social movement towards public and professional accountability that prescribes strategic and systematic planning. Research on cultural heritage management in the twenty-first century can – and does – produce an overriding system for drawing together the most successful elements from this 200-year-long odyssey of caring for heritage assets that is evident in many places nowadays. This journey is undertaken, in most cases, via a broadening of perspective (Table 1.1). It grows from (i) preserve – the initial effort to retain heritage assets; to include (ii) conserve – the effort to systematically care for them; and then incorporates (iii) integrate – the attempt to bring together holistically, fully and systematically – the notion of heritage management being part of all relevant governmental and non-governmental initiatives.

Within the larger framework informed by this broadening perspective, five specific sets of activities, corresponding to five groups of key indicators and carried out in many developed countries, could be identified. Experiences gathered from these countries show that they have moved through these five sets of activities before they reach a level of maturity in their CHM approaches. Indicators within these five phases can also be seen as basic tools or 'constants' in the process that a truly systematic and strategic CHM approach needs to undertake to be considered part of what intergovernmental organizations (such as UNESCO) and non-government organizations (such as ICOMOS) consider 'international best practices' in cultural heritage management.

Defining CHM's evolving framework

The study of cultural heritage management is a relatively new academic discipline and, as such, its theoretical framework (Figure 1.1) is still evolving. CHM appears to evolve through a process that is usually triggered by a (re)discovery of the value of culture and an ensuing and growing political interest. Five separate groups of activities associated with the broadening of perspective on heritage management can be identified in a typical framework of CHM: (i) an initial and continuing inventory-taking process; (ii) an initial enactment of protection legislation; (iii) an increase in professionalism; (iv) stakeholder consultation and participation; and (v) a review of the responsibilities of the professionals, other stakeholders and the state (McKercher and du Cros, 2002).[4] The *key* activities undertaken in each phase, as described in Table 1.1, are highlighted and summarized in Table 1.2. This evolving CHM framework provides the theoretical basis for the selection of the key issues to be examined in this project.

Table 1.1 Western frameworks and the historical development of cultural heritage management, tourism, planning and other considerations

Paradigms	Stages	CHM indicators	Tourism indicators	Planning and other considerations
Preservation (c.1800s–1960s)	Inventory	• Growing community interest • Documentation of heritage assets • Evolution from amateurs to professionals conducting work	• First organized commercial tour in 1841 (Thomas Cook) • Mass tourism arising in late 1800s	• Modernisation of cities • Early development of planning as a profession • Interest in idealized environments, e.g. garden city concepts • Rise of national parks and the conservation of natural areas • First intergovernmental organisations
	Initial legislation	• First-generation legislation to guide identification and protection of heritage assets • Focus on tangible but not intangible heritage • Creation of government heritage agencies • Little integration with other government agencies or laws	• Recognition of tourism impacts • Beginning of city and local government involvement in tourism planning • Recognition of the need to commodify heritage assets to be tourism attractions • First theme parks (Disneyland) • Boorstin's notion of 'contrived reality'	• A plethora of planning legislation and regulations (some of which conflict and overlap) enacted • Different political planning paradigms (e.g. socialist vs capitalist) • Out-migration to suburbs from inner city areas
Conservation (1960s–1980s)	Professionalism	• Heritage NGOs at all levels • Formalized codes of ethics, conservation principles in charters, etc. (and UNESCO's declarations and conventions)	• Tourism precincts initiated • Tourism NGOs • Tourism planning develops as a profession and discipline	• Restructuring of planning legislative framework and historic zoning developed to support conservation area protection

Table 1.1 (cont'd)

Paradigms	Stages	CHM indicators	Tourism indicators	Planning and other considerations
		• Development of heritage-related professions (public and private), quality assurance • Basic computerization of heritage data • Recognition of the linkage between urban planning and land use management (e.g. conservation areas, urban recreation areas, tourism precincts)	• Historic theme parks • Cultural tourism becomes a product category in 1975	• Planning NGOs • Development of standards and codes for planning • Advent of TDR, façadism and similar solutions for whole or partial building retention
	Stakeholder consultation	• Wide array of stakeholders emerge • Areas of conflict identified • More attention paid to community interests • Focus on gaining community support for strategies, such as adaptive reuse • Cultural heritage assessment included in EIA process	• Sustainable tourism development is established as an important planning concept • Cultural tourism identified as an important special interest type of tourism • Niche cultural tourism products appear	• Sustainable development arises as a concept • Environment Impact Assessment (EIA) • Urban consolidation • Restored buildings assigned higher real-estate value and return of high-income professionals from suburbs (gentrification) • Grass-roots environmental and urban activism • Gentrification of conservation areas has positive and negative impacts

Heritage (1990s+)	Review	• New understanding of responsibilities of stakeholders to heritage assets
• Recognition of multiple claims on heritage assets
• New or revised legislation
• Concept of 'integrated conservation'
• Rise of the concept of cultural landscapes
• Greater awareness of intangible heritage
• Broader range of tangible assets conserved (e.g. twentieth-century, colonial, industrial)
• Recognition that Eastern and Western views of authenticity and heritage differ
• Interest in government heritage agencies facilitating 'heritage development' in public–private partnerships
• Self-reflexivity: research, training and journals and other publications dedicated to understanding CHM	• Development of codes of ethics for sustainable tourism development and cultural tourism
• Integration of tourism concerns in wider planning framework
• Government facilitation of some sustainable tourism development projects
• Cultural tourism is fastest growing market segment, requiring more study	• New zoning overlays that put 'softer' controls on heritage assets
• Some cities try 'gentle gentrification' programmes
• Attempts to place an economic value on heritage
• Benchmarking of cities
• Increase in economic and cultural globalization

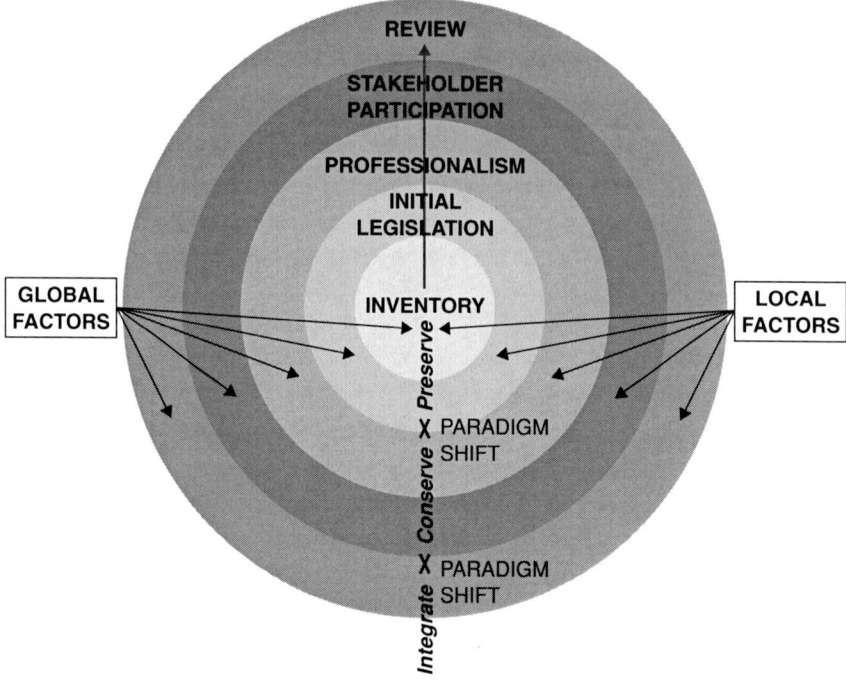

Figure 1.1 The theoretical framework of cultural heritage management.

This five-phase process of using various tools to preserve, conserve and then integrate heritage assets in and by itself forms a mature CHM approach. It begins with an initial recognition by academics, community leaders and politicians of the value of heritage and the need to preserve it. Once the value and scope of a jurisdiction's assets are acknowledged, the second phase involves invoking some form of legislation or policies to protect and conserve these assets. The creation of formal heritage departments or the establishment of heritage units in other government departments often coincides with this action. It is possible that in some cases, these two phases may occur concurrently.

The development of a strong emphasis on conserving such heritage assets forms the third and fourth phases. The third phase reflects increased professionalism in the sector and the corresponding policy decision-making process. Formal codes of practice and conservation charters are adopted, with countries typically becoming signatories to international charters. It is at this point that a wide array of different types of heritage professionals enters the sector, and university degrees and courses are created to train more professionals. Their disciplines include architectural

Table 1.2 Cultural heritage management's evolving framework

Phases	Key indicators
Inventory	• Growing community interest • Documentation • Evolution from amateurs to professionals conducting work
Initial legislation	• First-generation legislation to guide identification and protection of heritage assets • Focus on tangible but not intangible heritage • Creation of government heritage agencies • Little integration with other government agencies or laws
Increased professionalism	• Formation of heritage NGOs • Formalized codes of ethics, conservation principles in charters, etc. (and UNESCO's declarations and conventions) • Development of heritage-related professions (public and private) • Basic computerization of heritage data • Recognition of the linkage between urban planning and land use management by heritage managers
Stakeholder consultation	• Wide array of stakeholders emerge • Areas of conflict identified • More attention paid to community interests • Focus on gaining community support for adaptive reuse • Cultural heritage assessment included in EIA process
Review	• New understanding of responsibilities of stakeholders to CH assets • New or revised legislation • More integrated planning and practice • Rise of the concept of cultural landscapes • Greater awareness of intangible heritage • Recognition of other users of assets • New framework in place • Maturity

conservation (architectural preservation), archaeology, history, urban heritage planning, museum studies, artefact conservation, heritage engineers and landscape architecture, to name a few. Again, these two phases could occur consecutively or concurrently.

The fifth phase – review – reflects an even greater sophistication in cultural heritage management. The notion of the need to acknowledge the role of stakeholders, not only as interested parties but also as legitimate managers and co-managers of assets, has helped trigger a broadening of perspective that then promotes a greater integration of CHM into other frameworks and their proponents that are relevant to it. In doing so, more attention is paid to community concerns with the goal of achieving a consensus approach to management. This greater awareness usually means that a shift is needed to allow for greater integration in tools for CHM, such as existing legislation (McKercher and du Cros, 2002).

The model in Table 1.2 implies a sequential approach, moving from the first to the fifth phase. In reality, the three parts to the broadening of perspective on CHM are likely to occur consecutively but the phases and indicators within them could occur in any pattern. A fuller description of how these phases might occur in a scenario where they are consecutively connected is shown in Table 1.3. It also shows the evolving nature of some of CHM's most basic tools such as inventory-taking, which begins as basic documentation and list-making, to become the online-available resources that some public sector authorities offer today. It is hoped this model can also be used to describe approximately what changes in the CHM approach might look like for some countries that are only just coming to terms with caring for their heritage assets. It should be seen as an approximation of what actually appears on the ground, as local factors are likely to lead to differences in what praxis and concepts are adopted, rejected or refined over a series of shifts in focus.

However, it is not until all five phases are completed that maturity is reached. Given the diversity in the social, political, cultural and economic dimensions of the three selected case study cities, the activities associated with these phases have probably occurred at different paces and in different sequences, leading to observable variability in the type of CHM. In general, analyzing and understanding more about how these sequences have developed will allow CH managers and others in any place determine what is unique about their own situation. This approach should also generate cross-cultural and transnational comparisons of praxis that are more meaningful than those offered only through comparing the developing of single disciplines relating to cultural heritage management.

The influence of global and local factors

Given the notional framework described, what are the factors and underlying assumptions that have led to CHM's development in a particular place, and how have these factors and assumptions shaped it internationally and locally? Or, if viewed from another angle, what local and global factors have influenced the core concepts of what is promoted by international organizations, such as the International Council on Monuments and Sites (ICOMOS), as the current framework for ideal or best practice heritage management? Such management ideals are not created in a vacuum.

Table 1.3 The evolving framework for cultural heritage management: indicating how a regional tradition might develop its perspective and refine its practice over time

Preservation	Conservation		Integration
Inventory	Legislation	Increased professionalism	Stakeholder consultation	Review
Growing public interest				
Documentation of heritage assets	Initial legislation developed	Basic computerization		More access through computerization
Evolution from amateurs to professionals	Focus on tangible not intangible	Minor goal shift		New or revised legislation
				Greater awareness of intangible
	Creation of govt CH agencies	Some restructuring	Wide array of stakeholders emerge	New responsibilities to stakeholders; Government heritage agencies and PPP
	Little integration with other government agencies or laws	Some policies	Unclear pressure/some review	New relationships and referral procedures
		Heritage NGOs at all levels	Under pressure	New understanding of CHM and assets
			Areas of conflict identified; more attention paid to community interests	Concept of integrated conservation
		Formal codes of ethics, conservation principles, charter (UNESCO's declarations, conventions)	Join with SD/Envir. NGOs in some areas	Recognition of Western and Eastern views of authenticity
			Government adoption in briefs etc / NGOs aware of community interests	Broader range of heritage assets conserved
		Development of heritage-related professions (heritage industry), QA	CH in EIA process	Self-reflexivity
		Some recognition of linkage between urban planning and land use management (conservation areas, etc.)	Focus on gaining stakeholder support for strategies, such as adaptive reuse	Recognition of multiple claims on use of heritage assets
				Integrated conservation
				Rise in the concept of cultural landscapes
				MATURITY

MINOR SHIFT: SOME SUPPRESSION / DISCOURAGEMENT OF AMATEURS

MAJOR SHIFT: KEY POWER, STRUGGLE, GOVERNMENT / NGOs / DEVELOPERS

MINOR SHIFT: MORE STAKEHOLDERS EMERGE

MAJOR SHIFT: CRISIS IN PUBLIC FUNDING / BROADER SD PRIORITIES INCLUDING CH

One factor that permeates this research is that most CHM is heavily affected by the nature of the government structure with which it is linked. The overall political policy, the number of tiers and their inter-relationships and associated resources, the level of intervention in private sector affairs, and the inherent organizational culture of the civil service will all have some influence on how CHM is carried out. The degree of coordination, transparency, accountability and professional standards associated with this sector will inevitably have an impact on the nature of CHM in a particular place.

CHM is also influenced by change over time in land use management and business management paradigms, as well as by change in the study of the social sciences (Hall and McArthur, 1998; Ashworth and Tunbridge, 2002). Even so, because of these influences and its multidisciplinary basis, CHM is a strange hybrid – possibly even more so than environmental or business management. Sometimes general public-policy concepts are also incorporated, in order to institutionalize and integrate it more closely with land use planning within a civil administration. Hence, there is always some tension between what work is carried out in the general public interest and what reflects the needs of particular user groups, such as researchers, schools, community heritage organizations, tradition bearers, the tourism sector and developers, to name a few.

Importance of local factors to the development of CHM

With the recognition that CHM is a specific area of endeavour, comes the realization that it can differ in its philosophical concepts and practice geographically and culturally. Even international non-governmental organizations are subject to local influences in the development of their key tools, such as locally derived codes or charters of practice (see Bell, 1997). An example of this devolution is the development of the Venice Charter into regional charters, such as the Burra Charter and later the Indonesian and Chinese Charters, to fulfil local conditions (ICOMOS, 2005). Different ideas of what constitutes heritage, and different reasons for recognizing it as significant, can have their basis in the specific cultural, socio-economic and political policy-enabling environments of particular countries. ICOMOS is beginning to recognize this in the debate that began in Scandinavian countries and led to the *Nara Declaration on Authenticity, 1994*[5] and the findings of recent *Heritage@Risk* reports submitted by ICOMOS national chapters (Larsen, 1995; ICOMOS, 2004). The declaration modified the mainly Western-derived international framework in that it allowed a pluralist view of authenticity in relation to CHM to emerge, while the latter raises serious questions about the place of economic rationalization policies and nationalist sentiments in heritage practice.

The Pearl River Delta

Surprisingly, although much has been written regarding the use of heritage assets by individuals, groups and societies as well as more specific issues of such assets' technical conservation in different parts of the world, little has been published on how the broad system has been applied to their care in a way that can improve our understanding of regional differences in CHM approaches. This book fills that knowledge gap by comparing the essential elements of the current Western-based CHM tradition – which is generally regarded as the international generic ideal – with specific approaches to CHM in the Pearl River Delta, Southern China (Figure 2.1).

The notional framework described earlier forms the backbone of the book in order to understand change and the evolution of CHM in this region. Cultural heritage managers, planners, community organizations and others concerned with implementing or maintaining international best practice standards of cultural heritage management should find that this book will raise questions regarding their own everyday experiences in comparison.

The notional framework was applied to CHM approaches in three Pearl River Delta cities and then used to cross-compare the results. The cities comprise Hong Kong, Macau, and Guangzhou (once known as the treaty port of Canton). Although these cities are all located relatively close to each other geographically and have high populations of ethnic Chinese, they have very different historical, political, economic and cultural trajectories up until the re-integration of Hong Kong and Macau as Special Administrative Regions (SARs) within the People's Republic of China in 1997 and 1999, respectively. The nature of their previous development has given rise to the concern that regionally within the Pearl River Delta each of these cities could present a different face to heritage management and that it will be difficult for a proposed future integration to occur that can satisfy global ideals, political realities and local aspirations. The characteristics of the three case study cities are outlined in Table 1.4.

A number of issues specific to CHM are also relevant:

- The impact of legislative actions on the practice of heritage conservation
- The way specific codes of conservation practice have been used and their impacts on the efficacy of CHM schemes
- The degree to which there is a need, or opportunity available, for the training of heritage professionals

Table 1.4 Characteristics of case study cities

	Hong Kong	Macau	Guangzhou
Cultural/historical characteristics	• Ex-British colony now quasi-democratic with a legislative assembly, and administered with some autonomy as a Special Administrative Region (SAR) of PRC since 1997. • Other Asian cultures, in addition to local Chinese culture, influential in the city's development. • The large number of Chinese mainland immigrants (1949–1969) and descendants now facing dilemmas about cultural identity.	• Ex-Portuguese colony now administered as an SAR like Hong Kong since 1999.	• Capital of Guangdong province, PRC. Long history as a significant regional centre going back two thousand years. • Southern China was culturally and linguistically distinct from the North and sometimes only nominally under its control. • A strong role in trade as part of the Maritime Silk Route and then as the treaty port of Canton. • Lost ground to Shanghai after unrest in 1920s and later to the Shenzhen Special Economic Zone.
Economic characteristics	• Rapid economic growth 1972–1997 with laissez-faire policies. Companies 70% British until 1979–1985 when control diversified (taipans to tycoons). • Outsourcing of manufacturing to Shenzhen and the Asian financial downturn has affected growth and employment since 1997. • Tourism is the one industry still undergoing rapid growth.	• Slow economic growth, despite forecasts before handover. • Main areas of economic growth include gambling and tourism, with some businesses established recently as middlemen for mainland import/export. • Casino licences recently opened up to overseas operators, including some from Las Vegas.	• Increase in economic growth after 1989 with market liberalization reforms. • Both benefits and suffers disadvantages from its proximity to Hong Kong and Shenzhen. • Close Economic Partnership Arrangement (CEPA) has broadened the existing trade agreement to services as well as goods, which should aid cooperation.
Public sector characteristics	• Government reliant on artificially inflated property market that provides	• Government reliant on gambling tax as a	• Government undergoing devolution of authority with less central control

	• revenue as a compensation for offering low company and personal tax rates. • Urban planning (Planning Dept. and District Councils) just starting to flirt with more inclusive decision-making processes. • Heritage agency Antiquities and Monuments Office, low in government hierarchy, has been operating since 1976 with retrograde legislation.	• major source of revenues. • Cultural Heritage Department can designate ensembles of buildings. • World Heritage Area Inscription achieved for selected areas of older precincts.	• than previously, except in some critical areas. • Urban planning has promoted the redevelopment of areas that mixed industry, commerce and residential uses (heavy industry mostly moved out of city). Construction of new infrastructure and housing has had a major impact on vernacular inner-city architecture. • Municipal authorities comprise an interesting triangulation of power between the heritage agency, museums and university-based institutes. • Nationally listed sites require involvement of central authorities in Beijing. • Some interesting cases where the Mayor or Vice-Mayor have stepped in to save heritage assets.	• No strong heritage NGOs of the kind found in most developed countries. • No strong resident action groups.
Community awareness of heritage conservation	• No strong heritage NGOs of the kind found in most developed countries. • Some resident action groups established in recent years for environmental issues more than heritage ones. • Department of Education focus on Chinese heritage in syllabus is causing more demand for well-presented heritage assets, which has been answered more by building new museums than by better interpreted or protected sites. • Rise in day-trippers or domestic tourists to some heritage places in the New Territories.	• No strong heritage NGOs of the kind found in most developed countries. • Some resident action groups established in recent years with heavy involvement by local heritage professionals.		

- The way local communities have influenced heritage conservation programmes and activities
- The nature of stakeholder relationships and interactions pertaining to the management of cultural heritage assets, and the major constraints in reaching a consensus among the stakeholders
- The extent and the ways in which urban planning and environmental management policies have been an effective tool in protecting cultural heritage assets
- The impacts that have occurred from accommodating tourism product-development requirements on the nature of cultural heritage management.

Most importantly, the notional CHM framework assists in identifying and analysing the relative impact of global and local factors in shaping and influencing CHM practices within the Pearl River Delta case study cities. The cities were studied to ascertain if they developed with similar or different paces or sequences. This, to discovering significant variability in the type of CHM to be found in each city, and to showing how each has responded to CHM principles advocated at the international level.

It is hoped that this book makes a substantial contribution to understanding how CHM is practised in Asia and lead to a re-examination of some previously held assumptions about its development in the West as well. The results will be of relevance to any heritage and tourism professionals interested in acquiring an in-depth understanding of how local influences can interweave with those emanating from globally accepted practices. Accordingly, the book has been structured to give full attention to each of these conditions in Chapters 2 to 5. The concluding chapter draws the analysis back to the original question regarding the primacy of Western-derived notions of CHM practice in an Asian context and sums up the major implications and lessons for such notions that can be found in studying non-Western CHM practices.

Notes

1 In the United States, cultural heritage management is alternatively known as Cultural Resources Management or heritage stewardship.
2 The International Council on Monuments and Sites endorsed its first Charter on Cultural Tourism as early as 1976.
3 For example: the Southeast University of China, Tongji University in Shanghai and Tsinghua University in Beijing.
4 Although this model was developed independently and later than Ashworth and Howard's three-phase model (see Ashworth and Howard, 1999:42–50), the first three phases of these two models share some similarities. Both models confirm that there are great similarities in traditions of CHM in Western developed

countries. However, the McKercher du Cros model provides a more extensive framework and key activities.
5 The Declaration originated at a landmark conference on the topic of authenticity hosted by Japan ICOMOS in Nara that year. The conference addressed the issue of differing views on authenticity in regard to tangible and intangible heritage from Western and Eastern viewpoints.

2 The Pearl River Delta

One region, three systems

Hilary du Cros, Yok-shiu F. Lee, Alexandra Sauvigrain-McClelland, Euphemia Chow and David Lung

Key administrative characteristics of the case study cities

Local factors and conditions have been dominant in the early evolution of CHM in our case study cities. These factors will be identified and discussed in relation to the distinctive administrative characteristics of each of these three cities. Key events and significant changes in legislation that distinguish them as uniquely comprising three different systems of administration within one geographic region will then be delineated. That region is now recognized internationally as 'the Pearl River Delta' (PRD) as part of a deliberate policy to encourage more cooperation and integration. However, the three cities have developed very different administrative systems as a result of very different historical trajectories, which can make regional integration a challenging proposition. This chapter will investigate activities associated with the first two phases of the notional CHM framework: establishing inventories and promulgating initial legislation.

As the government is an important player in most CHM around the world, the administrative background and characteristics of the case study localities will be briefly outlined here in relation to their specific political, historical, social and cultural contexts. Three general administrative frameworks have been identified: British-colonial derived in Hong Kong; Portuguese-colonial derived in Macau; and the socialist-city-in-transition of Guangzhou in the Province of Guangdong.

The key turning points included the colonization and the eventual 'handover' to mainland Chinese control of Hong Kong and Macau (in 1997 and 1999 respectively). It should be noted that these events, together with the Second World War and the Chinese mainland's conversion to Communist control in 1949, have been the most significant events in the historical and political narratives of these cities. They have had a profound impact on how their respective administrative systems have developed in terms of political control, orientation and style.

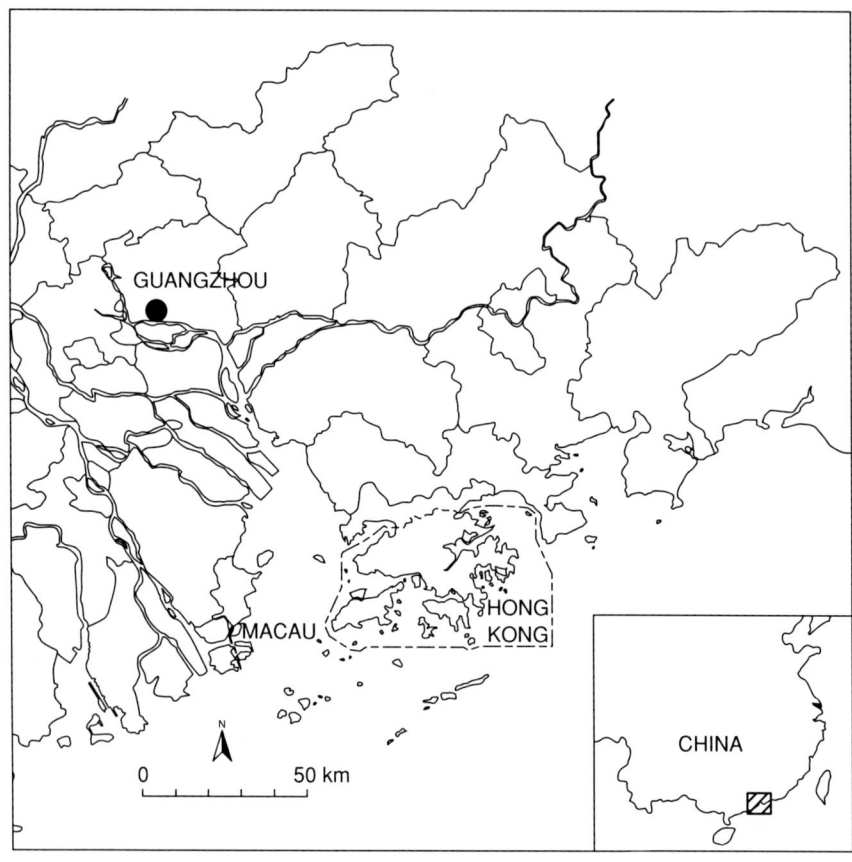

Figure 2.1 The location of the Pearl River Delta.

In the last thirty years, there have been many turning points in political visions that have influenced the development of Guangzhou, Hong Kong and Macau's administrative frameworks. Most of the development in CHM in these case studies has also occurred within this timeframe. There will be an examination of the reasons behind the establishment of formal inventories of tangible heritage assets and the promulgation of legislation for their protection. Before we turn to those reasons, however, the nature of China's traditional administrative framework should be briefly explored, because it provided the broad historical context for the earliest perspective on CHM – preservation – to evolve.

Public administration is not a recent concept for Chinese people. China has the oldest continuously active administration system, which can be traced back to the Qin dynasty (221–206 BC) at least. However, the competitive merit examinations, for which it is chiefly known, did not start until the Han dynasty (206 BC – AD 220). The dynastic form of Chinese bureaucracy – highly centralized and hierarchical – was centred on the educated elite of scholar-administrators (Dwivedi, 2003). Provinces on the periphery, such as Guangdong, were still answerable to the central authority but in practice were semi-autonomous (Garrett, 2002).

The recruitment of Qing dynasty officials formally came to an end in 1904. The culture of this massive bureaucracy has been almost exclusively Confucian-oriented. Confucius (*c.*551–*c.*479 BC) promoted a system of values that provided a basis for Chinese interpersonal behaviour. It stresses order, hierarchy, quality of relationships and respect for certain groups within the feudal system of the time. Modernization under Dr Sun Yat Sen after the 1911 revolution added an emerging educated middle class as a new partner. However, the Communist Revolution in 1949 destroyed this partnership by placing all commercial and production activities under state control.

After 1949, the administrative system on the mainland retained many features of the previous system, such as its organizational hierarchy (e.g., provinces, prefectures, counties, districts and functional units). The only event that has disrupted this system since then was the Cultural Revolution, when bureaucrats were designated as 'enemies of the revolution'. Restoration of the hierarchical administrative system after the end of the Cultural Revolution in 1976 gradually led to a policy of 'market socialism' – which allowed more autonomy to be given to lower-level administrative units to raise funds and administer goal-oriented policies (Dwivedi, 2003).

Hong Kong and Macau were established on the periphery of colonial empires with the necessary administrative frameworks to support their isolation. The administrative history of Hong Kong includes the establishment of offices managed by individuals sourced from Great Britain. Certain key officials even had their departments named after them (such as the Colonial Secretary's Office), thereby affirming their authority. Ho (2004) notes that their mission was much the same as that of the current government, and that was 'to maintain a stable government structure and develop the economic prosperity of Hong Kong' (Ho, 2004: 3).

The Hong Kong and Macau Special Administrative Regions (SARs) have been given fifty years to integrate with mainland China after the handover ceremonies were completed. At present, a Special Administrative Region is considered a type of local government directly responsible to the central government in Beijing. This interim political structure between the two SARs and the central government has been termed a 'one country, two systems' arrangement by Beijing (Tang in Miners, 1998). At the end of this fifty-year period, the two SARs will no longer be considered autonomous and will fully become a part of China's administrative system.

Establishing inventories

Most countries have witnessed a growth in community interest in the retention of and care for tangible heritage assets when they went through the process of industrialization. The surge in community interests in heritage assets logically leads to a desire to list and classify such items much in the way that early botanists and zoologists began to document species. Exploration of cultural practices and knowledge systems in distant places in the wake of world exploration and colonialism was reflected in the establishment of scholarly or learned societies. Museums were established for educational purposes, but often their primary function was to serve as repositories of ethnological collections of 'disappearing' ways of life and archaeological remains under threat from modern development. The early desire by antiquarians, learned societies, institutes, committees, museums, and/or universities towards the inventorying and protection of heritage assets will be investigated in this section.

The Chinese administrative system carried out the historical documentation of events in special 'gazetteers', which have since proved to be an important source of information for locating and assessing items considered to be of significance. Indeed, the ancient Chinese bureaucratic system had a fetish for recording all kinds of activities that now provide fascinating historical data. Today's Chinese heritage authorities claim that, around the late eighteenth century, the mid-Qing government was supposed to have developed a system for inventorying and registering 'cultural relics'. The 'four haves' that were enshrined in twentieth century legislation can be traced back to that time and they included measures to define the boundary of the relic, declare it with signage, create a site file, and designate a person or organization as principal caretaker. A few ad hoc programmes for recording heritage developed by universities or individuals occurred during the Republican period. But nothing systematic was undertaken until the Communist authorities commenced a nationwide inventory of cultural heritage assets in 1950, when all such activities were carried out by the state (Agnew and Demas, 2002: vii, 38).

Early inventory efforts: example 1 – archaeological sites

The Pearl River Delta witnessed the early development of inventory and excavation of archaeological remains, which in many cases had preceded interests in other tangible heritage assets. On October 22, 1928, the 'Center for Research in History and Languages within the Central Research Institute' was established in Guangzhou. This was the first academic organization established in Southern China that included a unit with a focus on archaeology. In 1931, under the encouragement of Xie Ying Bo, an archaeological organization called the 'Huang Hua Archaeological Institute' – the first of its kind – was founded in Guangzhou, on the current site of the Guangzhou Museum.[1] The Institute started publishing a journal called the 'Journal of Archaeology' and conducted a number of excavations in the outskirts of Guangzhou.[2] Despite the discovery of a Han tomb in the city's eastern suburbs by Hu Zhao Chun in the early 1930s, the progress of archaeological work in Guangzhou between 1929 and 1949 was in fact quite slow.

Meanwhile, a whole range of influences was at work in Hong Kong, in terms of shaping its inventory and excavation activities. A Jesuit priest, Father Daniel Finn, who probably received some training in the British Pitt River's tradition of archaeology, started excavating sites on Lamma Island in the early 1930s. After he passed away in 1936, much of what he excavated was sent to the University of Hong Kong's Museum and Art Gallery, and other unsorted material was kept in the Regional Seminary in Aberdeen (Finn in Ryan, 1958). As a part-time lecturer in Geography at the University of Hong Kong, Father Finn sometimes liaised with Shellshear, an anatomy professor at the same university, who was another early practitioner of archaeology in Hong Kong since the 1930s (Finn in Ryan, 1958).

Another key influence on the archaeological scene, following the Second World War, was Solomon Bard, who later became the head of the Antiquities and Monuments Office (AMO) in Hong Kong. Bard was one of the founders of The University Team that carried out archaeological survey and excavation work with Shellshear and others during this period (Bard, 1988). Other authorities working towards documenting archaeological heritage in Hong Kong included some local Chinese historians and amateur archaeologists, such as Cheng Kung-chu, Lo Hsiang-lin and Jao Tsung-i. Most of them published articles, books and lectures that provided the foundation of future work (Bard, 1999).

Cross-membership between the revived Royal Asiatic Society[3] and the university team was likely, as most members were connected with the University of Hong Kong, the Civil Service or some part of the colonial elite educated classes. In 1961, Bard gave a talk to the Society members about an axehead he found on Man Kok Tsui Beach on Lantau Island. Later, in the 1960s, the Society organized visits to cultural and archaeological sites on Lantau Island and the old villages in Aberdeen and Ap Lei Chau, which had not yet been redeveloped.[4]

More active in the discovery of archaeological sites in the 1960s was the Hong Kong Archaeological Society, which took over from The University Team in 1967. After the Antiquities and Monuments Ordinance was fully enacted in 1976, the government paid the Society a yearly subsidy of around HK$20,000 towards the employment of labourers on excavations. The Society still had to formally apply for excavation licences, but it shows

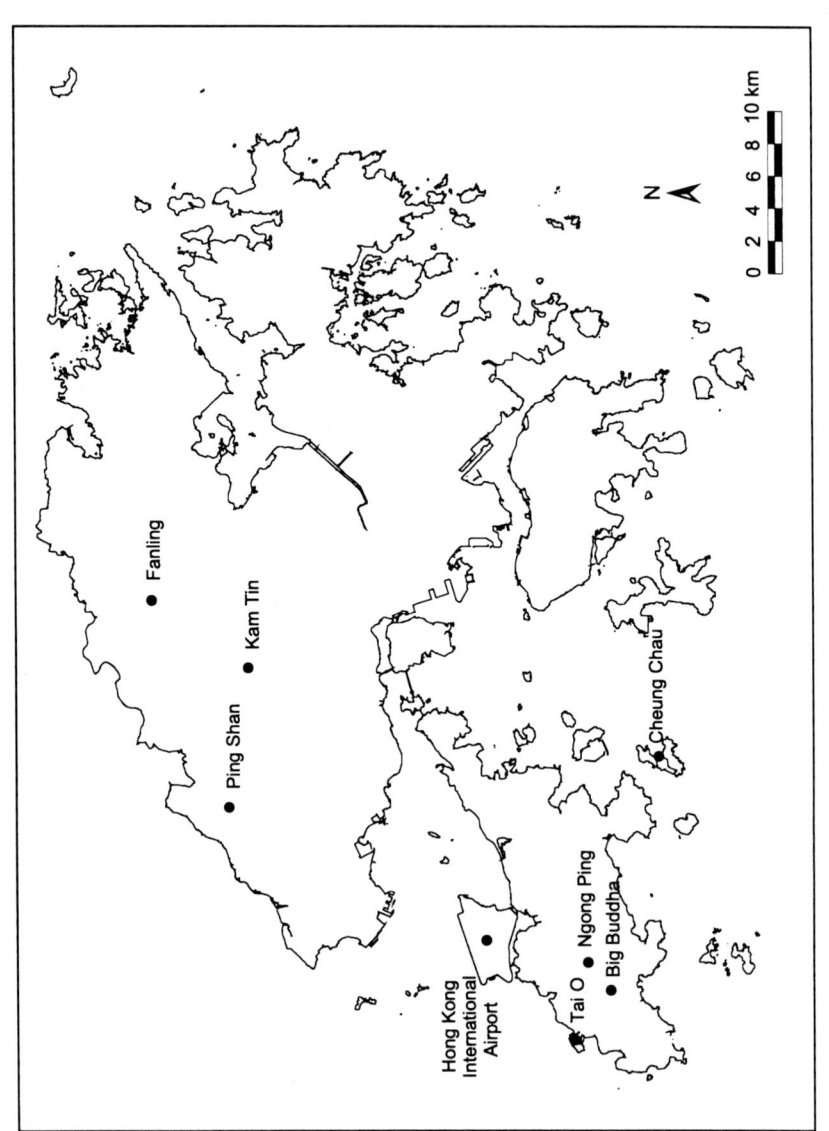

Figure 2.2 The location of places mentioned for Hong Kong.

that their efforts at public archaeology were welcomed by the AMO. The Society's work during the 1970s and 1980s has been regarded as pioneering by some local archaeologists, such as Au Ka-fat, who still works as a consulting archaeologist today (Au, 2004).

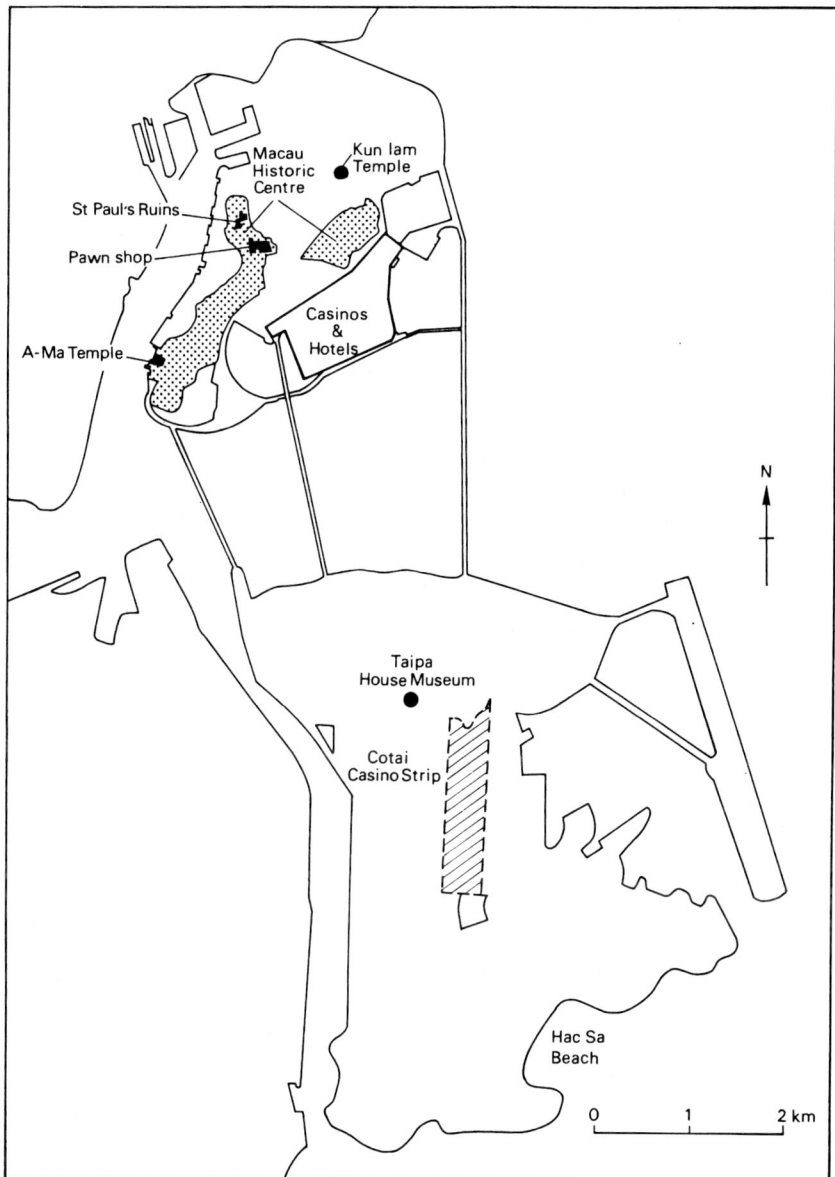

Figure 2.3 The location of places mentioned for Macau.

The Society has excavated outside of Hong Kong on some occasions. Maintaining a long-standing relationship with Macau, the Society had carried out some of the earliest excavations for the enclave in July 1972 and May 1973. The excavations had helped reveal materials from the Neolithic through to much later periods (Zheng, 1996). In October 1977, a group of archaeologists, engineers, researchers and students from Hong Kong participated in an excavation near Hac Sa Beach where coins and pottery fragments from the Qing dynasty (AD1644–1911) were found.[5]

Eventually, a sequence of at least five thousand years comprising that of the New Stone Age, the Bronze Age, the Qin/Han, Song, Yuan, Ming, and Qing dynasties was eventually confirmed for the Macau site of Hac Sa.[6] All of the work on this site was carried out with Hong Kong assistance, as no formal archaeological survey or excavation programme had been established in Macau before 1996 (Zheng, 1996).[7]

Early inventory efforts: example 2 – historic buildings survey

The Hong Kong Archaeological Society began stepping outside of archaeology in the 1960s, when it declared publicly its 'support for the conservation of Hong Kong's heritage in general, and of historic buildings in particular' (Bard, 1999: 5). Inventories of heritage assets were also being made, in a mostly ad hoc fashion, by some District Officers. For instance, one District Commissioner for the New Territories compiled a list of potentially declarable monuments as early as 1957 when efforts were being made at that time to draft a bill for legislation to protect them.[8] These lists were eventually handed over to the Antiquities and Monuments Office, when it was established in the late 1970s. In 1974, the Royal Asiatic Society (RAS, Hong Kong Branch) conducted a photographic survey of historic buildings in Hong Kong. When it was published six years later, however, some of the key buildings and much of the Western District had been demolished. The book noted that the aim of the original work was to 'record the Hong Kong scene of the present day, though with an emphasis on those aspects which are rapidly disappearing' (Topley in Royal Asiatic Society, 1980: v).

In Guangzhou, the Municipal Cultural Relics Bureau was established in 1951. Supervised by a vice-mayor, this was the city's first government office responsible for the surveying and excavation of cultural heritage, both below and above ground. The Bureau contained the following divisions/units: revolutionary, historic cultural relics, and historic architecture. In 1952, the Guangzhou Municipal Cultural Relics Bureau began its work in the surveying and collection of cultural heritage, in addition to carrying out archaeological excavations.[9] From 1966 to June 1970, all inventory and associated activities of the Bureau were stopped, due to the Cultural Revolution.

In Macau, not much action – such as the kind of community initiatives described above in Hong Kong – was happening. As in Guangzhou, it was the public sector that took up the cause. In December 1953, Governor Marques Esparteiro appointed a committee to register architectural heritage. In its early inception, the committee encountered opposition from members of the local community, particularly property owners, who even sometimes attacked members for daring to suggest they should retain and conserve historic buildings.[10] In 1960, this committee was replaced by a new task force whose objective was to 'research and to lay down appropriate measures for the protection of history and cultural heritage as a response to its importance'.[11] At this time, the task force did not have any legislative base to lend weight to its decisions, which would have made enforcement difficult. However, development pressures on Macau historic building stock were not as severe as those found in Hong Kong, which was by then entering a period of rapid economic growth. Neither city had any laws aimed at protecting heritage assets until the mid- to late 1970s.

Early inventory efforts: example 3 – museums and museum collections

Hong Kong has made many attempts at establishing collections and opening museums since it first became a British colony. Sir John Bowring,[12] Governor from 1854 to 1859, put forth the earliest initiative to set up a museum of 'cultural things' (Endacott, 1964: 105).[13] He later became one of the leaders of one of the earliest learned societies in the region – the Royal Asiatic Society.[14] Its China branch was established in Hong Kong in 1847, not long after the Hong Kong Club was set up. These two organizations formed the backbone of British colonial society life in Hong Kong, and provided a venue for the ruling elite to show some interests in Chinese culture and history.

At some point, the museum collection and its single curator was moved to City Hall, where the museum was later referred to as the 'old' City Hall Museum. It displayed 'Australian parrots, mineralogical specimens from Wales, old clocks, etc.' and was considered to be passé by 1938 when the first review of its role was conducted.[15] A small committee called the 'New Museum committee' was established in that year to consider plans to replace the City Hall Museum with a superior one. The proposal produced provided a candid window on the public's attitudes toward the British Empire, cultural heritage, museums and the Chinese population of the time. 'Cultural heritage' appeared to mean mostly cultural and natural specimens originating from the period prior to the arrival of the British in Hong Kong. Although the proposed museum had some modern features, it was still deeply routed in the natural history tradition of placing the cultures of 'other' alongside aspects of their natural environment (e.g., as in the collections of the Pitt Rivers Museum in Oxford). This tradition often led on to CHM being developed in parks organizations in 'New World' countries, such as Australia and North America (du Cros, 2002b). Indeed this museum proposal had originated from the Botanical and Forestry Department (1905–1941), which was later transformed into the current Agriculture, Fisheries and Conservation Department, with today's country parks falling under its jurisdiction (Ho, 2004).

However, the committee's intriguing plan never came to full fruition. The proposal was sidetracked before the war and the old museum's collection dispersed when the then City Hall was demolished in 1946. In 1948, the Governor, Geoffrey Northcote, supported the idea of constructing a purpose-built gallery as part of a new City Hall. Eventually, the New Museum committee's concept was subsumed into the Museum of Art, which was opened to the public in the newly built City Hall in 1965, where it stayed until 1991.[16]

Meanwhile, the University of Hong Kong was about to upgrade its Chinese library building where its historic Chinese scrolls and archaeological collections were housed. In 1963, a building donated to the university by Fung Ping Shan in 1932 was converted into the Fung Ping Shan Museum of Chinese Art and Archaeology. Ahead of the government, the university has been operating the longest continuously open museum in Hong Kong today. In 1994, an extension was built and the structure was renamed the University Museum and Art Gallery (UMAG, 2006). It was not until 1975 that Hong Kong developed and built the Museum of History.

In Guangzhou, the longest-serving museum is the Guangzhou Museum. Established in 1928, it is located in the historic Ming dynasty (AD1368–1644) structure of the Zhenhai Tower, which was once a part of the fort on Yuexiu Mountain in the centre of the city (see Plate 2.1). Although the reuse of the historic building as a museum has protected it from demolition, the structure has undergone some dramatic renovations. For instance, its internal wooden structure has been replaced by a reinforced concrete one in order to house the museum and stabilize the building (Mintz, 2001).

The museum was closed throughout the Japanese occupation period and the war years. It reopened in 1950 as a 'People's Museum' with a strong political theme. Even so, has developed its archaeological arm to undertake excavation and artefact collection. The museum was one of the main repositories for artefacts uncovered by archaeological work that was, and still is, under public sector control. Like many mainland public institutions, the Guangzhou Museum was closed again during parts of the Cultural Revolution. However, two things appear certain. First, it has managed to retain control of most of its collections,[17] and second, it has been an

Plate 2.1 Guangzhou Museum. (Hilary du Cros)

important facility in the inventory and deposition of the city's cultural property.

Most of the museum's collections have come from Guangzhou, and they were dated from the Neolithic period onwards and have been mainly accumulated over the last forty years (Mintz, 2001). Historical photographs, maps and other documents from Guangzhou's time as the treaty port of Canton also form a significant part of the collection.[18] In 1964, a special exhibition hall was added to the complex, to house and protect stone monuments and cannons that were removed from their original locations when the old city walls were demolished.

Macau also has an intermittent history of collection and housing of cultural property in museums. Its first museum has an interesting 'prehistory', as pointed out by a cultural anthropologist, Cathryn Hope Clayton. Prior to having recognizable museums with permanent quarters, staff and collections, it went through a series of phases not dissimilar in some ways to what had happened in Hong Kong. In the late nineteenth century, collections of commercial, sacred and maritime artefacts were sent to Paris and Portugal as part of the World Exhibition activities to mark Macau's significance as a Portuguese colony.

34 *Hilary du Cros* et al.

Proposals had been made for a permanent museum, but they were not acted upon even when they were backed by the Cultural Institute, an office created by the Macau government in 1920 to attend to cultural activities. Clayton (2003) connected the failure to build a museum to 'the atmosphere of total demoralization and defeat that reigned in Macau during that era' when the enclave was being out-competed economically by Hong Kong and Guangzhou. If it had succeeded, the Institute would have become the first public heritage agency in the Pearl River Delta charged with responsibility for the 'conservation of buildings and objects with historic, artistic or documentary value' (Clayton, 2003: 113). However, without strong government and public support, this early initiative failed.

The next phase in museum development in Macau reads like a saga of musical chairs. The collections were merged, split, partly sold off, moved and then relocated into three or four different buildings until 1960.[19] Clayton (2003) notes that the exhibits were not used to support colonial ideology, although this process of shuffling occurred during the 'high period' of Portuguese colonialism. In fact, the driving force behind the maintenance and enlargement of the collections was not the government, but a few individuals. As in Hong Kong, where amateur archaeologists and historians drove much of the advocacy for a permanent city museum, passionate collectors of cultural property lobbied each new governor with museum proposals until they were successful in 1960. In that year, the collections that were still extant became the basis of the Museu Luis de Camões.[20] The museum was opened to the public on 25 September 1960 as part of the cultural festival, Comemorações Henriques, coinciding with the end of the high colonial period and allowing the museum a role in serving a broader public than any institution previously (Clayton, 2003).

Comparative discussion

Of the inventory phase reviewed in each of the three case study cities, the Hong Kong tradition appears to be the most typical of the notional model outlined earlier. This impression may be due to a lack of information, as in the case of Macau, on early amateur, antiquarian and scholarly activities that are difficult to access at this distance. These activities may not have been recorded and they would probably not be retained beyond living memory for the pre-war period. However, some form of documentation of historical Chinese and colonial buildings must have been done by the community (for instance by the clergy) as well as by the government in Macau.

In Guangzhou, even before the arrival of Communism, which brought all such activities under state control, the fledgling Chinese Republican government was attempting to initiate some programmes through the

Guangzhou Museum and some of its institutes and universities.[21] After the revolution, the city developed the first public cultural heritage organization to record both historic buildings and archaeological sites. Although many buildings were no doubt documented for political purposes and archaeological sites were not always retained, the museum was the location of some of the first CHM activities carried out by a government body in Southern China.

However, what is surprising is the general lack of local historical societies and trust-like bodies in Hong Kong, despite the presence of some amateur and university-trained historians as well as the linkage with Britain. It is possible that there was not a critical mass of interested people to create such bodies (particularly given that many of the local Chinese population were recent immigrants from the mainland). Also, much of the type of genealogical work that historical societies generally undertake was (and still is) undertaken by indigenous clan organizations and other kinds of Chinese cultural associations.

In the Pearl River Delta, the general Chinese community in the early part of the twentieth century had little interest in maintaining tangible heritage assets, such as historic buildings and archaeological sites, as many were more concerned about basic survival. However, cultural heritage assets, such as temples and ancestral halls, were (and still are) in frequent use, and they are considered as part of contemporary culture rather than as cultural artefacts in a separate category requiring special care. For these people, Lowenthal's statement that 'every relic exists simultaneously in the past and in the present' holds real merit (Lowenthal, 1985: 241).

However, in Hong Kong, traditional-style residential buildings located in highly populated areas, where many of the newer immigrants had settled, had been replaced with more modern buildings and streetscapes comprised Western materials, such as concrete, without much of a backward glance. Consequently, the first antiquarians, heritage preservationists, museum curators, amateur historians and others to show an interest in Western-style heritage management were not indigenous. Often, in Hong Kong, initiatives were put forth by non-Chinese to document and preserve heritage assets before the wrecker's ball fell.

In Macau, the greatest gap pertains to the lack of support for the preservation of Chinese vernacular architecture and the institution of archaeological inventory programmes. It seems that most of the efforts were channelled into recording and preserving mostly Western-style aspects of the built environment and some Chinese temples. Interest in archaeological sites was haphazard and required support from expertise from Hong Kong. Museums struggled to maintain and exhibit publicly sponsored collections, while private collectors continued to push the government to make a greater commitment in this area.

Hong Kong mirrors this in some ways, in that collectors have had a role in establishing the University of Hong Kong's Museum and Art Gallery and later the Flagstaff Museum of Tea Culture. A former government arts administrator has commented that the Hong Kong civil service had an unspoken policy not to establish adequate visual arts and heritage galleries before the 1970s in case they inspired militancy. The performing arts, particularly the so-called 'Western high culture,' were always preferred over anything that might promote opposition to colonial rule, particularly during the Cultural Revolution (1966–1976) when social tensions were high.[22] However, it is likely that the most political aspect of cultural heritage at that time was the issue of ownership, particularly private property rights over historic buildings and (possibly) illegally acquired cultural property that originated from the mainland.

Initial legislation

At the end of the Qing dynasty, mainland China was suffering difficulties with the illegal removal and export of significant movable cultural property, such as antiques, paintings, scrolls, and sacred and archaeological artefacts. These items were mostly sold by or stolen from their owners/sites and left the country in increasing numbers. One of the last ordinances promulgated by the failing imperial government to protect such cultural property was introduced in 1909 through the newly instituted Ministry of Internal Affairs. Lai *et al.* (2004) suspect that the promulgation of this legislation was triggered by the removal by foreign expeditions of a significant number of items taken from the Silk Road sites (e.g. the Dunhuang scrolls).

However, in terms of the built environment, it was not until 1982 that the views of architectural preservationists, such as the famous architect Liang Sicheng, were included in the framing of relevant legislations. Chinese preservationists who had been active before the Second World War became active again in the 1950s and after the Cultural Revolution (Lai, 2004). When the central government was preparing to enact national legislation in the early 1980s, it took notice mostly of those preservationists working in Beijing. It is unlikely that authorities from Guangzhou had played much of a role in that legislation process.[23] However, modernization and urban growth occurring in Guangzhou would have significant impacts on China's tangible heritage. This realization might have helped influence the framing of the country's first effective national heritage protection legislation (Wang, 1998). Meanwhile, Hong Kong and Macau developed their respective initial legislations with only occasional reference to the mainland, as the possibility of their integration into the latter's legal and administrative system seemed, at that time, distant to the relevant colonial authorities.

Early efforts towards legislation

Although Britain had introduced various forms of heritage protection legislation since the passing of the first Ancient Monuments Protection Act in 1882, Hong Kong experienced an extensive prelude to the promulgation of its one and only heritage protection act – the Antiquities and Monuments Ordinance. The process began in 1957 when lawmakers were given the task of drafting the legislation. They were provided with examples of various laws sourced mainly from Commonwealth countries as guidelines. Bard (1999: 5) has observed wryly that the Hong Kong government, 'while recognizing the need of the new heritage legislation, had little taste for it'.

An early draft was completed in April 1957 but it was stalled, due to concerns about 'possible sensitivity in objection of the Chinese People's Government to acquisition by foreigners of Chinese antiques and objets d'art'.[24] Where this concern arose from is not entirely clear, but it seems to target movable cultural property more than 'monuments' in the sense of structural remains or historic buildings. Given the 'ambiguous' role Hong Kong has played in the dissemination and sale of cultural property from all over Asia when it became a key commercial centre, it is likely that the opposition to the ordinance was coming from private collectors, auctioneers and antique retailers. It is possible that they feared that one day the British administration of Hong Kong would end, and they would be left exposed to the tender mercies of the mainland government and possible repatriation of their collections.

In 1961, the bill was resuscitated because it was found that movable cultural property could be 'vested in the Hong Kong Government and not the British Government' by omitting the reference to the 1841 date of British settlement. Three years later, in 1964, the ordinance-drafting process shifted its goal towards the less contentious objective of establishing control over 'the archaeological discoveries in Hong Kong' and the preservation of such sites. By 1970, then, the definition for 'antiquities' had broadened to include 'any relic and ... place, building, sites or structure erected, formed or built by human agency before 1800'.[25] This cut-off date does not appear commonly in many other pieces and it appeared to be another attempt to allay the concerns of private collectors. Another possibility is that the early colonial period and late Qing dynasty heritage assets were considered to be not old enough or too commonplace to be worthy of special protection, and the government did not want to stand in the way of development within the more urbanized areas on either side of the harbour.

Finally, in August 1971, the bill to pass the ordinance was introduced in the Legislative Council.[26] However, while a Provisional Antiquities Advisory Board (PAAB) was established as per its articles in 1972, it took another four years before the Board's executive arm, the Antiquities and Monuments Office (AMO), was allocated resources to operate (Bard, 1999).

In Macau, the situation was much different. A piece of heritage legislation enacted in Portugal in 1953 was extended to Macau because it was considered then to be an 'overseas province.' In that same year, Macau's Governor, Jaime Silverio Marques, appointed a local committee to study and identify the enclave's 'national heritage.' Although the committee was local, the members were all senior Portuguese officials, who were trained in and had close links with Portugal. The Guia Fortress today still maintains a plaque, which states that it is a 'state property' and was the result of listing under the 1953 legislation. The structures that were 'designated' as National Heritage were mostly military fortresses and government/civil buildings (Macau Heritage Net, 2005). Unlike Hong Kong, no Chinese buildings were designated. This has become an ongoing issue for Macau, with complaints filed by local Chinese scholars to the *Macao Daily* from 1992 onwards, arguing that more needed to be done to protect Chinese buildings (*Macao Daily*, 30 March 1992, 26 July 1998).[27]

In 1960, the Governor in Macau then appointed a new taskforce to study and suggest protection measures for the designated structures. From 1960 to 1976 this taskforce made suggestions on designating other buildings, and these were made public.[28] It thus fulfilled a similar role played by the Antiquities Advisory Board in Hong Kong. However, both lacked an implementing agency to undertake systematic inventory work and conservation activities when they were first established.

In 1976, Macau enacted its first truly local heritage legislation – the Statutory Order no. 34/76/M – in response to Portugal pronouncing administrative and legal changes to the running of some of its overseas provinces/colonies. This Statutory Order recognized that the 'city of Macao, a meeting place of two civilizations and cultures, has characteristics that ... must be preserved in order to maintain the character that distinguishes Macao from the other population centres of the region in which it is located'. It also 'prescribes measures to allow Macao to evolve as a city without losing the heritage that, even today, gives it value, and to preserve and protect that heritage from depredation and modifications that could destroy this artistic and scenic value'.

This legislation was devised with more of a local emphasis, even though it borrowed heavily from the World Heritage Convention for definitions.[29] An increased awareness among local government officials about the importance of keeping historic buildings for the purpose of tourism development could have spurred the passage of the legislation at that juncture. The early 1970s were also a time when a number of historic items were destroyed and the preservation of Lou Lim Leoc Garden was one of the first indications that the government was listening to protests raised primarily by local tourism academics and the Pacific Asia Tourism Association (PATA).[30] In fact, two reports prepared by PATA on the need to develop new tourism strategies for Macau (1980, 1994) read more like heritage planning strategy reports than standard tourism planning documents.

A study of the initial legislation in Guangzhou needs to be centered on an analysis of the 1982 Law of the People's Republic of China on the Protection of Cultural Relics. This is because the two initial attempts at national-level heritage-protection legislation had failed to make much of an impact as a result of twentieth-century political and social upheavals. Legislation was and is still being developed and promulgated by the central government in a top-down approach to heritage management and other related matters. After the 1982 law was enacted, partly as a hierarchical response to the centralized administration and legal system, Guangzhou formulated its own city-level legislation that reflected aspects of the national law at the local level.

The promulgation of the 1982 law came after the intensively destructive period of the Cultural Revolution when many heritage assets were damaged or destroyed. For instance, in Guangzhou, the Chen Clan's Ancestral Hall suffered the removal and destruction, by fire, of 4000 years worth of ancestral tablets, along with all their genealogical information. The building itself survived, as it had already been converted into the Guangdong Museum of Folk Arts and Handicrafts (see Plate 2.2), which had some cachet with the Red Guards as 'a place for the people'.[31]

However, despite the promulgation of the 1982 law, cultural property items were still made available for sale to foreign collectors through the Canton International Trade Fair. China of the 1980s was a country that chased after foreign exchange; some international dealers were even invited to buy antiques by weight by the Ministry of Foreign Trade. This practice was finally stopped after the State Administration for Cultural Heritage (SACH) objected and pointed out that it contravened the 1982 Act protecting cultural relics (*SCMP*, 19 August 2000).

The Act's definition of heritage still bears the mark of its time, with its primary focus centered on cultural relics that are 'memorial buildings, sites related to revolutionary history, and memorial objects'.[32] The introduction to the legislation also reinforced this emphasis with a statement that says its purpose is to 'enhance the country's protection of cultural relics to facilitate research work, to continue the outstanding cultural heritage of our country, carry on patriotism and the traditional revolutionary spirit, and to build a socialist civilization'. Hence, there is a connection between heritage assets and policies for social engineering which is not found in the other two case studies, where heritage protection is done primarily in the public interest and is not given a clear political goal. Even so, the 1982 Act's definition of categories of heritage assets to be protected as cultural

Plate 2.2 Guangdong Museum of Folk Arts and Handicrafts. (Yok-shiu F. Lee)

relics is broad, including everything from historic cities to those 'underground and above ground cultural relics within the land and sea boundary of the country'.[33] As national-level legislation, its scope was widely defined so that it could be applied to a broad category of cultural heritage assets (although this does not include intangible heritage). The coverage of the 1982 national law's heritage definition is broader than that of Hong Kong's and Macau's closely prescribed ones. That the initial legislations in Hong Kong and Macau did not contain some provisions for protecting maritime sites is somewhat surprising, however, given the importance of maritime trade in the development of their economies.

Comparison of the three initial pieces of legislation

There could not be three more dissimilar laws despite their geographic proximity. Even so there are some commonalities. Authority in which the power to protect heritage assets in Hong Kong and Macau is now invested in senior civil servants, while mainland China has maintained a whole category of government offices dedicated to overseeing cultural heritage assets. And the authority is linked to the level of designation (e.g., the ultimate authority for authorising activities connected with a municipal designated cultural relic is a municipal-level cultural relics bureau official).

All the different legislation passed in the three cities refers to the government as the sole authority in deciding what cultural heritage assets are listed/protected/or deposited in museums. This is in line with most initial legislation found elsewhere around the world, although the listing procedures in some countries may include policies or amendments to allow for more community consultation in deciding what should be preserved.

In the three case study cities, the criteria for inclusion on a list, for declaration and the underlying statement of what heritage is considered to be of significance, though variously expressed, share some similarities as well. For instance, all include some elements of palaeontological or natural heritage assets with cultural heritage, even though Macau is the only one that goes further and protects settings and significant trees. This is not common in Western-derived heritage legislation, which usually makes separate provisions for fossils, geological features and other items of purely natural heritage value. Hong Kong has an anomalous time limit of 1800 for antiquities and relics, which seems redundant as it can be overridden by the criteria for declaring monuments. No protection of intangible heritage – or even the mention of it – was referred to in any of these three initial legislations, which is in line with most international practices for this phase.

While Macau and Guangzhou can designate groups of historic buildings, conservation areas or protection units, Hong Kong still can not.[34] By 1992, Macau had four types of designation to legally protect heritage items: monuments, buildings of architectural interest, classified areas and classified sites.[35] Along with special conservation areas, they add up to a total of 128 items occupying an area of 3.05 km^2, which represents a significant portion of Macau's compact 28.2 km^2 (Chui, 2001). However, any further addition to this list requires a special decree to be passed and, since then, only a few further designations have been made – none of these were proposed by NGOs and the community.[36]

Guangzhou can propose to list heritage assets found in the city to be designated protection units at either the municipal level or at the national and provincial levels, where the latter are considered to carry a higher level of significance than the former. For instance, any nomination that Guangzhou prepares to submit for World Heritage inscription would need to be put together first at the city level with funding sourced from the central government. The nomination would then need to be approved at the provincial level before it could be considered at the national level for inclusion on China's Tentative List. Once included in the country's Tentative List it would then have to wait for its turn to be put forward to the World Heritage Committee in Paris.[37] In the case of provincial- and national-level designation, the management of the asset may remain with the local government but the authority giving the approval would have to come from the corresponding level of the designation.

Hong Kong has followed the British practice of designating historic buildings and monuments into three grades. However, only structures categorized in grade I, being considered the highest, are deserved of declaration. Portugal has a three-tier system of 'National Monuments', those of 'Public Importance' and those of 'Regional Importance.' In Portugal, most structures fall into the second category (Ashworth and Howard, 1999), whereas key Macau monuments were designated as National Monuments.

Legal constraints on activities at protected/listed assets, excluding archaeological excavation, seem much the same across the three cities. Again, Hong Kong is a little unusual in that owners of heritage assets which were declared as 'monuments' would expect compensation for their loss of revenue associated with those assets – either in the form of resale value or redevelopment potential. This tacit understanding ensures that many monuments become basically public property or requiring a high degree of public involvement in their management once declared. Hong Kong is also the most sensitive to the issue of protecting private property owners' rights, offering an extensive appeal process. The appeal process was intended initially to offer some form of self-determination regarding the declaration of indigenous heritage assets, but it has since been used as a loophole by pro-development interests to avoid being required by the government to retain heritage assets for the public good.

Implications for the preservation of cultural heritage assets

In characterizing the three administrative frameworks of Hong Kong, Macau and Guangzhou in terms of their respective changes in last twenty-five years, it is notable that the Hong Kong civil service and its counterpart in Macau have changed the least. Hong Kong, in particular, has continued with little restructuring as it follows an 'executive-led government'[38] with only a thin veneer of ministerial portfolios and a partially democratically elected legislative assembly added more recently. This administrative set-up is supposed to be continually checked and assisted by numerous advisory bodies at many levels. This absorption of authority by the civil service and its special relationship with the private sector has been seen by many as an important source of Hong Kong's political stability (Lau, 1997; Hase, 2001). Since its inception, however, Hong Kong's Antiquities and Monuments Office has bounced around quite a bit within the bureaucratic framework, while Macau's Cultural Institute (now renamed the Cultural Affairs Bureau) has stayed put and grown stronger. In all likelihood, the latter's power is continuing to grow with the inscription on the World Heritage List of 'Macau's Historic Centre' in July 2005, ensuring that it receives an increasingly larger budget from the government to manage (at least) the World Heritage assets.

Market liberalization policies introduced in this period have had a major impact on the way the Chinese administrative framework operates in the city of Guangzhou. Ma and Chan (2004) describe this transition as being a move from the traditional Leninist totalitarian model to a much less monolithic entity with the notion of 'local state corporatism' forming a major component. As a result of fiscal reform, local authorities in China have been allowed to retain a part of the extra tax revenue they raise. The central government expects that this fiscal arrangement would motivate local authorities to develop entrepreneurial endeavours that benefit local communities. Individual senior cadres in local-level bureaus are expected to speed up the process of economic reform by taking up this responsibility.

In order to retain a type of federalism, the central government has instituted a type of rewards system designed to encourage officials to act responsibly, but which still gives the state a sense of central control. When the loyalty-based system was replaced by a performance-based system in the 1990s, an appraisal process was set in place to provide rewards or penalties to officials. Under the 'Target Management Responsibility System', officials can be rewarded financially or politically (e.g. given a promotion within the party). As such, archaeological sites have been saved from destruction by urban redevelopment because the reward system can be manipulated by concerned local officials to favour and entice actions that are in line with the direction towards conserving cultural capital (Ma and Chan, 2004).

Hong Kong and Macau are also moving towards a predominantly performance-based administrative system, but one aimed at a higher level of transparency for, and accountability to, the public. Hong Kong went through a stage where it invited more specialists to apply for civil service jobs in the 1980s and 1990s, which coincided with the greatest growth in the number of professional heritage staff for the AMO. This aspect of professional practice and its role associated with the next logical phase of the evolution of CHM in the case study cities will be dealt with in the next chapter. Examples of how stakeholders, such as local communities, are making their views known to heritage professionals and the governments are also included in Chapter 4.

Impact of global/colonial factors

It would be instructive to explore here how some international factors have influenced the formulation of the initial legislation in the case study cities. In the case of Hong Kong, the 1971/1976 ordinance was formulated prior to and quite separately from the process that went into the making of the UK's currently active legislation – the Ancient Monuments and Archaeological Areas Act (1979). Moreover, English Heritage (Historic Buildings and Monuments Commission for England) did not come into being until 1984, a year after the National Heritage Act (1983) was enacted. Hence, these events have all come too late to have any impact on the 1971/1976 Hong Kong ordinance, particularly with regard to influencing it to extend protection to heritage assets with some kind of area or group designation. However, legislation allowing for the designation of conservation areas within the English town planning process has preceded Hong Kong's ordinance and the lack of inclusion of this provision in the latter is therefore somewhat problematic.

The models for developing the regulations associated with the Hong Kong ordinance were taken from Australia and Israel/Palestine. These pieces of legislation and their regulations were heavily oriented towards archaeological heritage rather than the built environment, possibly because most of the first lists produced included many such sites and amateur archaeologists were pushing much of the preservation effort. Moreover, Solomon Bard, whose main expertise was archaeology, was the person given the task by the PAAB of sourcing relevant legislation as a model for implementing the ordinance.[39] His experience in Australia through working at the Australian Museum in Sydney probably accounted for his decision to source a selection of its state legislation as one model. One could only speculate on Bard's choice of Palestine's as another model, which possibly had something to do with his Jewish heritage (even though he was raised in China).[40]

The British thinking behind architectural conservation began in the nineteenth century, with decisions made to preserve historic buildings mostly in terms of satisfying political motives and not always influenced by their historical value. In other words, decisions to preserve or retain buildings were often made in reaction to public sentiment. Overall, such buildings were seen as more functional than symbolic. Sauvegrain (2001: 27–28) has made some comparisons with France in this respect. She found that the French tended to see such assets as being more like 'witnesses of cultural transmission in themselves'. This is an interesting comparison as Britain and France were colonial competitors of a higher order in the region than Britain and Portugal. The French were not so heavily focused on archaeology as the British and they had tried to link preservation of heritage assets in its colonies with themes that helped define their colonial history. In this way, it is not dissimilar to Portugal's relationship with Macau. Macau started off with national legislation that listed its most significant colonial sites in 1953 on a national list in Portugal. It then developed local laws that protected a broader range of assets as it gained greater independence in the 1970s.

In the case of Guangzhou, it is possible that the 1982 Law of the People's Republic of China on the Protection of Cultural Relics might have some similarities to earlier Soviet legislations in that it advocated the protection of sites of 'memorial buildings, sites related to revolutionary history, and memorial objects'. However, without any information one way or the other to confirm this connection, this category of heritage significance could just as easily have a uniquely Chinese Communist Party origin. For many years, China was sensitive about how its laws are translated into other languages, so finding out more about the origins of the 1982 law still requires some thawing within the State Administration for Cultural Heritage.

Notes

1 Feng Yongqu, editor, Special Issue Number 3 of the *Guangzhou Research Institute on Heritage and Archeology: A Collection of Works on Fifty Years of Archeological Work in Guangzhou* (Guangzhou shi wenwukaoguyanjiusuo zhuankan zhi san: Guangzhou wenwu kaoguji – Guangzhou kaogu wushinian wenxuan), Guangzhou Publishing House (Guangzhou chubanshe), n.d.: 3.
2 Available at Southcn.com website: www.southcn.com/news/gdnews/hotspot/dzgdwhhm/jscj/200309171504.htm
3 See note 14, below.
4 Public Records Office file HKMS170-1-30 Royal Asiatic Society History, Press Cuttings.
5 *Illustrated Chronicle of Macao* (Aomen quan jili), Shanghai People's Publishing House (Shanghai renmin chubanshe), 1999: 189.
6 *Illustrated Chronicle of Macao* (Aomen quan jili), Shanghai People's Publishing House (Shanghai renmin chubanshe), 1999: 252.
7 Some mainland Chinese archaeologists were invited to survey Macau by heritage authorities as a goodwill gesture. They mainly concentrated their efforts on the islands of Coloane and Taipa, avoiding urban areas and Portuguese/Macanese sites. Interview with Stephan Chan, Cultural Affairs Bureau, Macau, February 2006.
8 Public Records Office 684-3-26: Antiquities and Monuments Bill.
9 Feng Yongqu, editor, Special Issue Number 3 of the *Guangzhou Research Institute on Heritage and Archeology: A Collection of Works on Fifty Years of Archeological Work in Guangzhou* (Guangzhou shi wenwukaoguyanjiusuo zhuankan zhi san: Guangzhou wenwu kaoguji – Guangzhou kaogu wushinian wenxuan), Guangzhou Publishing House (Guangzhou chubanshe), n.d.
10 Interview with Stephan Chan, Cultural Affairs Bureau, Macau, February 2006.
11 'The History of Heritage Conservation in Macau', available at website: http://macauheritage.net/Education/CycloDE.asp?id=69
12 Bowring also authorized the construction of the Central Police Station's earliest buildings, which are now being considered for a heritage tourism development project (see Chapter 4).
13 It was likely similar in nature to geographical collections made by Pitt Rivers and Christie during the same period (see Chapman, 1985). The Pitt Rivers Museum in Oxford is an example of how such items were often displayed as it is almost a 'museum of museums'.

46 *Hilary du Cros et al.*

14 The Hong Kong branch of the Royal Asiatic Society was founded in 1847. The main Society was founded in 1823 in London 'for the investigation of subjects connected with and for the encouragement of science, literature and the arts, in relation to Asia'. Most of its work was done in colonial branches. The Hong Kong branch grew out of the Medico-Chirurgical Society in 1845. (Speech by Professor of Chinese Studies, F.S. Drake, compiled on the occasion of the Inaugural Meeting of the revived Hong Kong Branch of the Royal Asiatic Society, on 7 April 1960, The University of Hong Kong). Telephone interview with Julie Chan, April 2005.
15 New Museum Committee Report, 11 January 1938, Hong Kong Botanical and Forestry Department files, 1938.
16 Letter from D.J. Sloss, The University of Hong Kong Temporary Office in London, to Mark Young (PCMS)18 July 1946; Public Records Office files 1948–1951; press clippings on City Hall in Public Records Office files 1953–1954; Christina Chu, Chief Curator, Museum of Art, personal communication, 2000.
17 Guangzhou officials noted in an interview undertaken in January 2005 that there were some suspicions that the Kuomingtang took some pieces away with them to Taiwan towards the end of the Civil War in the late 1940s.
18 All three cities have just recently collaborated over a travelling exhibition that highlights maritime trade in the PRD with some of the most intriguing artefacts coming from the Museum of Guangzhou's collection that reflect its role as a treaty port. When it was in the Museum of Macau, the local students were most interested in the dictionary of 'pidgin English' intended for Cantonese go-down (warehouse) and dock workers who could read Chinese. The dictionary gave the English words in phonetically designated Chinese characters.
19 See Clayton (2003: 115–116) for details of this saga.
20 Not even this museum made it to the present day unscathed. It was closed in 1988 and its collection packed up and put into storage until the 1990s. The Museum Maritimo de Macau opened in 1987 and has managed to stay operating. Several other smaller museums have also been established without closing after 1960. One is the site museum Museu Arqueológico das Ruínas de S. Paulo.
21 These learned institutions were likely to be some of the earliest of their kind in China, because of Guangzhou's role in the establishment of the new Chinese Republic in 1911.
22 Ada Wong, public lecture, given 4 May 2005, The University of Hong Kong.
23 It is likely that Guangzhou was the site of the enactment of some of the earliest heritage legislation in China, with the passing of one of the early acts to protect cultural property, probably done by the government of fledgling Republic.
24 Public Records Office, file HKRS 684-3-26.
25 Ibid.
26 Memo from the Secretary of Home Affairs to C.S. Goodair, Public Records Office, file HKRS 684-3-26; Minutes of the Executive Council Papers: Public Records Office, file HKRS 261-3-350.
27 After 1984, special decrees were needed each time there was a new heritage designation, so the list was effectively closed to all those who could not afford the time and money to set this in motion. Chinese buildings and items would only be recommended for such designation by the government.
28 Only single designations could be made up until the new decree in 1976.
29 Interview with Stephan Chan, Cultural Affairs Bureau, Macau, February 2006.
30 Interview in 2004 with Jose de Sales Marques, Mayor of Macau 1993–2001.
31 Interview with Vice-Curator of the Guangzhou Museum.

32 From an English translation by Ivan Ho, Architectural Conservation Programme, The University of Hong Kong.
33 Ibid.
34 This is despite conservation areas being a common designation in the United Kingdom (Larkham, 1996).
35 A large number of Macau's monuments are churches. They are required under legislation guidelines to undertake conservation works, but they can send a request to heritage authorities (currently known as the Cultural Affairs Bureau) for assistance (according to Stephan Chan). At least one of the Chinese Temples, Kun Iam (Buddhist Goddess of Mercy), is privately owned by an individual, who can make similar requests but usually tries to fund the works by himself.
36 Interview with Stephan Chan, February 2006.
37 World Heritage Site nominations have been rationed to one per country per year. The competition between provinces to be each year's contender has become intense in China as they are linked inexorably with local-level economic development aspirations in most officials' minds. Macau did well to get through the process as fast as it did.
38 The Chinese government liked the previous arrangement under the Crown colony government and the way it generated economic growth, so they decided to keep it. However, it was renamed as being an 'executive-led government' (Lau, 1997: 40–41).
39 Public Records Office, files HKRS 684-3-81.
40 One might also speculate further that he saw the indigenous villagers as being somewhat treated like the Palestinians in their relationship to the British.

3 The rise of professionalism

Hilary du Cros, Yok-shiu F. Lee, Alexandra Sauvigrain-McClelland, Euphemia Chow and William Logan

The previous chapter discussed the way heritage assets have been documented and protected in the first stages of the CHM approaches identified in the Pearl River Delta. This chapter focuses on aspects of their care in the last fifteen years. The nature of the pressure arising out of rapid economic growth on heritage assets will be examined, and the imperative of each city to establish a unique cultural identity in China's latest transitional phase will be highlighted. How these localities within China have dealt with and are dealing with change and the maintenance of core cultural values is examined closely.

Key economic, political and social characteristics

The case study cities have changed their perspectives on heritage and its utilization since the enactment of initial heritage legislation and establishment of associated government authorities to administer it. In recent years, a number of events and activities have stimulated and prevented improvements in CHM in the case study cities. In particular, heritage and its management have been closely influenced by debates about the three cities' respective cultural identity and how it is linked to economic development. As the heritage analyst Barbara Bender once commented, heritage is 'never inert, people engage with it, re-work it, appropriate it and contest it. It is part of the way identities are created and disputed, whether as individual, group or national state' (Bender in Harvey, 2001: 336). Alternatively, UNESCO's Regional Advisor for Culture in Asia and the Pacific, Richard Engelhardt, notes that 'in this stormy world, we rely on our heritage to anchor us to the ethical values we have evolved and which we call our cultures' (Engelhardt, 2004).

Hong Kong's experience of being a part of the 'motherland' has been ambivalent at times. Hong Kong survived the challenge of the Asian economic downtown that occurred almost immediately after the handover from British to mainland Chinese control in 1997. Although the downturn has had a more direct impact on the lives of the populace, the handover was a cause for concern in that it meant possible change to civil, social and economic freedoms with the implementation of the new Basic Law. The passing of colonial control has allowed some examination of cultural identity in retrospect and in present-day public life (du Cros, 2004). Meanwhile, Macau's official line is that everyone is now 'Macanese' culturally,[1] a special mixture of cultural groups that is unique to Macau. It is a mixture that has developed over a longer colonial period than that for Hong Kong, which still classifies non-Chinese born in Hong Kong as part of the expatriate population. 'Macanese' is a term that appears to be used differently depending on to whom one is speaking in Macau. However, schools in both cities are now apprehensive about the politically correct way to approach teaching colonial history. Guangzhou considers itself in competition with other Chinese cities on the mainland for resources, tourism and investment. Developing a unique cultural identity can help it 'benchmark' itself in this environment, and it has been included in policy more for economic rationalist reasons than for a great concern over cultural diversity or cultural heritage.

After the handover, Hong Kong began promoting an image of itself to outsiders as a progressive and predominantly Chinese cosmopolitan society (Culture and Heritage Commission, 2002). It is a myth or impression that the government and its advisory bodies are trying to present, not just to outsiders, but also to its own population in order for them to feel more secure about their identity and place in relation to mainland China. Although Hong Kong has a British colonial history, it could be argued that it is far from cosmopolitan, with over ninety-five per cent of the population being ethnic Chinese, many of whom do not speak another language besides Cantonese or Mandarin. Meanwhile, cities on the mainland itself, like Guangzhou, have no such qualms.

It could be argued that Hong Kong is incapable of establishing its own national myths as it has gone from being a colony of one country to being a semi-independent territory of another. However, any community can develop its myths or any self-governing territory its 'national' myth during the de-colonization process. In fact myth-making is often an important tool used by revolutionaries (e.g., maintaining social cohesion in Vietnam after the war).

Nevertheless, Hong Kong is earnestly seeking one to underpin its cultural identity. Cultural identity can be defined as a 'snapshot of unfolding meanings relating to self-nomination or ascription by others... it relates nodal points in cultural meaning, most notably class, gender, race, ethnicity, nation and age' (Barker in du Cros, 2004: 154). It can be expressed through symbols and discourses so that the national myths of city-states are not only established to support political and economic ideals, but also to be tools of cultural representation. These representations, when mixed with loaded symbols, can evoke a passionate response from members of society as it clashes with some aspects of their cultural identity – one that is private and not based on the publicly fostered national myth.

In Hong Kong, the colonial period set the scene for current attitudes to cultural and heritage management. The end of British rule came officially at midnight on 30 June 1997. The colonial derived legislation has been shown in the previous chapter to have certain deficiencies. Alternatively, the market liberalization process and administrative reforms in China have had a major impact on CHM over a longer period. Its economy is on an accelerating trajectory to a full market economy, further boosted by China's accession into the World Trade Organization in December 2001.

Market liberalization comprises three major sub-processes: the correction of market disequilibria, the privatization of state-owned enterprises and services; and international trade liberalization (Kirkpatrick and Lee, 1997). Such liberalization necessarily requires massive restructuring away from a previously closed and tightly government-regulated economy. The economy of the People's Republic of China has already undergone a dramatic reform and growth since the liberalization process was initiated by Deng Xiao-Ping's 'Open Door' policy in 1978. A study by the World Bank in 1997 found that China's economic growth in the 1980s and early 1990s was the fastest in global economic history (Campanella *et al.*, 2002). Its recent accession into the World Trade Organization (WTO) will further accelerate its growth and the liberalization process. Changes associated with both are considered likely to have an impact on China's stewardship of heritage assets.

In connection with this transformation, privatization of some cultural heritage government agencies and the impact of this on the training and careers of bureaucrats will be explored for Guangzhou. The creation of civil society in the West that has accompanied such economic change requires the production and availability of professionals who come from a university background (Freidson, 1994). However, China's Communist Party has been historically apprehensive of intellectual elites and the potential power they might wield. It is an interesting question as to how far university arts faculties on the mainland and even those established in earlier colonial times for Hong Kong and Macau will be allowed to go, to train heritage professionals to think critically in order to contribute more to the modern world than just their fields of technical expertise.

This section will examine whether opportunities for self-expression and activism in relation to the retention of heritage assets have opened up as a result of this process in the three cities, particularly in Guangzhou, a city that was one of the first to open up to global influences after the Cultural Revolution, and one that continues to court foreign exchange

Plate 3.1 'Shamian the Romantic European Culture Island' billboard on the northern side of Shamian Island in Guangzhou. The Shamian Island Street Management Office hopes that it can attract tourists of all kinds and related businesses to the location with various promotions. (Hilary du Cros)

(see Plate 3.1). Also, this section will examine the question of whether there have been opportunities for non-government organizations, the media and individuals to have a meaningful role in urban planning and CHM decision-making processes as these cities adopt (or not) international best practices regarding stakeholder participation.

Increased professionalism

The need for greater technical expertise and critical thinking in this phase is usually underpinned by mutually agreed sets of professional principles and ethics. This is a feature of many local approaches to CHM in Western countries. It marks the change towards a more heritage specific administration that can follow a proactive policy of heritage management with a long-term vision for conservation (the conservation perspective). Mature CHM is more than just trying to maintain the status quo and certainly not a reaction-based management system. Vision, leadership and long-term planning should ensure that priorities are set to allow heritage assets to be enjoyed by future as well as by present generations. CH managers who are also heritage professionals with such a purpose should be able to follow a logical process to manage their duties. They can be employed in the public or private sector or even by non-governmental organizations. Heritage professionals could also become increasingly common in the private sector as consultants, whether they have worked previously in the public sector or not. NGOs that may employ heritage professionals for CHM-related work include indigenous, tourism or conservation organizations. What they all usually have in common is a concern with maintaining professional standards and ethics, along with some university-based training in a heritage-related discipline.

Opportunities for locally established professional training can affect how CH managers and other heritage professionals undertake their duties. Also, the influence of international and regional heritage IGOs and NGOs for professionals can be important in relation to what kind of principles they apply to heritage management projects. UNESCO and ICOMOS, the International Council of Museums (ICOM) and the International Centre for the Study of the Preservation and Restoration of Cultural Property (ICCROM – established in Italy by UNESCO in the early 1960s) have an extensive influence on the development of CHM internationally. UNESCO's conventions and declarations have varying impact on government policies regarding heritage assets for sovereign states that are signatories. The use of ICOMOS- and ICOM-generated codes of conservation practice, establishment of university-level training and standards for professional practice and accountability can have implications for the kinds of CHM found in the case study cities. Some minor administrative restructuring and indications of greater sophistication in the undertaking of routine activities are also of interest in this context, such as inventorying heritage items and dealing with other government departments. All these factors will be analysed and compared in this section in order to define unique local characteristics. The notional model for CHM applied in this book has no set order for the appearance of sub-indicator activities and so a roughly chronological approach will be undertaken here when activities are not happening concurrently. It should also be remembered that it is likely that many such activities are still ongoing. In particular, many NGOs for heritage professionals are still debating what ethics to follow, and new charters or principles are added as the framework continues to evolve.

Training available for heritage professionals in the Pearl River Delta

The development of heritage-related professions (public and private) has been intermittent in the Pearl River Delta, and so many CH managers in the area have received training overseas. There have been problems associated with the area's attitude to intellectuals or colonial policies that have had a direct or indirect impact on locally available tertiary courses in particular. In relation to the core heritage management disciplines of public archaeology, architectural conservation and public history, their integration within a university environment has not gone smoothly. There are clear political, historical, economic and cultural reasons for the current situation which will be explored briefly in relation to a number of key universities. This is a phase that all cities are still struggling with in some way.

Guangzhou's tertiary sector

The oldest university in Guangzhou is Zhongshan University, originally known as Guangdong University. It is also one of the oldest of its kind in China. It was founded in 1924 by Dr Sun Yat-sen (also known as Sun Zhongshan), the founder of modern China. It was renamed Zhongshan University in 1926 in commemoration of Dr Sun after his death. It is also known outside of China as Sun Yat Sen University.

The 1930s saw rapid developments in the university which in 1931 had five Schools (Arts, Law, Science, Agriculture, and Medicine). It established the Engineering School in 1934, together with the Graduate School which began to take in graduate students in 1935. During the Second World War, the university was forced to move from one place to another, to Luoding in Guangdong, to Chengjiang in Yunnan, and to Pingshi, Dongjiang, and Lianxian County in Guangdong. It was moved back to Shi Pai, Guangzhou in 1945 when the war was over.[2]

In 1952, the university was restructured to conform to the nationwide plans for reorganizing schools and departments under the new Communist government. As a result, the Schools of Engineering, Agriculture, Medicine and the Teachers' College were separated from Zhongshan University, which was then made into a comprehensive university specializing in the liberal arts and sciences. In the same year it moved from Shipai to Kangleyuan, the present Guangzhou Southern Campus (Sun Yat Sen University, 2005).

In the province of Guangdong, the only institution involved in architectural conservation is the South China University of Technology. Its work in conservation began with the work of Lu Yuan Ding, who at the time was the Director of Architectural History within the Department of Architecture. His focus lay more on the typology of historic buildings and the building form. His student, Cheng Jian Jun, is now also heavily involved in conservation. Cheng's focus lies more on the materials and techniques in architectural conservation. Cheng does not conduct formal training on this subject. Like other professors who have an interest in conservation matters, he conducts informal studio groups for students. The students can then participate in conservation projects under the guidance of such professors. Conservation projects are usually those tendered by the government authorities as contracts.³

Archaeology has been formally recognized by the tertiary sector for a while throughout China. It had been established as an undergraduate major at Beijing University in 1952 and then at another ten universities, including Zhongshan University. The latter conducted courses in archaeology within its history department. This reflected the discipline's early obsession with confirming the details of historical documents with tangible evidence (Lu, 2002). Zhongshan University established a separate Department of Anthropology with a major in archaeology in 1981, one of the earliest departments outside of Beijing (Chiao, 1993). Tracey Lu (now at the Chinese University of Hong Kong) was taught in its Department of History and was one of their first archaeology students after the Cultural Revolution.⁴

Hong Kong's tertiary sector

The Chinese University of Hong Kong first ran anthropology undergraduate courses in the Department of Sociology in 1973. They were initially taught by Barbara Ward from Cambridge University, who had been visiting Hong Kong for nearly 30 years before that to undertake field recording. The Department of Anthropology then became an independent unit in 1980 (Chiao, 1993).⁵ Archaeology started at this institution within the Anthropology Department with Tracey Lu in 2000, but not as a full independent degree. In the same year, Hilary du Cros started teaching courses on archaeology and on cultural tourism.⁶ These courses were given between 2000 and 2005 within the Department of Geography at the University of Hong Kong,⁷ which had also been the home of Solomon Bard's field schools in the 1970s and Father Finn's archaeological courses in the 1930s. The courses have had some impact on graduates that have taken archaeology courses offered at the Chinese University of Hong Kong or the University of Hong Kong, as some of them have subsequently been employed by the Antiquities and Monuments Office.⁸

Courses in Chinese history, languages and culture had been a feature of Hong Kong's universities prior to the Second World War. The University of Hong Kong was the first to establish an Arts Faculty. A history of the university states that it was 'the only institution in China with Medical, Engineering and Arts faculties in which the degrees were comparable to that obtainable in London' (HKU pamphlet, 1913). The university originally hoped to become a key institution training civil servants for China, but this option was closed off in the 1920s. The vision was for an Oxbridge equivalent, but with a heavy emphasis on producing graduates for the public service and professions (The Newspaper Ltd, 1933).[9]

The university was officially opened in 1911, but an Arts Faculty was not included until 1913 at the request of the Chinese community (Lugard, 1910). Even so, it originally covered economics, chemistry, physics, mathematics, history, and English and Chinese languages and literature (HKU pamphlet, 1913). Lugard's vision for the university was also strictly secular and apolitical. Apparently, subjects like philosophy, political economy and abstract science were perceived to possess the potential to cause unrest amongst the indigenous populations of British imperial territories and they were therefore not offered in the university. This decision was probably also influenced by the fact that problems had occurred in India, which was at that time still a colonial possession (Chan and Cunich, 2002).[10]

Between 1913 and 1966, the Chair for the Chinese Department was held by a mixture of Chinese and overseas scholars. From 1966 onwards, the Chair's occupants included Professors Lo Hsiang-lin, Ma Meng, Ho Peng Yoke and Chiu Ling Yeong. Professor Lo was a graduate of a private Guangzhou University and he moved to Hong Kong in 1949 and was an influential member of the first Antiquities Advisory Board (School of Chinese, 2006, Chu Hai College, 2006). Before he died in May 1978, he was a vocal advocate on the Board for the preservation of both Western and Chinese historic buildings.[11] Concern about such buildings and their history has also been shown by those in other Asian and Chinese Studies departments and centres in Hong Kong and Macau.[12]

The university established the School of Architecture in 1950. Architecture students were encouraged to document colonial architecture, and this had, for example, led to the production of a report on Murray House in 1967.[13] When David Lung returned to Hong Kong after gaining a postgraduate degree in architecture from Oregon University in 1978, he was the first to set up courses on traditional Chinese architecture as the department turned its research focus towards Hong Kong.[14]

David Lung was also the first director of the Architecture Conservation Master's and Graduate Diploma Programme initiated in 2000 by the department. This is the first course specifically on architectural conservation established in Hong Kong that draws on international best practice principles. Its purpose is to encourage graduates in heritage-related fields to upgrade their professional skills in a way that views CHM as a system. It offers more than practical experience in conservation planning by giving its students an intellectual framework within which to base their work. It has also established an informal network of students, alumni, lecturers and guest lecturers through which news about heritage management events, such as conferences and seminar can be disseminated. In 2005, this course was complemented by a continuing education certificate programme focused specifically on CHM and offered through the university's School of Professional and Continuing Education (SPACE). This programme was designed to offer a lower-order graduate certificate course on CHM that could introduce graduates to general concepts and encourage them to then undertake more detailed studies as part of the Architectural Conservation Programme.[15]

SPACE (in conjunction with the University of Sydney) and the Chinese University of Hong Kong are the only places where programmes in museum studies can be undertaken in Hong Kong. Even so, no detailed study of the conservation of movable cultural heritage is possible in Hong Kong and students still have to travel abroad for this specialization. The director of Hong Kong's Museum of History prefers this arrangement for his staff. The museum also shares expertise with personnel from museums on the mainland, particularly Guangzhou, in planning new museums.[16]

Macau's tertiary sector

The first tertiary institution in Macau was established in March 1981, originally as the privately owned University of East Asia (UEA). It was founded by Ricci Island West Limited. UEA started with several three-year undergraduate degree programmes. English was the main medium of instruction and most students came from Hong Kong. To meet the demand for local human resources during the transition period of Macau returning to China, the Government of Macau established the Macau Foundation to acquire and manage the university in 1988. Subsequent restructuring led to the establishment of the Faculties of Arts, Business Administration, Social Sciences, and Science and Technology.[17] English has remained the main medium of instruction, in addition to Chinese and Portuguese.

In 1991, under a new University Charter, the university became the public University of Macau. The university was primarily aimed at attracting more local students to fulfill the needs associated with the transfer of sovereignty of 1999. The university offers undergraduate, master's, doctorate and 'Bacharelato' (higher diploma) programmes (University of Macau, 2005). Some of its academics, such as Cathryn Hope Clayton, have published studies on Macau's cultural heritage and identity (Clayton, 2002, 2003). Although a Macau Studies Research Centre exists in the university, there appear to be no formal undergraduate courses on archaeology, history or cultural studies that relate directly to Macau.[18]

Macau has had little interest in developing university-level courses or a research programme on archaeology or architectural conservation, possibly because little local history has been taught in schools. This situation

58 *Hilary du Cros* et al.

was lamented in 1996 by Zheng Weiming, a lecturer in Chinese Studies at the University of Macau. He identified a broad range of themes for archaeological study in particular, including prehistoric tombs, the historic development of industries and some aspects of maritime history that could benefit from archaeological investigation but had been (and continue to be) ignored by the universities and the government (Zheng, 1996). In 1999 there was still no archaeology taught in Macau's universities, although since then a vocational course has been set up by the Macao Museum of Art (*Macao Daily*, 30 June 1999).

In addition to universities, Macau has several other tertiary institutions that are publicly – or privately – funded. Most were established in the 1980s or 1990s. The Institute of European Studies offers a course on Macau's history; and a graduate diploma in Cultural Tourism is offered in conjunction with the Institute For Tourism Studies.[19] The most recent innovations for Macau in relation to CHM-related training and courses are the advent of a heritage management specialization offered by the Institute For Tourism Studies (IFT) Bachelor of Business Management programme.[20]

Of the three cities, Macau has been the slowest to adopt a tertiary level CHM programme to cater to the interests and needs of its locally educated middle-class professionals who might have a concern with local heritage. That most professionals were trained in Portugal and employed in the civil service may explain this deficiency.

International organizations have recently taken a role in enhancing regional cooperation on capacity building and professional training by the staging of training seminars in connection with the network known as the Asian Academy for Heritage Management. The network is a UNESCO initiative, supported by most of the universities with heritage-related courses in the Asia-Pacific Region (IFT, 2005; UNESCO, 2004). Aside from this network, there are opportunities emerging in the future for Hong Kong and Macau universities to undertake more training and interaction with each other and those in mainland China with regard to training heritage professionals.

Background and career paths of CH managers in the PRD

Museums in Guangzhou appear to employ a number of heritage professionals. It is difficult to find out much about the early history of professionalism in this group as the first generation of museum curators after 1949 have all retired. In 1953, the State Administration of Cultural Heritage (SACH) organized the Second National Archaeological Training Course for all lower-level cultural officials in China. It was held in Beijing with a class size of one hundred[21] which included Mai Ying Hao and Au Ka-fat. Mai went to on to become an archaeological curator at the Guangzhou

Museum, and Au later became a private archaeological consultant in Hong Kong (much later after he emigrated there). Au had also obtained a degree from the History Department of the Huanan University of Education prior to attending the course (Au, 2004; Mai, 2004).

Many of the current generation of senior staff in Guangzhou, however, started work or study during the Cultural Revolution. Even so, most of them now have earned university degrees. Some have upgraded their skills or have encouraged younger staff to further their studies, for instance, by taking a museum major offered by Peking University. A Vice-Curator at the Guangzhou Museum of Art observed that the standard of heritage professionals in mainland China has been continually rising. She noted that her staff had taken a course on museology/history of art, which included management of collections, research, and techniques in setting up exhibitions.[22]

Generally speaking, Hong Kong's CH managers have usually spent some time in an overseas university. Exceptions are Louis Ng (current Executive Secretary of the AMO), Joseph Ting (Chief Curator at the Museum of History), and W.K. Chan (Hong Kong General Chamber of Commerce and the Hong Kong Conservancy Association). These individuals gained all their under- and post-graduate degrees at either the University of Hong Kong or the Chinese University of Hong Kong. Many urban planners, architects and archaeologists currently working in Hong Kong have acquired their degrees, diplomas or more from overseas institutions. Not surprisingly, many of these qualifications obtained before 1997 were granted by British universities. York and London universities appear to be the favourites because they offer courses in specific heritage subjects, such as public archaeology, architectural conservation and museum-related studies.

In Macau, most of the original middle and senior management staff of the Culture Institute (now the Cultural Affairs Bureau) came from Portugal and were trained there. Only the few current staff, who were trained in Portugal, are familiar with the Portuguese language and how the system worked. This can be a problem for accessing previous records, if they are not also prepared in Chinese. Staff from the Cultural Affairs Bureau noted that this situation has discouraged the involvement of the local Chinese community in researching public history as most historical records need translation.[23]

Career paths in PRD heritage management

Career paths for CH managers in Guangzhou and Hong Kong usually involve some time working in museums for those with a background in history, anthropology or archaeology. The administrative reforms have allowed more acknowledgment of merit and expertise in the career paths of museum professionals in Guangzhou and across China. The career path now has five ranks:

> Rank 1: Requires at least a 'basic' university degree, minimum of one year's work before promotion
> Rank 2: Assistant museum curator, three years' experience with some publications and exhibitions considered satisfactory before promotion
> Rank 3: Middle management, five years' minimum experience with two major exhibitions and/or two excavations[24]
> Rank 4: Vice-researcher (like a lecturer) with five years' minimum experience
> Rank 5: Curator (like a professor).

The original system had more emphasis on seniority and it used to require five years in each rank, before applications for promotion could be made. Now the emphasis is placed on work performance and achievement, which allows for gifted professionals to (theoretically) reduce the time before they can be promoted. Even so, the standard required to attain a promotion is rated by two criteria: work achievements and research findings. This is why most museum professionals achieve a middle management position, as 'research findings' (e.g. the publication of monographs and essays) to make the next grade are harder to obtain.[25]

In Hong Kong, most CH managers seem to move from museum to museum, or to the AMO and back again, as their careers progress. There appears to be little in the way of a clear career path beyond becoming a 'senior curator'. Even so, hardly anyone has left to become a consultant, probably due to the still generous conditions that the civil service in Hong Kong provides for its staff. Architects and urban planners who have an interest in heritage are more likely to move straight into private practice from university. At present there are no practices that rely entirely on heritage conservation work. Those businesses with an interest in it support themselves on contemporary architectural design and urban planning projects. This situation is probably the result of the small size of Hong Kong's heritage industry and the general lack of requirement for such expertise by government and the private sector in contrast with cities such as London, Sydney and New York. The mainland has potentially a much larger private sector for such work, but it is currently being constrained by government policy against a private consulting industry developing for such projects.[26]

Internal restructuring of government agencies

With so much CHM professional practice occurring within the government sector, it is worth exploring how it has developed in the PRD in the last thirty years. The earliest restructuring after local legislation was introduced occurred in the administration of duties within Macau. Hong Kong's restructuring, as will be seen, followed later. The need for increased professionalism was reflected in the Macau government's revamp of the Standing Committee's role and resources in 1982. The Cultural Property Bureau (later renamed the Cultural Heritage Department) within the Culture Institute was to become the 'outlet through which conservation policies in Macau could be implemented. It transforms conservation ideas that were only conceptual in the past into accomplishable missions' (Macau Heritage Net, 2005). By this, it means that heritage assets would be subject to a conservation planning process (in the case of tangible heritage assets such as buildings and archaeological sites) and priorities would be set. The role of the Cultural Heritage Department was to implement Decree Law no. 56/84/M and Decree no. 83/92/M.

In 1984, Article 1 of Decree no. 56/84/M, the Committee for the Defence of the Architectural, Environmental and Cultural Heritage (Comissão de Defesa do Património Arquitectónico, Paisagístico e Cultural) was created to replace the Committee for the Defence of Macao's Urbanistic, Natural and Cultural Heritage. Compared with the responsibilities of the previous Committee, those stipulated now are much more precise:

(i) Issue opinions on the classification of sites
(ii) Issue opinions on the delimitation of classified complexes, sites and areas
(iii) Issue opinions on adaptive reuse
(iv) Issue opinions on whether preferential rights should be exercised in cases of alienation of sites
(v) Provide technical support for all works carried out on classified sites, with the right to suspend any unauthorized work or authorized work that is being carried out incorrectly or defectively
(vi) Issue opinions on any ordinance plans, urbanization projects prepared by both private and public entities that may interfere with the classified sites
(vii) Collaborate with other public and private entities to ensure that city plans and ordinances take into consideration the cultural values
(viii) Issue opinions on the organization, methodology of inventory
(ix) Issue opinions on the promotion of the cultural and educational values of the heritage, not forgetting its social and economic importance.

In addition to these administrative duties, CH professionals have endeavoured to keep in touch with the practice of others inside and outside Macau. Opportunities for professional debate on CHM have been limited, but not entirely missing. In the first conference of the Architects Association of Macau in 1987, one of the four agenda topics was conservation. It suggested that the government utilize tax incentives and transfer of develop-ment rights mechanisms to encourage private owners to cooperate with the government on conservation matters.[27] The first conference on the culture of Macau, sponsored by the Cultural Institute (now the Cultural Affairs Bureau), was held in July 1988.[28] Professional debate on the nature of heritage has also been productive. Macau has added new CH categories of heritage and made readjustments to its Classified List. In 1992, under the terms of Statutory Order no. 82/92/M, the category of 'Buildings of architectonic interest' was created. Buildings included in this category include any structure that 'through its original architectonic quality is representative of an important period of the evolution of the Territory'.

This period included some growth in the inventory actions of Macau's CH managers. The list was increased from 89 to 128 items, and protected areas were clearly delineated on maps, which are an integral part of Macau's legislation on heritage conservation. However, no further additions were possible without another decree being issued. This makes updating the list with new items very difficult and protracted.

Another major change came in 1992: an architectural works arm was added to the Cultural Institute, allowing it to carry out its own conservation works projects on buildings without requiring assistance from an outside department.[29] The AMO in Hong Kong is still required to involve the Architectural Services department, administered by another ministry, in any public conservation works project.

An awareness of the gaps in the CHM for Macau sometime in the early 1990s initiated the addition of a new public museum to the Institute's administrative structure. The planning for the Museum of Macau began in April 1995. It was a transition-era project initiated by the government prior to the 1999 handover, and it was also necessary to plug the gap caused by the demise of the Museu Luis de Camões in 1988 (see Box 3.1 below).

More resources have been allocated to CH managers in Macau since the last decree in 1992. Below is the current allocation of staff (as of February 2006) showing the ratio of professional to clerical and other positions in the Cultural Affairs Bureau, as compared with that before 1998. Despite the addition of parts of Macau to the World Heritage List as 'The Historic Centre of Macau' inscription in July 2005, and an increase in duties and responsibilities that this entails, resources have actually decreased for management since the handover. The only other restructuring change was a superficial one that occurred in May 2005, when the Institute was renamed the Cultural Affairs Bureau in English, although its Portuguese and Chinese names have remained unchanged.[30]

> **Box 3.1**
> **Museum of Macau: an example of early CH administration and adaptive reuse in Macau**
>
> The museum's construction was initiated in September 1996, and it was opened on 18 April 1998. The design was ambitious, and it had its critics. An extensive survey had been made of all possible locations for the museum, including the Monte Fortress – a historic fortification built by the Jesuits in 1626, on the peak of Monte Hill, perched high above the city centre. It was selected by the government as the site for the new museum on the basis of its symbolic and historical location.
>
> The museum building is an example of local Portuguese attitudes to adaptive reuse that included the removal of much of the original interior of the Monte Fortress. It can be accessed by an escalator from ground level to the third floor above the base of the fort. Its total area is 2,800 square metres, of which about 2,100 square metres is exhibition space. The administrative building, which already existed just outside the fortress, was joined to the museum by way of a tunnel, with escalators that pass under the walls. It contains the technical and administrative offices of the museum as well as the management and technician centre, security headquarters, and auditorium. In 1998, under Decree no. 31/98/M, the Museum of Macau was incorporated into the organizational structure of the Cultural Institute.

Hong Kong's restructuring of CHM administration has occurred over a period of similar length to that of Macau. Staff appointment issues, however, were at the core of the problem with the government's slowness in establishing the Antiquities and Monuments Office (AMO) in the first place. However, restructuring has been positive, in part, and led to AMO eventually gaining more staff and resources.

It began with an inter-departmental committee, with the Municipal Services Branch of Urban Services investigating a restructure for AMO in the late 1980s. There was a proposal by the AMO to upgrade the Executive Secretary from 'curator' to the rank of 'chief curator' in order to 'improve the quality of an existing service and assume full responsibilities'.[31] The Executive Secretary, according to an AMO report, 'will oversee all its professional functions in relation to the search, identification, preservation and display of Hong Kong's cultural heritage'.[32]

> **Box 3.2**
> **Comparison of staff allocation in the Cultural Affairs Bureau before and after 1998**
>
> | *Prior to 1998* | *2006* |
> |---|---|
> | Total 18 people | Total 14 people |
> | (6 Portuguese, 1 Brazilian, 11 Chinese) | (1 Portuguese, 13 Chinese) |
> | 7 architects | 5 architects |
> | 2 civil engineers | 1 civil engineer |
> | 1 conservator (mural restoration) | 1 education, liberal arts background (major in Chinese) |
> | 1 researcher (art history background, previously a curator in Portugal) | 3 draughtsmen |
> | 1 secretary | 1 secretary |
> | 1 clerk | 1 clerk |
> | 1 chauffeur | 1 chauffeur |
> | 1 office assistant | 1 office assistant |
> | | Plus student interns year round |

A discussion paper on heritage management in Hong Kong was also tabled at a meeting of the Antiquities Advisory Board (AAB) in 1989. It resulted in AMO being split into three clear sub-sections that are still evident today: architecture, archaeology and education (which also handles AMO's public relations functions). The AAB also reorganized its sub-committees in a similar way. The transition period prior to the handover also witnessed some changes as more staff were employed, although the number of professional staff has increased slowly.[33] Low salaries for administrative staff and others without professional qualifications meant that more of these could be engaged than is common in most Western countries' CHM administrations. Such a high number of non-professional staff is also common in Macau.

Training for professional staff, particularly the archaeologists, was a concern in this period. Neither the University of Hong Kong nor the Chinese University of Hong Kong (CUHK) were interested at the time in providing local courses, even inter-mural ones, to upgrade field techniques. In the meantime, the AMO organized a short course by itself in January 1991. Later, the AMO sent its staff (including architectural curators) to undertake studies in Britain.[34] Eventually, the advent of the Architectural Conservation Programme and some CUHK courses in the last few years have allowed some members of the staff to gain or upgrade their skills locally.

Membership in international organizations and use of charters in conservation practice

Overseas links were established during the colonial and transition periods for Hong Kong and Macau and these links have continued into the postcolonial phase. However, the nature of these links has undergone some change of focus. The two cities have become less reliant on sourcing expertise or training from their colonial masters than they had once been. Since the mid-1990s, which marked the end of the transition period for both Hong Kong and Macau, a greater interest has developed in UNESCO programmes and its advice. The UNESCO Heritage Awards were one of the first initiatives to attract attention in the region, with the restoration of the Jewish synagogue Ohel Leah in the Mid Levels in Hong Kong winning an award. Although the conservation architectural consultants were sourced from Australia, the work was supervised by Hong Kong's Architectural Services Department and the AMO.[35]

This international involvement can also be seen in how UNESCO was involved in the conference organized by the AMO, AAB and the Lord Wilson Heritage Trust on tourism and heritage in 1999. However, it was not until 2004 that UNESCO co-hosted a conference in Hong Kong. This conference was focused on 'underwater heritage', with the aim by UNESCO of promoting a recent initiative to protect such heritage in the region. It coincided with AMO's growing interests in the protection and management of such heritage items, such as those affected by the development projects in Penny's Bay (prior to the Disney theme park development). And AMO (on the advice of AAB) invited maritime archaeologists from the mainland and occasionally from the United Kingdom.

On the other hand, the application of key international charters of conservation principles seems to be more widespread. Interviews with heritage officials and academics in Guangzhou revealed that they were familiar with the 1964 ICOMOS Venice Charter. Some of the younger officials had only just heard of the China Principles when interviewed in late 2004.[36] It is otherwise known as 'Principles for the Conservation of Heritage Sites in China'. This document was devised as a collaborative project between the State Administration for Cultural Heritage (SACH), the Getty Conservation Institute in Los Angeles, and the Australian Heritage Commission (now itself restructured as part of Environment Australia). The Australian Heritage Commission was involved as the process of developing the China Principles has followed the Burra Charter – Australia's regional version of the Venice Charter – rather than the Venice Charter itself, as a starting point.

The introduction to the China Principles notes that China's socialist market economy presents new challenges for conservation and the underlying values of heritage sites. It provides the first guidelines for heritage practice for Chinese heritage under the mainland system. That is, its definition of heritage significance follows that defined in the 1982 Relics Protection Act and it does not include any guidance on stakeholder consultation (Sullivan, 2001; Agnew and Demas, 2002). David Lung, who made some informal comments on the translation of the document, considers it a sound document but still untested in most of China.[37] SACH has recognized the difficulties posed by getting local officials to take notice of the Principles and is seeking to give them more statutory weight (Agnew et al., 2005).

Stephen Chan from the Cultural Affairs Bureau had observed that Macau's policy on the use of charters can vary. He saw it as important to 'keep in line with the Venice Charter and the China Principles, but it is more important to handle projects on a case by case basis'. He followed the China Principles in cases involving Chinese structures 'because [they] don't want to Westernize the structures'.[38]

The usage of conservation principles in Hong Kong also varies. Some heritage professionals use the Principles, others use the Burra Charter, and some use nothing at all as there is no stated requirement for local studies.[39] There is no one set of principles that seems to be widely endorsed. Many people interviewed stated they would like to see Hong Kong develop its own version, as Australia did. However, no one appears keen to undertake responsibility for initiating a process to do this, as it would be a difficult task to complete without the backing of an active local chapter or sub-chapter of ICOMOS.

Establishing a local sub-chapter of China ICOMOS for Hong Kong and Macau has been a difficult process in itself. Heritage professionals have recognized that the differences in the legal/administrative systems between the two SARs on the one hand, and the mainland on the other, would require some kind of separate body to be set up for the SAR professionals. They have liaised extensively about the issue with key China ICOMOS representatives in Beijing (who are also employed by SACH).[40] Networking and other activities necessary for increasing the professionalism of CH managers has been hampered by the lack of such a peak interdisciplinary heritage non-governmental organization in the Pearl River Delta.

Public–private sector relationships and professional ethics

Each city has a different arrangement for the conduct of public–private sector relationships and this inevitably has an impact on the professional ethics exhibited. Since 2002, the public sector in Hong Kong has been under pressure to be more accountable to the public, with new political reforms introduced. Unfortunately for CHM, this initiative coincided with revelations about corruption within the upper echelons of the Antiquities and Monuments Office. The Executive Secretary, the Senior Archaeological Curator and members of an archaeological consulting company were all arrested in an operation codenamed 'Greendike' in April 2002.[41] This situation has created a tense working environment for those who remained in the AMO, until their colleagues went to trial in early 2005. Even so, all official proceedings, particularly the letting of archaeological contracts, continued to be carefully scrutinized. For the first time, the AMO had to devise a system for undertaking such tasks that would be transparent and in line with other government practices of accountability. Other new measures were also instituted by the new Executive Secretary.[42] The AMO has set out to streamline many of its administrative processes in answer to the ICAC review of procedures and new civil service requirements for greater transparency and accountability. However, there has never been an open debate about the nature of professional ethics in Hong Kong in regard to CHM, and there may not be for a while as the allegations have made this a sensitive topic.

Overall, the ICAC investigation may have contributed to AMO being passed over by the government in favour of the Tourism Commission as the facilitator of two major heritage development projects, namely the development of the declared historic buildings of the former Marine Police Headquarters Compound and the Central Police Station Complex. It certainly has not helped its profile with the rest of the government according to some heritage professionals, who deal with these agencies on a regular basis.[43]

Problems have also occurred with locally born heritage consultants and professional ethics. Only limited support and guidance has been made available towards peer regulation from a small number of professional associations, which are formed by architects, planners and landscape architects. These associations count heritage management activities as of small concern to their members.[44] Little support from the AMO, AAB or professional associations is given to consultants working in difficult situations, especially those projects where their professional views differ from that of their developer clients (who are often backed by other parts of the government). Locally born consultants may not be confident enough without the backing of a professional heritage NGO to cause ripples,[45] which could become an emerging problem for increasing professionalism. A stronger overall CHM professional heritage association of the stature of ICOMOS or a sub-branch of ICOMOS is needed to promote professional ethics, codes and charters. That is, provided that such an organization can establish true autonomy from the public sector. Even so, the AMO has taken an active role in improving professionalism in both public and private sectors by adopting a new set of internal management measures, and increasing professionalism has been identified as one of its major targets over the next few years.[46] This same issue barely comes up in Macau, however, as there is no formal EIA system requiring independent assessment of CH assets and because there is not much private heritage practice of any kind.[47]

Hong Kong academic Ka-ho Mok, who has studied professional autonomy in China, notes that Chinese professionals have to balance professional freedom with intellectual independence. Often they have attempted to break the conventional order and go beyond the 'approved' boundaries (Mok, 2000). The authors of this volume have encountered a few individuals similar to this description in Guangzhou. They usually tend to be older, senior male academics, or they are retired senior officials who were active in pre-Cultural Revolution times. They often have strong opinions which they will offer very candidly in public about heritage and use their age and seniority as a buffer against any reprisals. Some are affiliated with semi-independent research institutes that can undertake consulting work for the government.

The type of consulting work undertaken in Guangzhou is generally in the area of architectural conservation, urban heritage planning and archaeological salvage excavation or site clearance for (re)development.[48] Many of these semi-independent institutes and museums are still really public sector-based, despite increasing privatization of *danwei* (work units). There is some risk of placing professionalism under pressure with added temptation for corruption (stealing from museums, artefacts for sale on the black market, etc.) but privatization could eventually offer an attractive alternative to a career path that rewards merit-based promotions over long service.

In Guangzhou, an understanding of the attitudes towards professional ethics and treatment of CH managers was gained from talking to people working in the Guangzhou Museum and the Guangzhou Museum of Art. These two institutions differed greatly in approach to staff and collection management. The former held staff directly responsible for the safety of the collection and its security. There was a fire in 2003 and the museum staff were penalized. They are unable to go on long holidays in case something goes wrong. The curators are expected to take it in turns to be caretakers at night. Much of this relates to a financial decision not to employ a professional security company, which the Guangzhou Museum of Art did. The official we interviewed at the Guangzhou Museum said that she intended to take her turn to watch that night, which would make for a very long working day. She would be there with a museum caretaker and was worried that they would be no match for very determined thieves or well-organised ones (possibly from overseas).[49] Even though this museum is considered a privatized *danwei*, it still has an in-house party secretary as a representative of the Communist Party overseeing administration.

Other issues for increasing professionalization in Guangzhou include the lack of staff with specialist conservation materials expertise and the difficulty with employing them as consultants. This is recognized as a problem by the Nanyue Kings Tomb Museum that is trying to conserve artefacts for the long term, but not so much by work units that are actively excavating. These specialist skills are not available or easily acquired in the Pearl River Delta. Some are only found in those professionals trained overseas and/or working in Hong Kong (e.g. metal conservation). Guangzhou officials have little opportunity to experience innovations in this area, because there is still little interaction with professionals from outside the PRD or regular use of conservation principles/charters. Even so, ICOM's code of ethics for museum professionals has been filtered down to them by a central authority for museums in Beijing.[50] For officials dealing with historic buildings, the greater use of a set of conservation principles that advocates following a set process in planning (which is also focused on intrinsic values) would strengthen the linkage between planning and the protection of a wider range of heritage assets.[51] It is likely that any charter on the management of intangible heritage that follows international declarations by UNESCO and ICOMOS is not an immediate priority. There is an economic rationalist argument, however, related to tourism, that could be made for developing it specifically for China and the huge impacts domestic tourism is making on this category of heritage asset.

Refinement of inventory practices in line with international development

One of the indicators for increased professionalism involves measuring the amount of progress undertaken in refining some of the activities begun in earlier phases (see Table 1.3, earlier). One such example is the transforming and updating of hard copy for the site registers so that information can be more readily accessed on computer. Computerization in some countries has included a basic transformation to a simple database and then later upgrading it to a Geographical Information Systems relational database for greater efficiency. A certain level of professional expertise is expected in the updating of information and the creation of a database. Box 3.3 outlines how updating existing information on archaeological sites and historic buildings was conducted for Hong Kong and the efforts so far to eventually transfer this information to GIS.

The example in Box 3.3 indicates that, even with the best intentions, some projects related to this sub-indicator have undergone their share of problems, possibly because of the nature of the definition of heritage contained in the Ordinance and the culture of the public service system that administers it. Significantly, it reflects much of the uncertainty of the

Box 3.3
Refining inventories of tangible heritage assets: Hong Kong 1991 onwards

- 1991: AAB review the situation with existing records, particularly the 1982 survey of archaeological sites by retired museum curator, Brian Peacock. Debate whether results should be made public.[52] AAB also reviews the floating cut-off date for the age of historic buildings and archaeological sites considered significant or able to be declared under the Ordinance.
- November 1995: AAB first discuss a territory-wide survey of historic buildings. A report has been commissioned to be produced by Dr Peter Drewet, Member of the British Institute of Field Archaeologists, on how to proceed for archaeological sites.
- Report by Drewet advises on strategy and noted that previous survey by Peacock was saved on computer disks that were not updated and eventually mislaid for several years.
- AAB recommends in June 1996 that the archaeological survey be reduced to eight months to be undertaken by eleven teams, each led by a principal investigator with not less than three years field experience and university training.
- October 1996: AMO advises AAB that team directors do not necessarily need specific university qualifications, just 'local heritage knowledge', and the ability to undertake some photogrammetry for computerization.
- AAB are also advised in October that the historic buildings survey should divide Hong Kong into four areas, and it still needs 'historic criteria'. Work for this survey will also use a new recording form. Team directors should be 'very experienced in conducting researches (sic) or very knowledgeable in local history, local architecture or related fields'. The survey is estimated to take two years and include only buildings built before 1950. Proposal to secure funds from the Hong Kong Jockey Club charitable fund.
- A progress report to AAB in May 1997 noted that the archaeological survey had been underway since September. However, some consultants are still being sought besides Dr Drewet, and Hong Kong and mainland consultants.
- Post-handover in September 1997, around 1,200 buildings documented. Proposal to engage two mainland teams to assist from Tsinghua University in Beijing and Shenzhen. Notes some trouble with villagers (not formally or informally contacted to take part)

- and lack of standardization of terms between teams. Proposal is made to engage a computer consultant for data collected.
- November 1998: AAB memo notes that both surveys should be a starting point for a 'well structured conservation strategy'. However, a second season of archaeological survey appears to have been authorized and funded out of the money set aside for computer consultants. First season found twenty new sites and re-surveyed a hundred sites.
- December 1999: Heritage and Tourism conference paper by AMO staff on the archaeological survey project notes that 207 sites had been confirmed by its completion. There are close to 9,000 historic buildings confirmed in the historic buildings survey (less than one per cent have been fully declared and protected under the Ordinance).
- 2004: PCCW telecommunications company engaged to computerize survey documentation for AMO. As it is constrained by civil service regulations, only HK consultants approved by the government could be engaged, whether they have set up site registers on computer before or not.
- At the time of writing, AMO is still perfecting a GIS database for its inventory of tangible heritage assets. Researchers and others who require site information are still given paper files.

time – when Hong Kong was caught between two masters in the transition from British to Chinese sovereignty. This is evident in the composition of the survey teams, which included British, mainland and Hong Kong professionals in order to cover all contingencies. Problems for the actual computerization and establishment of a best practice GIS database also show strong evidence of local factors (e.g. government guidelines on tendering).

In Macau, after the handover, the Cultural Affairs Bureau re-assessed in 2000 the conservation status of tangible cultural heritage. As part of this initiative, a group of mainland archaeologists were invited to survey areas for new archaeological sites. The emphasis was placed on Chinese sites outside the colonial period and on non-urban areas. The CAB has medium-term and long-term plans to include more investment in the GIS system and in the internet, so that the cultural heritage of Macau will become more widely known throughout the world.[53] Again, this seems to be closely linked with tourism initiatives as has been the case in the past, which is a form of transparency, although it does little to aid awareness amongst the local Chinese population, some of whom do not use computers.

The Cultural Heritage Department of the CAB has carried out surveys of the buildings and sites, setting up computerized files of maps, detailed plans, rigorous drawings of each monument and other documents relating to the conservation projects. All of the twelve items first included in the World Heritage nomination proposal have dedicated information files that are constantly updated and reviewed. In 2005, CAB was encouraged by UNESCO to include more items in the proposal, which may not be quite as well documented but could be covered at a later date if funding is not lacking (see Box 3.2, above, on staff resource allocations).

Recognition of the linkage between urban planning, land use and CHM

Guangzhou and Macau are the best cities in which to see this sub-indicator operating effectively. First, an examination is warranted in how CHM policy is now connected to urban planning policy since the key turning point of the discovery in 1995 of the Nanyue Palace. The palace archaeological site is located in the centre of Guangzhou (see Plate 3.2 and Box 3.4 below).

Plate 3.2 The Nanyue Palace Site excavation in Guangzhou was still in progress when the authors visited it in early 2005. The site is massive and also includes a Qing dynasty shipyard. (Hilary du Cros)

Box 3.4
The Nanyue Palace archaeological site's role in integrating CHM into urban planning in Guangzhou

- A tomb for one of the Nanyue kings had already been discovered in the early 1980s, so local archaeologists knew that the old city was archaeologically sensitive. One Han official had worked out and written down where the palace was 18 years after the palace and city had burned down. Guangzhou archaeologists were aware of such historic details and ordered monitoring of any construction.
- In June 1995 construction workers, watched by archaeologists from one of the public archaeology institutes, drilled holes into the site they had acquired from the government for constructing a long-distance communications building for a China/Hong Kong/Macau joint venture development (Ma and Chan, 2004).[54]
- When the 'Pan Yu' stones were discovered and publicized by the archaeologists, the developers became 'very aggressive'. Guangzhou Cultural Bureau (GCB) was 'so shocked' at what was going on that they went immediately to the Provincial Administration and reported it.
- The GCB and the Mayor Li Ziliu then appealed directly to Beijing, and officials from the State Administration for Cultural Heritage (SACH) arrived to have a look at stone tablets and other remains located in the preliminary excavations.[55]
- In 1996, SACH listed it as being one of 'the ten most important archaeological finds for 1995' for the whole of China.[56]
- In 1998, it was designated as a national-level site, which included later phases of occupation associated with the garden and shipyard (the earlier discovery of the Nanyue Tomb is part of a separate listing).[57]
- It became known as the Museum of the Palace of the Nanyue Kingdom in 1999.
  Part of the site is still under the Telecommunications Bureau's earlier buildings in one section (not demolished yet).
- More money is required to pay compensation to the Telecommunications Bureau when they get around to demolishing the aging 1960s buildings to excavate more of the site.
- Despite the fame it has enjoyed, the Telecommunications Bureau still disagrees with them about whether this is the best use of 'taxpayers' money'.[58]
- However, as a result of the discovery, archaeological assessment has become more commonplace prior to any development in the old city area, with work occurring at a more intensive level than just monitoring.

The palace site required a payment of 500 million yuan from the municipal government as compensation for the developers to give up their project site. The municipal government also paid another 100 million yuan to cover the costs of excavation. In regard to this palace site, the mayor was quoted as saying, 'what Guangzhou lacks is not high-rise buildings, but culture'. This support from the mayor's office assisted the heritage authorities in fighting pro-development government authorities. Officials at the Guangzhou Culture Bureau (GCB) now view the site as one of their best heritage assets, and one which gives them prestige and power within the local administration.[59]

Overall, the GCB defines its role, since the palace discovery, as managerial rather than proactive. For instance, when they get referrals from the municipal planning department they act by seeking advice from experts about the sites and assist in facilitating resolutions to any disputes. Feng Yong Qu from the Guangzhou Municipal Institute of Cultural Relics and Archaeology observed, during interviews, that Guangzhou has 'a fast pace of development, with around 3,000 sites under construction in any one day. Development pressure still dictates the strategy for urban archaeology, although increasingly developers are expected to pay.' The developers have to check for archaeological sensitivity of certain areas in the city with officials. The government has drawn up a plan of 'hot spots' in the city and a government enforcement team is supposed to check construction sites for relics during soil removal.

Much of this work is regarded as rescue archaeology and, as seen by Feng and his colleagues, considered 'passive work' whereas research archaeology that keeps remains *in situ* is seen as 'active work'. He was regretful that he was not asked to do much active work by the authorities.[60] Zhang from the GCB has observed that the 'overall problem for Guangzhou's heritage conservation is that the Central Business District has not moved much in the last 2,000 years'. China's booming economy is pushing up real-estate prices and putting increasing pressure on much of its tangible heritage, such as historic buildings, vernacular architecture and archaeological remains.[61]

Macau's real-estate industry began to boom in the late 1960s. In 1969, thirty-two buildings, totalling 140 storeys and amounting to MOP$4.4 million, were completed. In 1970, fifty-two buildings, totalling 243 storeys and amounting to MOP$7.1 million, were completed. The increase in the monetary value of newly completed floor space between 1969 and 1970 was over 60 per cent.[62]

Macau, however, is the only one of the case study cities to have introduced fiscal incentives for conservation and adaptive reuse. These measures were incorporated within 1984 Decree no. 56/84/M and comprise:

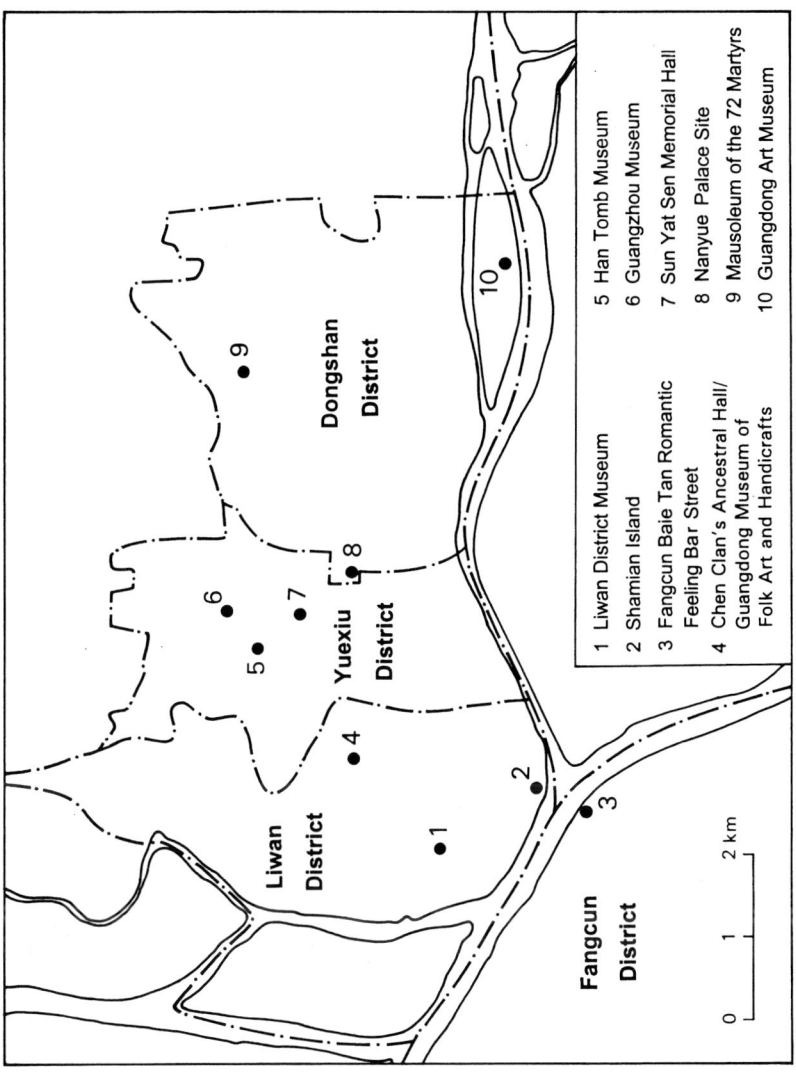

Figure 3.1 The location of places mentioned for Guangzhou.

1 Exemption from urban property tax for those designated buildings that undergo those conservation works that meet approval and which costs more than 50,000 patacas.
2 Reduce taxes paid by industrial or commercial establishments by half if they carry out conservation works that meet approval and which costs more than 50,000 patacas.
3 The sum spent on the conservation and recuperation of classified buildings may be deducted, for a period of ten years, from the complementary tax to be paid by the party who have borne this expense. If complementary taxes do not apply to the party involved, the amount can be deducted from his/her income tax, for a period of five years.
4 Classified buildings are exempt from Conveyance Tax and Succession and Donations Duty.
5 Import of materials and equipment for the conservation of classified buildings is exempt from any taxes.

The process is now administered by the CAB. The parties that are to benefit from the incentives first make an application accompanied by sufficient proof as defined by the Bureau. At their request, the CAB will, within fifteen days, issue a document certifying the state of conservation of the building involved.[63]

In Hong Kong, the linkages between urban planning, environmental impact assessment and CHM are governed more by policy than legislation. From 1999 onwards, the AMO has been under pressure to deal with the growing number of Environment Impact Assessment referrals and assessments. The inclusion of heritage assessment as part of the implementation of the 1997 Environmental Assessment Ordinance was seen as a step forward by many CH professionals.

Prior to the enactment of EIA legislation, the AMO oversaw whatever work was required under a loose system of referrals of planned projects on mainly public land. Some of this work was conducted by consultants with varying degrees of accreditation in their specialist fields. One of the largest of these projects was that for the Hong Kong International Airport in the early 1990s. Even then it was recognised that professional expertise was required in the private sector to undertake the assessment and site-clearance work. The later legislation was formulated by the Environmental Protection Agency after some consultation with the AMO and the AAB in the mid-1990s. Its enactment forced the AMO to update its list of non-statutory graded buildings and address problems that had developed since the early days of the initial legislation with definitions of what might be considered heritage.

Is more integration through implementing recent urban renewal procedures evident?

Meanwhile, heritage conservation advocates in Hong Kong have hoped that the transformation in 2000 of the Land Development Corporation (LDC) into the Urban Renewal Authority (URA) under its own ordinance would mean a new era of integration of CHM within urban planning. The LDC had briefly flirted with adaptive reuse and urban renewal in a few projects, including that of the Western Market building in Sheung Wan. Some heritage professionals interviewed had great hopes of the URA, believing that its establishment might represent a key turning-point in the greater integration of urban planning and CHM. In the six years that it has been operating, the URA has experienced some lessons on a number of heritage and planning issues, not least of which is how to deal with community pressure groups, as will be seen in the next chapter. However, it has been partially hamstrung by a government requirement that it is revenue-generating in its redevelopment efforts.

One final key player in the administration of urban planning that has a bearing on CHM in Hong Kong is the Town Planning Board. It meets more frequently, and has more power than the AAB to influence the conservation of historic buildings. Interviewees note that there have been instances where building projects have come before the TPB for consideration before the AAB is even aware of them. This has serious implications for the long-term planning and the ability of much CHM in Hong Kong to be truly proactive instead of reactive.[64] The TPB has now opened its meetings to the public, which could have some interesting consequences for heritage advocates, although it is yet to allow formal public consultation on its planning applications. From July 2005 onwards, the meeting minutes have appeared on its website (Town Planning Board, 2006). The AAB has also been under pressure by the media to do the same, and to defend or improve the kind of professional expertise it has access to in making its decisions.[65] Macau is slowly implementing a similar program of renewal, but with some of its own unique features to avoid the problems with owner/tenant compensation that Hong Kong has suffered. Whether these will be more successful, however, is difficult to ascertain at this stage. In any event, they cannot be any worse than some of the stories regarding this issue in mainland China that have been published in both mainland and Hong Kong newspapers, where dissatisfaction has been intense.

Implications for understanding the impact of global and local factors

The case study cities are still working their way through the sub-indicators in this phase. Part of the problem may be that they mostly operate independently from the rest of China for the most part – even Guangzhou – and have to rely on local resources. More than this, there is the problem that heritage professionals administer their duties as officials or act as independent private practitioners in urban environments under intense development pressure from the booming economy in each city and are at risk of having decisions and ethics questioned. While CH managers and other professionals are struggling to deal with these pressures, it is difficult for them to stop and evaluate how well they are performing and where further professional training may be useful.

In order to understand the impact of global and local factors on the development of heritage professions in the PRD, it is necessary to explore the availability of local versus overseas professional training as a first step in this section. This is not originally a sub-indicator in the notional model, but should probably become one as a way of understanding how professional expertise in CHM and ethics are shaped in any one place.

Inevitably, the kind of educational backgrounds most current CH managers have will have an impact on their work. For instance, until fairly recently, Hong Kong's secondary school curriculum did not include much discussion on local history and culture (Poon and Wong 2005, 2004), nor did Macau's.[66] It was a problem that various authorities, such as the Lord Wilson Heritage Trust in Hong Kong, have worked hard to change. It would also explain why more specialist heritage courses have not been set up at the various universities. Accordingly, the universities have their own unique priorities for the development of locally focused heritage courses, as a result of their historical and cultural contexts (as discussed earlier). That fact, combined with the social, cultural and historical underpinnings of some of the universities providing most of the local training, has put differing emphases on the importance of local culture and its management for future generations. While the various government administrations are encouraging their employees to develop their professional expertise, there are still limited resources or opportunities to do this locally.

In interviews, CH managers and others were asked about what sets of conservation principles they used and what they thought of CHM as a term. This line of questioning revealed much about their backgrounds and aspirations in terms of engaging with international best practice. Guangzhou and Macau officials had applied the Venice Charter more often than others. However, this may change as the China Principles become more widely known and refined over time. Hong Kong had a slight preference for the

Burra Charter over these other two sets of principles, but many practitioners also expressed a desire for a locally derived charter that recognized local legislation over that of the mainland as a point of reference. Many of those interviewed liked to use the term 'cultural heritage management' to describe what they were involved in, but did not use it commonly, preferring the terms 'cultural relic conservation' (Guangzhou) or 'heritage conservation' (the other cities) instead.

The computerization of heritage asset inventories could be used as an example to understand the influence of local and global factors on refining established tools of heritage management (as per Table 1.3). Macau, with the smallest heritage inventory (in terms of the number of tangible assets) and most IT expertise, was ahead of the other two cities in this regard. Despite a greater overall budget for heritage spending, Hong Kong has had difficulties in systematically dealing with this aspect of heritage management. It is hoped that when it has a system in place, it could move on to making much of its inventory publicly available through online internet access, as is the case in Australia, the United States and Macau. Beijing may be the only city in China closest to having a similar system, but it may be many years before this is seen as a priority anywhere else in the country, given the massive demands placed on government financial resources just to retain and conserve heritage items.

Creating and building linkages between urban planning and CHM in the Pearl River Delta appears to require an advocate actively campaigning for the concept of heritage conservation. In the case of Guangzhou, it was the city's mayor and SACH – a mixture of state and local advocates that raised the awareness of retaining ancient urban archaeological sites. Such sites were eventually viewed by others as giving Guangzhou's continuous history a tangible marker. Even so, the huge financial payout to another government department and to private developers meant that a plan for predicting and identifying areas of archaeological sensitivity was a necessity. Guangzhou is the only city out of the three to have developed such a plan that requires regular pre-development testing and monitoring of construction projects located inside the city's 'hot spots'.

Meanwhile, in Macau, more overt linkages between CHM, tourism development and urban planning have been developed earlier than those evident in Hong Kong. Some anecdotal evidence suggests that not everything appears as it does on the surface. While some Hong Kong authorities sometimes envy the substantial amount of political will supporting pro-heritage conservation in Macau, Macau authorities covet what they perceive as being the broader community support that Hong Kong has received for its efforts. It is likely that both cities are still in a state of flux regarding measures implemented by government authorities towards maintaining such linkages between departments. How these activities are

80 *Hilary du Cros* et al.

going to be undertaken and how the support of the private sector and the rest of the community is being sought will be discussed in the next chapter, in relation to the ongoing debate about the importance of nurturing economic versus social capital.

Notes

1 Notes from a CHM research workshop in Macau, June 2004.
2 Such upheavals in the operation of the older universities on the mainland are not uncommon, although most suffered their greatest disruptions during the Cultural Revolution.
3 Interview with Ho Yin Lee of the Department of Architecture, University of Hong Kong, June 2005.
4 However, she is not directly involved in CHM other than to teach courses in archaeology or analyse plant remains from several major excavations, since she moved to Hong Kong in 2000. She is a specialist in the origins of agriculture in China, completing her doctorate on Chinese agricultural practices at Australian National University in Canberra in the late 1990s. She is one of the few archaeologists in the PRD that has achieved the trifecta of working and studying on the mainland, Hong Kong and overseas.
5 The university was also a participant in an information organization of anthropologists known as the South China Research Circle. It began after the Conference on the Study of Regional Society of Southern China in 1980 in order to promote an interdisciplinary and cross-border approach. It has over the years supported academic activities, and gathering and the exchange of information, particularly as China re-opened to outside influences. One special area of interest has been clan organization in Hong Kong's New Territories, although studies reach from Guangdong down to Vietnam (Cheung, 2004).
6 Cultural tourism is also offered as part of a Master's programme by the School of Hotel and Tourism Management at the Hong Kong Polytechnic University. This course has a stronger marketing focus than the University of Hong Kong's one but does include some CHM concepts.
7 At the time of writing, it is unlikely that the archaeology course will continue to be taught, because of du Cros's relocation to Macau, as the other professionally trained locally based archaeologists are all employed full-time in the private sector as consultants.
8 Observations by Hilary du Cros and information gathered from interview with Tracey Lu, July 2004.
9 A certain amount of paternalism is evident in this statement by Sir Cecil Clementi, Governor of Hong Kong and Chancellor of the University, in his address to the Royal Empire Society in London towards the end of 1935, 'the University of Hong Kong should become during the course of the 20th century a famous seat of Chinese learning, to which men throughout the 18 provinces would look . . . as Englishmen look at Oxford and Cambridge . . . for authoritative guidance in the study of their language, their literature, their history, their archaeology, their folklore, their religious beliefs, and the whole fabric of their civilization' (Clementi in School of Chinese Studies, 2006).
10 The university still lacks a sense of political consciousness as can be seen in the nature of the student societies on campus. Some recent postgraduates seeking to

engage more with post-modernist theories of cultural heritage studies have gone overseas.
11 Public Records Office: AAB files 24 April 1977 and 19 June 1978, respectively.
12 The Centre for Asian Studies is one of the earliest multidisciplinary cultural research centres in Hong Kong and was established in 1967 at the University of Hong Kong. Its latest research includes social and oral history projects about the development of Hong Kong (Centre for Asian Studies, 2004). Scholars from the University of Macau and the Inter-University of Macau have also undertaken some research (e.g. Zheng, 1996; Clayton, 2003).
13 Public Records Office: AAB files 19 January 1973.
14 Interview with David Lung, April 2004.
15 Other relevant training for CHM has been provided by the Centre for Urban Planning and Environmental Management (CUPEM) at the University of Hong Kong, which was established in 1980. It has produced graduates with interest in stakeholder consultation as part of their community planning courses. They have found employment in public and private sectors and have become involved in advocacy work with non-governmental organizations concerned with heritage, such as the Conservancy Association.
16 Interview with Joseph Ting, July 2004.
17 Four-year programmes have been proposed for Hong Kong universities, also starting 2007.
18 A Master's programme in Public History was set up in late 2005 by the Inter-University of Macau that includes some heritage-related subjects. The Inter-University is a privately funded university that charges student fees.
19 This might be the result of a pre-handover increase in cross-border cultural exchanges, such as conferences and exhibitions held in the previous year (see *Macao Daily*, 30 July, 14 September, 26 November, 17 December, 1998).
20 The Institute For Tourism Studies in Macao, with the support of the European Union, has also established the Macao–Europe Centre for Advanced Tourism Studies (M–ECATS) in May 1999. This centre monitors trends in tourism and hospitality, and designs courses answering to the changing needs of the industry. The centre offers courses in 'Sustainable Tourism Planning and Development' and 'Heritage Tourism'. There is also a Higher Diploma in Cultural Tourism programme, which has the aim of 'producing diploma graduates who are culturally aware and equipped with skills to work in areas such as festivals and events, travel and tour agencies, guiding, museums, cultural heritage ... in addition to other cultural tourism initiatives' (IEEM brochure, 2005). Cultural tourism is only just beginning to be taught at the university level in Hong Kong and Macau.
21 Feng Yongqu, editor, Special Issue Number 3 of the Guangzhou Research Institute on Heritage and Archeology: A Collection of Works on Fifty Years of Archeological Work in Guangzhou (Guangzhou shi wenwukaoguyanjiusuo zhuankan zhi san: Guangzhou wenwu kaoguji – Guangzhou kaogu wushinian wenxuan), Guangzhou Publishing House (Guangzhou chubanshe), n.d.
22 It was one of the courses offered by Hong Kong museums to build linkages with the mainland.
23 Interview with Stephan Chan, January 2006.
24 Some museums as well as institutes, which are still all public-sector institutions, are responsible for archaeological excavations. Museums are the repositories for material afterwards, so this is logical.
25 Interview with Chen Ying, Vice-Curator of the Guangzhou Museum of Art, 20 January 2005.

26 Sullivan (2001) notes that Chinese officials took a healthy interest in the private heritage industry in Australia when they visited. They seemed 'impressed by the quality and dedication of people working in the industry [and] the wide use of the Burra Charter by private practitioners, their adherence to it in debating heritage issues with their clients, and the mutual support provided by Australia ICOMOS' (Sullivan, 2001: 17). Instituting the China Principles and encouraging their adoption widely by all levels of the administration may be the first step in instituting a private industry in China, as the first practitioners of it will inevitably come from its ranks.
27 Illustrated Chronicle of Macao (Aomen quan jili), Shanghai People's Publishing House (Shanghai renmin chubanshe), 1999: 286.
28 Illustrated Chronicle of Macao (Aomen quan jili), Shanghai People's Publishing House (Shanghai renmin chubanshe), 1999: 293.
29 Interview with Stephan Chan, February 2006.
30 Macao's cultural heritage is currently protected by the two main protective measures of: 'The Basic Law of the Macao Special Administrative Region of the People's Republic of China', Decree Law no. 56/84/M and Decree no. 83/92/M relating to the 'Defence of the Architectural, Environmental and Cultural Heritage', and Decree no. 7/91/M relating to 'General Regulations for Urban Construction'.
31 The background to this request was that by 1987, the AMO comprised nine posts and was looking for this upgrade and another 15 positions to deal with an increasing workload, much of which was coming from site clearance and development-approval work (AMO report March 1988). During this period and up until 1989, the AMO was in constant conflict with certain archaeologists in the community, their pressure groups and the Antiquities Advisory Board for change (Memo by Alex Yip, Executive Secretary after Solomon Bard).
32 AMO report to the Department Establishment Committee, Municipal Services, March 1988.
33 AAB and AMO records between 1987 and 1998.
34 AMO report on heritage management to AAB March 1991.
35 Needless to say, the principles used were those of the Burra Charter.
36 Interview conducted at Guangzhou Cultural Bureau, December 2004 of a panel of senior officials from the Bureau, local museums and the Guangzhou Cultural Heritage and Archaeology Research Centre.
37 Interview with David Lung, 12 April 2004.
38 This comment indicates that a regional version of the Venice Charter might ultimately be more popular than the Venice Charter, in that Chinese CH managers may feel a greater sense of ownership and local applicability.
39 Hilary du Cros's observations and interviews with David Lung and Pamela Rumball Rogers, 12 April and 18 May 2004, respectively.
40 Interview with David Lung, 12 April 2004 and 16 March, 2005.
41 ICAC website Press Release 25 April 2002 – accessed 26 April 2002, http://file:// C:\WINDOWS\TEMP\triLDLJF.htm; *South China Morning Post*, 26 April 2002, Hong Kong.
42 Ng has a doctorate in History from the Chinese University of Hong Kong and was transferred to the AMO from the Museum of History.
43 Interview with Pamela Rumball Rogers, 18 May 2004.
44 Interview with David Lung, 12 April 2004.
45 See 'Decades for Police HQ's Greenery to Recover', City Section 1, *SCMP*, 3 January 2005.

46 Interview with Louis Ng, 25 May 2004.
47 At the time of writing the Institute For Tourism Studies (IFT) has just been directed by the Minister for Social and Cultural Affairs to investigate the significance and impacts of a redevelopment proposal for a Western-style building. IFT was advised to hire consultants with advice from UNESCO to undertake what is basically a study of local heritage significance and that the consultants need to come from outside of Macau. The CAB has not been given a major role in monitoring the study for no stated reason, but will provide some informal advice. It is likely that any private practice in Macau is still a long way off, should government clients continue to follow this kind of strategy, possibly because they consider Macau a very 'closed' community.
48 Interviews conducted with heritage authorities in Guangzhou, 2004–2005 and those interviewed for other projects (see du Cros, 2006).
49 Interview with Guangzhou officials on 20 January 2005. The museum cannot afford to insure collection pieces and staff have gone to jail if any are stolen possibly because more senior officials cannot discount the possibility of it being an 'inside job'. Pay scales for staff are lower than those for officials still in fully publicly funded positions and they often have to find their own funding. No doubt all this can add to temptation to steal for some less professional staff.
50 Interview with Chen Ying, Vice-Curator, Guangzhou Museum of Art, 20 January 2005.
51 Although it was not openly stated in the interviews, it is likely that some officials in Guangzhou who were interviewed do not have formal heritage skills and are more likely to have only had some brief training in archaeology or general heritage administration. Exceptions to this might include museum curators who require history, fine arts and other skills in order to mount exhibitions.
52 This is relevant to the next chapter's discussion of stakeholders and inclusiveness. It is interesting that at no time did the AAB think of involving the community directly in the project in any way.
53 Cultural Affairs Bureau, World Heritage Nomination Document, 2003.
54 Information also gathered from an interview with Guangzhou Cultural Bureau officials on 7 December 2004.
55 Ibid.
56 Retired archaeologist Mai Ying Hao, Honorary Director, Guangzhou Museum remembers that after the SACH visit in 1995, the mayor received more respect from gainsayers about his view on heritage conservation – particularly as they compared it favourably with stone architectural ruins in Ancient Rome, stating that it was the first of its kind found in China.
57 Criteria for this include its age, link to Linguan civilization and extensive nature (they are still looking for more of it). The municipal government thinks it is significant as it reflects an early start to the economic history of the region.
58 Interview with Mai on 8 December 2004.
59 Ibid.
60 Interview with Feng on 7 December 2004.
61 Interview with J.J. Zhang on 7 December 2004. Zhang had only just been transferred into the post of Assistant Director at the Guangzhou Cultural Bureau, but had been involved in other aspects of heritage management, including planning for the Historic and Culturally Famous Cities Bureau in Guangzhou.
62 Illustrated Chronicle of Macao (Aomen quan jili), Shanghai People's Publishing House (Shanghai renmin chubanshe), 1999: 130.

63 However, some building owners are still not interested. A Portuguese-style house behind the Portuguese Military School has been deliberately neglected by its owner rather than renovated in the hope that the CAB will allow its removal. In May 2006, its condition had become so parlous that the government was forced to put up emergency scaffolding on the street-facing façade as a safety measure, and reroute traffic after a series of thunderstorms were causing its masonry to crumble.

64 When the author du Cros first visited the AMO on arriving in 1999, the people she spoke to all seemed to be buried under paperwork for the EIA process, and reacting to heritage site preservation issues that flared up like 'bushfires' rather than trying to anticipate where problems might occur. Lack of computerization of resources and other problems with the system made this reaction less efficient than expected, given the number of staff and number of assets being managed.

65 At the time of writing, the decision to retain or demolish the Central Market on Hong Kong Island had just been put before the AAB and the *SCMP* noted that it made the decision 'behind closed doors' and attacked it for this lack of transparency yet again (*SCMP*, 18 May 2006).

66 Stephen Chan, interviewed in February 2006.

4 Economic growth and cultural identity

Hilary du Cros, Yok-shiu F. Lee, David Lung and Lynne DiStefano

The development of more inclusive management practices is the key to initiating a progressive change to the review phase, the last segment of the notional CHM framework outlined in Chapter 1. In the West, recognition of the role of many different sectors in CHM was brought overtly and covertly to the attention of the heritage profession and bureaucratic circles by the media and community advocacy in a lot of cases. Meanwhile, successful cases of stakeholder consultation and involvement in CHM are characterized by an emphasis on transparency and the use of a carefully planned process for issue resolution. This section will examine if there are, on the part of the case study cities, similar or different issues and strategies arising in relation to key debates on heritage management and site projects to ascertain the degree of global and local influences on their development.

Emergence of a wide array of stakeholders

A wide range of stakeholders has emerged in recent years in each of the case study cities in the Pearl River Delta. Hong Kong has encountered some vociferous stakeholders immediately after its handover and Guangzhou may have only just begun to deal with such an issue now (more over land compensation matters than actual heritage concerns). However, the types of stakeholders whom CHM authorities may have to listen to, regarding heritage management decisions for Southern China, now include:

- indigenous organizations (clan- or community-based)
- heritage and conservation non-governmental organizations
- individual heritage professionals (academics and consultants)
- schools and youth groups
- private property owners, developers and landlords
- tourism marketing boards, tourism operators and service providers
- religious authorities that manage temples and other places of worship
- small business owners
- private owners of temples (Macau only)

86 *Hilary du Cros* et al.

- building occupants and tenants
- government departments and related bodies (for planning, urban renewal, tourism, transport, environmental management, property management, public works, lands, country parks, communications and services, education, etc.).

A general model of stakeholder relationships found in democratic, market-based cities (du Cros *et al.*, 2005) is presented below as a starting point:

1 The public sector, which initiates and administers laws, policies, principles and guidelines for the conservation and use of heritage assets; steers the strategic development of tourism, inventories and circulates knowledge and information pertaining to the assets; sets conservation priorities; formulates conservation education programmes; assesses archaeological potential; facilitates conservation and heritage development projects and provides incentives for adaptive reuse of buildings and the transfer of development rights.
2 The private sector, which can identify the tourism market potential of certain sites; provides entrepreneurship and capital for the retention and conservation of assets (including those undergoing refurbishment for adaptive reuse), gentrifies some urban areas, builds tourism attractions and may make philanthropic donations.
3 Non-governmental organizations (NGOs) and intergovernmental organizations (such as UNESCO), which can represent a wide range of interests; can facilitate and fund conservation works; be a vocal advocate for retention of assets; provides mechanisms where heritage assets can be purchased by private individuals (subject to rules that are consistent with sustainable use) and increases awareness through education and training programmes.
4 The community, which if permitted to represent its own interests, has the potential to promote greater equity in the distribution of benefits realized from development of heritage assets.

The affiliation of non-governmental organizations with government departments or other bodies presents a strange history in the Pearl River Delta. mainland China has been careful in establishing a control system for many of these organizations that can be classified into two main types: independent NGOs (that have been set up separately but are affiliated with a government partner) and government-organized non-governmental organizations (GONGOs) where the government sets up these bodies, and most members are current or retired officials.

China ICOMOS is a classic example of a GONGO. The establishment of a sub-chapter combining Hong Kong and Macau has been fraught with difficulties, because there are differences in style and membership between that of the SARs and mainland China. However, for Guangzhou, as with the rest of the mainland, there is a strictly designed system still in place for registering such organizations. Most heritage NGOs that the authors heard about in Guangzhou appeared to be concerned about intangible heritage, such as the preservation of Cantonese opera or puppet performances. Even these groups have a limited influence on CHM. Many retired officials have tried to assist tradition bearers in raising their profile with government agencies. They have also assisted in fundraising activities. One example is the Chinese Puppet Group that had found a home in one of the Xiguan houses in the Liwan district, close to the tourist precinct of 'cuisine and antiques streets'.[1]

In Hong Kong, the main advocacy organizations are often required to register with representatives of functional constituencies in order to have their views heard before the Legislative Council (Legco). They can also use councillors to present bills to change laws that affect heritage assets or bring issues to the government's notice. So far little of this has been successful in relation to heritage conservation. The Antiquities Advisory Board (AAB) is the other body that should embrace heritage conservation advocacy as part of its role. However, it has been dogged from its inception with a position in the system that allows it little influence on government policy. On the other hand, its meetings remain closed to the public and it rarely reports on its activities publicly, unless it is asked by the media to respond to a site-specific preservation controversy. In 1995, a motion was put forward by several members of the AAB to open its meetings to the public. This was defeated, however, because of the fear that only the more recalcitrant members of the public would attend and these were people who had hotly criticized its past decisions in the media.

Stakeholder consultation: local conventions versus international best practices

International best practice principles enshrined in many recent codes and charters are used by most countries to guide and support local policies and regulations that guide local practice. Often inclusiveness and self-determination principles drawn from such an international source have to be re-interpreted in some way or adapted to local conditions to be applied widely (e.g. the China Principles). Arguments have also been made that the involvement of non-professionals requires some education programmes to either raise public awareness or allow conservation principles to be adopted at all. In this regard, Hong Kong, of the three case study cities, was the first to start education campaigns and, given recent debates reported in the media, it appears that this has made a discernable impact. In particular, the community's awareness of heritage in Hong Kong, prior to the handover in 1997, had received a huge boost from the government media broadcaster Radio Television Hong Kong (RTHK) and the Lord Wilson Heritage Trust.

From 1982, RTHK had been working at raising community awareness about Hong Kong's history and heritage. Their first specialized effort was the TV series *Archaeology and Antiquities*. It was well-received, despite being what programmers termed a 'minority-demand' programme in a fringe timeslot. The series was repeated several times before a new one was completed in 1984. Koo Kai-fai, the Senior Executive Producer for the station, noted that the year 1984, with the signing of the Sino-British Joint Declaration live on TV, was a turning point in the local audience's appreciation of local history. The government also backed this up with a campaign to 'Get to know the place you live' to breed a sense of belonging in Hong Kong's still predominantly migrant population. In the post-Tiananmen Square era, a wave of out-migration from the colony spurred more government education programmes via the media, including one titled *Hong Kong Yesterday, Today and Tomorrow* (Koo, 2004).

In 1995, the Lord Wilson Heritage Trust (LWHT), with support from the AMO, sponsored RTHK to produce a thirteen-episode series entitled *This Home of Ours*. With a strong heritage-conservation message, this series gave an overview of archaeology and conservation works on historic buildings. It also encouraged the public to visit heritage assets after watching the programme. Videotapes of the programme were distributed to the schools. RTHK and the Department of Education have since produced heritage-related programmes specifically for children and schools. RTHK was also involved in other transition-era projects, such as the Heritage Year (Koo, 2004).

Transition-era projects and stakeholder involvement

During the transition to Chinese sovereignty, the Macau government was sometimes reluctant to organize public consultations because it did not want to deal with the *kai fong*, which are neighbourhood-based organizations. The government's reluctance may stem from the fact that these organizations have been criticized for trying to exercise too much influence and drown out other stakeholders. Some government officials are still critical of the motives of the *kai fong*, believing that they are only active for political gains.[2] However, the *kai fong's* and the general community's awareness about the benefits of heritage conservation changed with the pedestrianization of Leal Senado Square in 1986 and the subsequent increase in sightseeing tourists in recent years. The economic benefits emanating from heritage attractions have changed people's attitudes towards conservation. More support has come from these stakeholders after the 2003 induction of the Free Independent Travellers (FIT) scheme (which allows Chinese mainlanders to visit on individual visas) as people realized that conservation could be profitable. The rent and property values around the Square have increased, and this has impressed some of Macau's more materially minded stakeholders, who have been cashing in on the gentrification of this area.[3] Now the *kai fong* would like to see the benefits spread more equitably to other parts of Macau, and are keen to see that other heritage assets be also publicly recognized as having tourism potential (du Cros and Kong, 2006).

Heritage tourism was helped by government policy, particularly that of actively 'asserting an identity', which was a central theme of the Portuguese government's cultural policy in the transition era. A paper given by CH managers from the then Cultural Institute described Macau as a 'tiny territory lying in the wide region of South East Asia, [so] the asserting of its identity has to be assumed with even more care, not only because of this particular period of transition, but also because it always has been a place of transit for the most of its population' (Durão et al., 2004: 92). Although this concern appears to be similar to that shown by the Hong Kong government regarding cultural identity, the way Macau's cultural policy was tied to heritage conservation efforts started much earlier and was given a higher priority. In the transition period, the Macau government spent HK$48 million on conservation activities, with most of this money used on building conservation projects in 1995 and 1996. The works were not as expensive to fund as those carried out in Hong Kong, however, and the Macau government was able to fund projects to assist the restoration of privately owned buildings as well as public ones. By 1997, they had restored sixty private buildings and thirteen Chinese temples, and provided funding for other work on several churches. The government had also occupied and upgraded the interiors of historic buildings for its own offices (not just CAB, but other departments as well) – a practice not yet common in Hong Kong. Although CH managers see this as a compromise in that many of the old interiors have been gutted and replaced by modern office facilities, it is one they were willing to make to keep the exteriors intact for greater visual appeal because, as they conceded, 'buildings must adapt to new realities' (Durão et al., 2004).

Meanwhile, heritage authorities in Hong Kong were taking a different approach during the transition period. They were trying to raise local awareness of the value of heritage assets in relation to strengthening Hong Kong's cultural identity prior to the 1997 handover by instigating heritage education and publicity projects. Key amongst these was Heritage Year 1996–97, which was intended to help mark the twentieth anniversary of the full enactment of the Antiquities and Monuments

Ordinance in 1976. This was carried out with a generous budget of HK$7.68 million from the Lord Wilson Heritage Trust and implemented by the AMO with advice from the AAB. Other sponsorship was also sought by a fundraising taskforce, and the Hong Kong Tourism Association[4] also played a role in coordinating some activities. The idea grew from the successful undertaking of a School Heritage Festival by the LWHT, the Department of Education and the AMO in 1996. It aimed to publicize conservation activities amongst schools by hosting a drawing competition, exhibitions, heritage tours, workshops and public lectures by AMO staff.

The Heritage Year was carried out on a larger scale with the assistance of five individual taskforces. A prelude to the activities occurred at the Chinese New Year in the form of an entry in the annual parade in Central of a 'heritage theme bus accompanied by a 150-foot long golden dragon manned by clan members of six villages in Wang Chau, Yuen Long' (Chiu, 2004: 58). The opening ceremony featured the Chief Secretary for Administration, Anson Chan, and her appearance indicated that the support for the initiative was coming from the highest levels in the civil service.

The popularity of the events led one commentator to remark that although he expected such events to be non-profit making, their popularity in this case had allowed the ticket-selling events to break even. Unlike the Hong Kong museums that have been undertaking little in the way of merchandising their permanent exhibitions,[5] the Heritage Year organizers produced a plethora of merchandise and they sold reasonable well. Exhibitions for the Heritage Year continued to be displayed at the AMO's offices in Nathan Road for almost twelve months after the event.[6] This exhibition also included archaeological artefacts from the Ma Wan excavation, with a sequence dating back nearly 6,000 years to the Middle Neolithic. It was promoted as being a highly significant discovery because it showed that Hong Kong had 'a profound tie with the mainland' early on; it was a 'successful joint excavation with the mainland archaeologists;' the 'mainland experts recognized Hong Kong's achievement'; and as part of Heritage Year it 'heightened public awareness of local history' (AMO, 1997). The whole tenor of the interpretation struck one of the authors as being very much caught up in a kind of 'handover fever'.

Overall, the impact of Heritage Year on stakeholders is difficult to measure. It is likely that it has helped raise the profile of CHM and that of agencies associated with it among other parts of the government and the greater community. It also provided an opportunity for AAB members to travel to Beijing to meet their new masters and ascertain their attitude to CHM administration in Hong Kong. It was a pivotal trip for the AAB members who took part. Beijing expressed concerns about the lack of a strong movable cultural property protection in Hong Kong and was not so much concerned about other issues. Some CH professionals had been worried that SACH would want to see less emphasis placed on the preservation of important colonial sites and even possibly the removal of symbolic ones, such as Government House. Instead, SACH's attitude toward the city's heritage assets was that 'Hong Kong should preserve its own integrity'.[7]

Guangzhou is still part of a centrally planned system of CHM with SACH at the top trying to filter down various initiatives to the local levels of management. As China makes the transition to a socialist-style market economy, a cultural identity is emerging with a distinctly Han Chinese Confucian flavour. The country has been subject to various national heritage education projects, with the objective of forging social unity foremost in mind, and it utilizes heritage assets as an important tool. In the 1990s, China's cultural policy strongly emphasized the use of heritage as a way of generating national pride in Chinese achievements, thus ensuring social cohesion (Sofield and Li, 1998). SACH has promoted, through various education programmes, the importance of heritage preservation as supported by the 1982 National Cultural Relics Protection Act (amended 2003). The definitions of heritage outlined in the law are still used as the basis of all programmes that aim to 'raise common understanding among the public of the importance of the protection of cultural heritage in order to have more exemplary deeds of protection of cultural heritage'. Even so, there have been problems protecting movable cultural heritage. SACH acknowledges that these problems include 'stealing from ancient tombs and museum collections, and smuggling of cultural relics' (Hou, 2004: 166).

Guangzhou's heritage authorities have translated this directive into changing attitudes to heritage conservation amongst the community in their own way. In September 1996, construction work revealed twenty-three tombs from the Han to Qing dynasties, located at Hengzhigang on the northern outskirts of the city. Archaeologists who arrived from the local institute to salvage the sites found that they had already been extensively looted.[8] The situation was publicized in order to provide a lesson to the public about how destructive this activity can be and what a great loss it is for present and future generations. This incident was reinforced in the public's mind when compared with remains, such as those dated from the Nanyue period, that are well preserved. The programmes have concentrated on bringing the issue down to the local level, as being one of city civic pride, and drawing the public's attention to the laws that protect heritage assets (Huang, 2004). However, campaigns of this kind are not always effective with some elements of the community, who have not benefited as much as they would like from the region's economic boom.

At the macro-level: post-colonial cultural and CHM policies

Of the three case study cities, Macau is the only one that has developed a cultural policy with a statutory underpinning. Of course, cultural policies containing references to cultural heritage do not necessarily have to have a statutory basis to be successful or widely endorsed by all stakeholders. Macau's cultural policy is contained within the 1989 Decree no. 31/89/M. It recognizes that increased collaboration among government departments is needed for the execution of Macau's cultural policy. The decree provided for the Committee for Culture to be established, stipulating that the membership would comprise the Secretaries of most of the Government's bureaus, together with representatives from the major culture/art groups. The Committee was given the right to advise on the planning/research/categorization of Macau's natural and cultural heritage as well as the physical boundaries of conservation zones.

The first indication after the handover in Hong Kong that macro-level policy was being considered for heritage came in the 1998 policy speech given by its first Chief Executive Tung Chee-hwa. In this speech, he stated:

> To foster a sense of belonging and identity, we need to promote our heritage, which is a valuable cultural legacy. This involves the protection of historic buildings and archaeological sites, of which some are more than 6,000 years old. . . . We need also to look at ways for better presenting to the world our distinctive heritage.[9]

This policy speech gave tourism stakeholders the invitation to promote tourism by using Hong Kong's heritage assets. A 'heritage tourism taskforce' was established in early 1999 by the Hong Kong Tourism Association to facilitate this task (du Cros, 2000). However, the supply side of the equation which requires adequate commodification of appropriate heritage assets as tourist attractions (including the interpretation of heritage values) was not clearly recognized by the authorities as a task that requires special CHM input (McKercher, Ho and du Cros, 2004).

As the issue of post-handover cultural identity and the community's view of it assumed greater importance in the late 1990s, the Hong Kong government then tried to establish a cultural policy to respond to these concerns. Similar to Macau, the transient nature of the city's population – which contains many new immigrants – has always had a role in influencing how Hong Kongers view their city and its heritage. The government realized that heritage assets could assist in providing a greater sense of attachment to the city as 'home' for all residents, not just a place to live and work. However, the government also recognized that there was still an opportunity for heritage to become a revenue-generating medium, through tourism. A special group, the Culture and Heritage Commission, was thus established in 2000 with the mission to enhance the quality of life of Hong Kong people; to foster a sense of belonging and establish a cultural identity amongst the public; and to develop Hong Kong into a centre of international cultural exchange through activities such as tourism (Culture and Heritage Commission, 2002).

The Commission immediately produced a consultation paper on promoting cultural development in Hong Kong that received a favourable reception from the public. Some submissions from the community on the paper revealed a 'longing for a bright future in the development of culture in Hong Kong' (Home Affairs Bureau, 2001). The use of the word 'longing' could also be taken to refer to those submissions that revealed a deep frustration with Hong Kong's poor record on heritage protection and the promotion of locally based arts. However, the Commission was wound up in 2003 after producing only one more position paper that reprised public sentiments, such as 'West Kowloon for the people of Hong Kong, not only for tourists' and 'HK people's cultural identity should start from local culture'.[10] The tension about whether heritage was being managed principally to show off to outsiders, or whether it should be managed primarily for local consumption, began to emerge more clearly than it ever had before amongst heritage stakeholders.

Critics felt that the crux of the position papers had been ignored by the government, despite being based on two rounds of comprehensive public consultation on cultural policy for Hong Kong. Their main concern continues to be that decisions are being made daily by government regarding the arts and cultural heritage without any cultural blueprint as a background for policy and strategy that is endorsed by the community. Other authorities considered the Commission a 'toothless tiger' that had little chance of implementing change within the government towards better heritage protection.[11] The public have also expressed frustrations, primarily through the media, at the government's current approach toward cultural heritage. It seems to favour heritage development projects that are likely to bring in some financial reward for the government or landlords/developers.[12] One critic has campaigned for greater community involvement, and has recommended a tripartite committee comprising the public, private and community sectors to oversee cultural heritage projects, pointing out that a culture policy could act like 'glue to hold together all the disparate parts for a better civil society'.[13]

Planning processes, policy and stakeholders

It is a curious fact that many current projects for arts/heritage development in Hong Kong are not managed by the Home Affairs Bureau (HAB), despite the fact that it was given the responsibility under legislation to manage cultural heritage in Hong Kong. For instance, West Kowloon is being managed by the Housing, Planning and Lands Bureau, and the Tourism Commission is facilitating the prime heritage development projects of the former Marine Police Headquarters Compound in Tsim Sha Tsui and the Central Police Station Compound. Day-to-day planning decisions are now being made about heritage assets that should, but in reality do not, relate to an overall cultural policy. Most of these decisions are made by the Town Planning Board with only minimal reference to the AAB and the Education and Manpower Bureau, although they occasionally speak out.[14]

Economics plays the greatest role in the way the Hong Kong government deals with heritage stakeholders on all levels. It is likely that this situation will not change because of the way that the government's land economic policy has structured Hong Kong as a low-level income tax haven to encourage high consumer spending and business investment. But salary tax is still gathered, and there has been talk of a Goods and Services Tax to broaden the tax base. The government raises tax on land by having a monopoly on supply, and planning can often occur as an offshoot of this mechanism (Lai, 1997). The government has used its control over the release of land for sale to developers over the years to artificially force up land prices, as the developers are required to pay the government a specific premium or land tax depending on the intended use. Notably, land likely to be developed for commercial purposes or expensive housing has the highest land premiums attached to its sale. Much of this land is located in urban areas, specifically on Hong Kong Island, where the least amount of tangible heritage has survived in urban areas in comparison with the rest of the SAR.

The land premiums collected through public land auctions provide the government with most of its revenue. In the 1980s and early 1990s, this revenue was increased dramatically as a consequence of low interest rates, which led to high inflation rates and fuelled land speculation activities, resulting in high prices paid to government by developers at auctions. Even so, in November 2002, the government froze public land sales for 13 months, and this helped push premiums up even further when small sites close to the CBD came up for sale at the end of this period (Lai, 1997; Lung 1999; *SCMP*, 9 March 2004).

In addition, the Urban Renewal Authority (URA) plays an important role in making residential land available for mixed or solely commercial development and sale. Much of these activities occur through the demolition of older building stock slated for 'renewal'. It is therefore not surprising that the process of reviewing heritage-protection measures that might affect this system of urban redevelopment would be accorded a low priority in certain quarters of the government, unless the tax base is

Economic growth and cultural identity 95

broadened.[15] Moreover, given that the URA is also supposed to derive much of its income directly from such redevelopment projects and sales, critics thus argue that this provision would force the body to compromise its claims regarding heritage preservation.

Stakeholder concerns raised in the consultation process for the Culture and Heritage Commission did have one consequence for CHM that could eventually lead to an updating of the legislation. After the Commission folded, HAB continued the process of developing a policy for the built environment (but so far has ignored any overarching cultural policy within which the former might fit). It is possible that this has been spurred by the public's response to the Commission's previous enquiries and a report by Civic Exchange, a non-profit think tank that recommended that the whole system needs an extensive overhaul (Chu and Ubergang, 2002). HAB was aware at the time that the 1976 Ordinance needed reviewing, and had begun this process in 2001 by establishing a special policy review unit by seconding staff from the AMO and other agencies to undertake an in-house appraisal of its problems. However, the first opportunity for public consultation on these issues did not arrive until the publication and release of the Built Environment Conservation Policy Review in early 2004.

Although the Built Environment Conservation Policy Review could be considered an instance of public consultation to engage CH stakeholders (see Box 4.1), it does not constitute an effort that will push Hong Kong into the next phase of 'Review' according to the notional model in Chapter 1. This is because it still does not seriously deal with the basic problems that are inherent in its initial legislation, especially in light of economic pressures described above. Hong Kong is a city that is unique amongst its international/regional counterparts in having only one piece of legislation to protect heritage assets – one that no stakeholders or any other pressures have yet succeeded in having adequately amended, integrated or replaced, after thirty years.

Specific attempts to amend the 1976 Ordinance that would broaden its heritage definitions, or allow group listings or restructure and replace or upgrade AMO/AAB are still urgently needed, if the HAB is serious about conducting a real review and overhaul of heritage management in Hong Kong. Meanwhile, after at least six years of public consultation, concerned authorities have commented that 'Rome still burns'.

At micro-level: areas of conflict identified, then more attention to community interests

Hong Kong is a protracted example of this sub-indicator in that ever since the demolition of key historic buildings in the 1970s and 1980s, there have

> **Box 4.1**
> **Policy review stage 1: example of stakeholder consultation on CHM policy (Hong Kong)**
>
> A brief bilingual consultation document about the 'Built Environment Conservation Policy Review' was made available to the public in February 2004 and enjoined them to respond to its key issues within three months. At the time it was issued, there was no mention of a second stage for consultation. Nor was there information submitted in it about the length and nature of the process at this point. After the submission date had closed, the HAB noted that the results would be publicized. However, when these results were made available, suddenly a second stage of consultation was proposed (possibly in response to submissions that critiqued the vagueness of the initial effort). At the time of writing it still has not been carried out.
>
> Three basic questions were broached: What should we conserve? How do we conserve? How much and who should pay?
>
> The summary of responses to the first question showed that respondents have moved beyond official definitions of heritage under the Ordinance and wanted these broadened to include intangible aspects, group listings and recognition of social significance of heritage assets. Submissions regarding the second question showed that there was considerable division amongst stakeholders regarding the amount of intervention they expected from government, particularly in relation to controls on private property owners' rights and redevelopment. Several options were proposed for restructuring AMO/AAB into something new and more efficient, but they all pointed to a 'single authority [that] may remain with the Home Affairs Bureau, or vested in another bureau if deemed more appropriate or be an independent entity with appropriate statutory power'.
>
> Answers to the last question were also very telling of local conditions in Hong Kong. Most stakeholders do not realistically expect that the government can bear the sole cost of heritage conservation in the way that the 1976 Ordinance intended. The HAB reported that 'most respondents opined that since heritage conservation is for the good of the community and future generations, the whole community should contribute and bear the cost collectively' (HAB, 9 November 2004).[16]

been heritage advocates trying to retain historic buildings in the public interest. In Macau and Guangzhou, there was really little interest in heritage amongst non-government stakeholders at this time. Even in Hong Kong, publicly and privately owned buildings have suffered from the prevailing community view that older building stock should not impede progress in prime locations or that 'skyscrapers that symbolize modernity [should replace] antiquated tenements or *tong lau* [which are] an eyesore for many' (*SCMP*, 30 March 2004).

Over the years, the AMO concentrated its efforts in the rural parts of the New Territories where development pressure has been less intense. Again, it still had to deal with private property owners and indigenous villagers and convince them that heritage conservation was not just in their interest, but also for the good of the whole community.[17] The AMO decided to set up a series of heritage trails in 1991 with the Ping Shan, Yuen Long as the pilot study (see Box 4.2). The Ping Shan area was selected by the AMO

Box 4.2
AMO learns about stakeholder consultation the hard way: the Ping Shan heritage trail

In 1991, the AMO organized a working group to plan the trail, comprised of relevant government organizations, including those for the district, tourism, transport and planning.[19] It, however, did not include a representative from the Tang clan, the local indigenous landholders. The group probably did not think that this was unusual at the time as many government projects were carried out in this way. Initially, the villagers welcomed the trail and assisted with works to set up signage and undertake the opening ceremony.

Once the trail was opened in 1993, the Tang clan began noticing visitor impacts. The trail had no visitor management plan with actions to mitigate social and physical impacts of an increase in visitation on the community and its heritage assets. Added to this was the revival of a historic resentment against the colonial administration that had never really disappeared since the Tangs were defeated in battle in April 1899 after the British accession of the New Territories.[20] The colonial administration had established a police station soon afterwards on the hill above Ping Shan's ancestral hall. This act was believed to have disturbed the area's *Feng Shui*, a Chinese traditional system of understanding cultural landscapes and settings. Any bad luck from this point on was attributed to the presence of the station (Cheung, 1999).

> Sidney Cheung (1999), a local anthropologist based at the Chinese University of Hong Kong, identified four groups of stakeholders in the dispute: AMO/AAB, the Hong Kong Tourism Association (now Board), domestic tour organizers and the Tang clan. As the transition period to the handover unfolded, the Tang's aggravation at government interference rose. Just before it erupted at the AMO and HKTA, it had been directed at the other parts of the government which had requested that Tang ancestral graves located elsewhere in the Territory be exhumed for a land-reclamation project. Three more departments were involved – Lands, Planning and Environmental Protection – none of which was known for its cultural sensitivity at the time.[21]
>
> The problem emerged in 1990 and was not resolved until 1997. Because of the conflict over the graves, the Tang clan closed three key monuments on the Ping Shan heritage trail in May 1995. This action made visitation to the trail less than satisfactory for visitors, which provided the clan with a bargaining chip against the government as a whole.[22] In June 1997, the AMO negotiated a special heritage agreement to reopen some of the historic features. One of the clauses in the agreement was the conversion of the police station to a site museum for the trail after the relocation of the traffic unit currently in residence. Compensation for the grave exhumation in the total amount of HK$1,840,000 was eventually accepted by the Tang clan.[23] Some more attractions were eventually opened and further work undertaken in 2004 on some buildings, which indicates that the AMO, the ASD and the Tang Clan have mended some bridges. The Police Station museum that was opened in 2005 to satisfy indigenous concerns concluded the issue for the government.

initially because of its 'easy accessibility by public transport, concentration of interesting features all within easy walking distance and the likelihood of local support for the historical structures to be open for public viewing'.[18]

The historic features of the Ping Shan trail comprised: Tsui Shing Lau (Hong Kong's oldest Buddhist pagoda), the local Tang Clan's ancestral hall (the largest in the New Territories), Sheung Cheung Wai (a walled village containing some new village houses thanks to the Small House policy), Kun Ting Study Hall, and the Hau Wong Temple, as well as a number of Chinese buildings of lesser importance and the village well. At the time, the pagoda was still set in farmland and the area was yet to have the West Rail and other developments encroaching upon it. There was access by light rail and minibuses (which require some local knowledge) but otherwise the AMO's assessment of its value for the project was fairly accurate at the time. Money was donated by the Hong Kong Jockey Club, the Lord Wilson Heritage Trust, and the Tang clan to prepare the buildings. The trail was 1.14 km long, with panel displays in some key buildings and brochures available in both English and Chinese.

The saga over the Ping Shan heritage trail vividly demonstrates how poor attention to process and planning in stakeholder consultation can have long-lasting consequences, particularly when so many different government and quasi-government organizations are involved. It is a lesson that the whole government, not just the AMO, can attest to, particularly after the July 1 public demonstrations against its administration in 2003 and 2004, which have made the government more sensitive to the issue of inclusiveness. Even so, subsequent July 1 demonstrations have been seen by some as a protest against a lack of inclusiveness in overall government decision-making as Hong Kong is only a partial democracy.

Indeed, town planning and urban policy often appear to have little to offer concerned heritage stakeholders in Hong Kong. One recent example of such a problem relates to one of several redevelopment projects proposed for Wanchai.[24] The urban district of Wanchai continues to be the subject of EIAs, urban renewal plans and subsequent debates about the role of Hong Kong urban inhabitants in these planning processes. It is a mixed residential and small-scale commercial area and is one of the oldest districts on Hong Kong Island. It is immediately adjacent to the Central Business District (CBD), a site of much redevelopment and land speculation for many years. Wanchai previously relied on a buffer zone provided by police and military facilities located between it and the CBD for a while, which could be considered the only evidence of long-term planning. But since the mid 1980s, the government has allowed many privately sponsored developments, including harbour reclamation and office blocks, such as the Hopewell Centre (Figure 4.1), to overwhelm this buffer. Most of these projects have been approved without an opportunity for public consultation. Away from the harbour, older sections are currently under pressure because there has been a rise in land values after the Asian downturn was concluded and the subsequent boom began in the economy.

Guangzhou is dealing with the same issue of public consultation, but in its own unique way. Shamian Island is an example of Guangzhou's implementation of the strategy of adaptive reuse towards heritage conservation of historic buildings (Figure 3.1). A piece of reclaimed land, it was set aside as an enclave for foreign residents in Canton after China was forced to sign the Treaty of Tientsin in 1858 by British and French armed forces. It continued to have a troubled history of poor race relations in the early twentieth century in Guangzhou. The area is now an exclave of Western-style buildings that have high aesthetic values based on

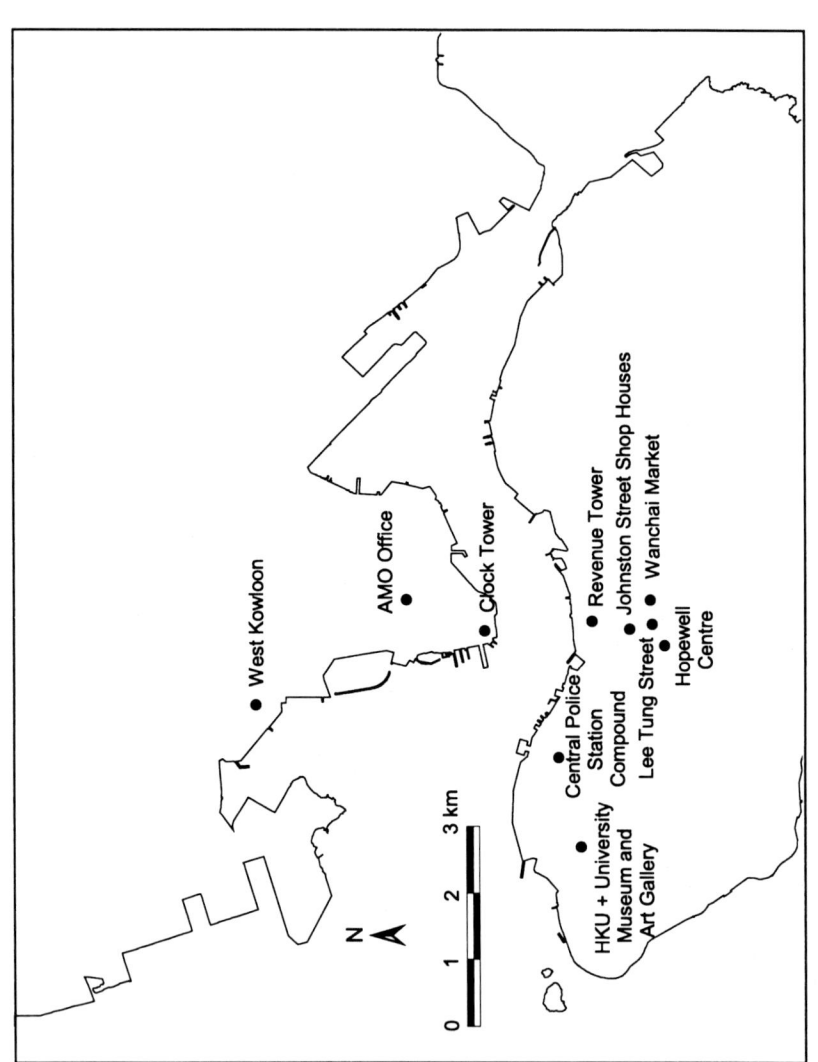

Figure 4.1 The location of places mentioned for urban Hong Kong.

their exotic architecture and layout. The street plan was always more spacious and European in nature than old Canton. The wide central avenue now includes playgrounds in the middle of its parkland with high recreational values as well (see also Plate 3.1). These values are now considered ripe by local authorities for exploitation for tourism development purposes.

Shamian Island was awarded the National Heritage Protection Unit designation in 1997. It has fifty-three classified historic buildings, as individual sites and as a group. The protection for the buildings as a group is very strong. No building can be demolished or heavily modified without permission from the State Administration for Cultural Heritage in Beijing. However, the conservation policy is simple: at the lowest and most grassroots level of government the protection unit is cared for by the 'street committee' – the 'Working Committee of the Chinese Community Party of Guangzhou Liwan District Shamian Street'. It works to annually review the use of the buildings and make approvals, but will seek advice elsewhere when needed, even from state officials in Beijing.[25] The street committee's budget includes rental income derived from commercial buildings, at around 2 million yuan, and this money was the primary source of reinvestment into daily conservation work. It also receives money from the municipal government for special projects (through a competitive project approval system).[26]

There have been some adaptive reuse projects of varying success implemented in Shamian. Some of the best have been carried out by Hong Kong property developers in the form of conversion of buildings to restaurants and bars. Some limited work has also been done on the buildings by the street committee, which makes it difficult to argue that the neighbourhood is actually gentrifying. It is, in fact, analogous to maintaining the status quo conservation-wise after a long neglect. A few buildings have now been converted to house shops, art galleries, offices and showrooms for import/export businesses. The street committee stated that Shamian has twenty large and small restaurants for tourists. International cuisine is now part of the mix. All businesses applying to set up in Shamian have to show the committee how they will fit with its latest view on development. Given that the Secretary recognizes that the tourists only need the 'five haves: eat, stay, tour, shop and sight-see', this may not be too difficult.

One of the impacts of the Cultural Revolution was an increase in the density of occupation as buildings were divided up into small family flats with improvised kitchens and other facilities, effectively taking in more people than the infrastructure could accommodate. The street committee has been implementing measures to reduce the local population density. A policy was actually introduced in 1996 that said that once the residents leave the neighbourhood, they could not make new applications for residential housing. The authorities have undertaken to relocate many families out of the area, with financial compensation, to reverse some of these impacts. The local population has thus been reduced from around 10,000 in 1996 to about 4,800 at the end of 2004. An increasing number of buildings are becoming vacant as people move out, and the authorities are actively looking to convert them for business or tourism uses rather than upgrading them as residences.[27]

Strict restrictions have also been put in place to limit the remaining residents' use of the historic buildings. For instance, they are required to submit any proposals for interior renovations to the 'building management committee' within the street committee. The authors noted that there are efforts to inform the community but not necessarily include them in the decision-making processes. Signs announcing tourism plans in Chinese intended for the local community were identified near the waterfront, but there was apparently no opportunity for the community to respond to these plans in return.

The Secretary of the street committee has a strong economic rationalist viewpoint, stating that it 'must use [Shamian's building stock] and not think of it as a museum', but looks for projects that are aiming at 'reasonable utilization'. He tries not to move too far away from the original use when assessing approvals. There is a policy to demolish or rework newer buildings to fit in better with its vision of Shamian's architectural style.[28] The street committee would also, in particular, welcome the return of the original inhabitants, particularly European businesses and Hong Kong banks. This is in the hope that they will take on some responsibility for the conservation of their original buildings and provide the much needed revenue through rents that can be used for the conservation of other buildings. The street committee would like to reach a 'global exposure' of its mission, which it sees as being essential for the future of Shamian.[29]

The public relations Vice-director of the White Swan Hotel[30] observed that the local authorities, particularly the street committee, have gone through three strategies in trying to develop Shamian Island for tourism:

- Lan Kwai Fong model.[31] With help from Allan Zeman, a pilot project has helped yield a few bars. The street committee stopped encouraging this model as there were concerns that this approach would make the area lose its ambience as a family attraction.
- Xintiandi (from Shanghai) model.[32] This was tried only briefly, possibly because they could not get investors interested.
- Current model. This approach highlights Shamian as a 'business and cultural heritage tourism island that has a continental European ambience'.[33]

The street committee secretary stated that they have adopted the third model, which allows the growth of tourism to be centred on the conservation of cultural heritage assets. This approach is apparently welcomed by one major stakeholder, the White Swan Hotel, which views Shamian Island as an 'exotic place within Guangzhou'. At the moment, the hotel draws fifty per cent of its occupation from Western countries, and most of its guests are families. If Shamian Island becomes 'too touristy' with too many bars, then it could create a 'sleazy' atmosphere and ruin the park-like and family-friendly ambience (and no doubt the quality of life of the local families as well) and, in turn, the guest-drawing power of the hotel. Thus, it is not surprising to see an agreement reached by both the street committee and one of Shamian Island's major stakeholders to follow the least disruptive approach to heritage conservation.

Overall, Shamian Island is still positioned very early in the 'tourist area life-cycle' which holds that, as tourism develops, places go through a series of stages, from discovery to decline (Butler, 1980). The paste was still drying on the new billboard that the authors saw in December 2004, where a large poster, facing the city, was put up to proclaim Shamian as a 'Romantic European Culture Island' (see Plate 3.1). The street committee is not concerned about the views of the local community in particular, but it is actively looking for stakeholders with the resources to appropriately convert and reuse historic buildings that are within its care.

Stakeholders and private–public partnerships

Among the three cities, working with the private sector directly on the adaptive reuse of buildings has been undertaken most successfully in Macau. An example of a local type of private–public partnership between stakeholders for the adaptive reuse of buildings is the Tak Seng On Pawn Shop. This building came up for redevelopment in 2000 (see Plate 4.1). The owner's proposal was referred to the Cultural Heritage Department (located within the CAB), which feared that the proposed interior changes would reduce its intrinsic cultural significance. The pawnshop's storage tower had been designated in the last intake in 1992 under Decree Order 83/92/M and it was considered as a structure of architectonic interest. Accordingly, the architectural guidelines released in 1994 by the Department advised that the tower must be protected and no additions made to its height. However, at that time, no stipulations were made about interior alterations.

The Department's representatives made an on-site assessment in 2000 and recognized that the interiors had a high degree of integrity and contained evidence of its historical use as a pawn shop, bank and other commercial activities. This evidence was documented, and negotiations

Plate 4.1 Macau's Tak Seng On Pawn Shop interior in 2003, after restoration. (Hilary du Cros)

began formally with the owner, Yinghe Development Ltd, in March 2001. Fortunately, the owner shared the Department's view that the structure should be conserved and that it was important to Macau's cultural identity and history. Taking advantage of funding programmes in place for such partnerships, the owner and the government formed a partnership to carry out conservation work on the property. A few years later it was re-opened as a pawn shop museum with shops on other levels. In the first five years following the opening, the government would use and manage part of the ground floor as a temporary museum. After that period, in 2006, the owner resumed control of the property. A waiver of property tax was used as an incentive for the owner to continue to maintain the property under agreed conservation and maintenance guidelines, with a certificate granted each year that work has been evident. This conservation project received an Honourable Mention in the UNESCO Pacific Heritage Awards in 2002.[34]

The review phase: PRD cities and mature practice

Specified under the notional Western-derived framework, the last phase of 'Review' should be evident with the creation of a more proactive, transparent, integrated and accountable system for CHM. It should provide for a new understanding of responsibilities on the part of stakeholders to care for CH assets and point to new ways to bring in stakeholders in the process of generating public policy on CHM and urban planning. Undertaking successful stakeholder partnerships is one part of these activities, but this often requires administrative and legal changes to allow such partnerships to be formed in the first place.

Often the 'Review' phase in many countries requires new or revised legislation to amend or repeal the first generation heritage-specific legislation, and to enhance the across-the-board efficiency of public CHM practices. This should include, in particular, a greater recognition of intangible heritage, as most initial legislations around the world tend to be lacking in their coverage of this category. This is not surprising because, in most cases, the inception of such laws was primarily influenced by the disappearance of tangible heritage.

Although CHM in the Pearl River Delta appears to be still working its way through the last two phases of 'Increased professionalism' and 'Stakeholder consultation', it is possible that it may be close to entering the fifth phase of 'Review' in regard to providing laws or policies to protect intangible heritage. This aspect will be examined in relation to each of the case study cities with regard to rising concerns about cultural identity, and the economic realities that these communities have to deal with in their respective transition positions. But first, the question of what constitutes intangible heritage in this region is briefly discussed here.

Intangible heritage found in urban settings in Southern China generally comprises:

1 Historic businesses (family, long-term, icon) that have a sense of continuity, having survived upheavals and other factors to remain *in situ* or in a particular neighbourhood.
2 Business clustering (markets, street-focused, artisan's quarters, precincts) which is related to the intangible concept of grouping related businesses together, usually in the same street. It is possible that it is an idea that goes back to early urbanization and city planning concepts for China.

3 Religious customs (festivals, shrines, temples, *feng shui* beliefs and influences) as practised by indigenous villagers and more recent arrivals of all kinds. Beliefs and influences, such as *feng shui*, can also be seen in the construction and layout of certain buildings and landscapes in South China.[35]

4 Oral history, stories and associations (memories of long-term residents, collective memory) including all the folklore and stories that are important for the cultural identity of a group or even a city.

5 Arts and cultural performances (street/theatre, puppet shows, Cantonese opera).

6 Cuisine – that includes local variations on broad-based styles and locally developed examples of the preparation, presentation and consumption of food and drink.

7 Languages and other forms of cultural expression (e.g. Cantonese words for which there are no Chinese characters, as they are slang words only used in everyday dialogue).

Among the three cities, Macau has had the longest formal recognition of intangible heritage and measures for its management. In 1984, when the Standing Committee was restructured as the Cultural Institute, it was expected, in addition to managing its tangible heritage, to 'assist in drafting and implementing the Territory's policies on culture and academic research by organizing activities relating to Sino-Portuguese cultural interchange and by disseminating and stimulating an interest in Portuguese language and culture in this part of the world'.[36]

In 1984, the government of Macau issued a new law governing the protection of Macao's cultural heritage, giving clear and complete definitions, categorizing heritage into material cultural heritage and immaterial (that is, intangible) cultural heritage, setting detailed rules and regulations governing the protection of each of the classifications. The Decree issued in 1984 defined immaterial cultural heritage as 'those values which form part of the cultural tradition of the Territory but are not found in material form. They should, however, be the object of graphic and audio-visual recording for the purposes of preservation and propagation.' However, the ongoing close inter-organizational linkages between cultural heritage and tourism authorities would have ensured that the 'propagation' aspect of the decree's definition would require inputs from the then Cultural Institute, not the sporting or leisure bureaucrats of Macau's administration, which is contrary to the practice found in Hong Kong currently. In Hong Kong, the AMO is positioned within the Leisure and Cultural Services Department under the Home Affairs Bureau, which tends to view the appreciation of local intangible heritage as something akin to sport. This approach used by the HAB can be seen with their recent promotion of aspects of the Cheung Chau Bun Festival, as shown below.

Cheung Chau is one of Hong Kong's outlying islands, and as such has retained a strong sense of its own identity and culture (Figure 2.2). The Cheung Chau Bun Festival is celebrated to placate 'hungry' or restless ghosts of people who were either killed by pirates or died from a plague. Some local islanders also believe that the ghosts are the spirits of all the fish and animals eaten during the year. This group also see the event as ending a fast from eating seafood and meat. The variety of beliefs about the meaning of the festival reflects the multicultural nature of the island community which comprises the descendants of the Tanka and Hoklo (fishing communities), Hakka (farmers) and more recent Han Chinese arrivals from the mainland. The island has also been a haven at various times for notorious pirates and retired senior colonial officials.

The festivities are carried out after Buddha's birthday in May. They are supported by a series of ceremonies with both Taoist and Buddhist aspects to them. The festival is expected to last for eight days in all, and its key dates are selected by divination. It is mainly known for the 'procession' of effigies of the local gods Pak Tai, Tin Hau, Kwan Hung, Hung Shing Tai Wong and Kwun Yum (also known as the 'Floating Children' parade) and the bun tower ceremony. Cantonese operas are staged near the main temple to Pak Tai, the Ocean God, and Lion Dances are held in front and as part of the procession. Aside from the Cantonese opera, which is carried out by a travelling troupe which goes to all the remaining indigenous villages in Hong Kong, the other ceremonies are conducted by the local people of Cheung Chau (Cheung Chau Tour Guide, n.d., HK Magazine, 2005).

The procession was originally accompanied by a 'bun scramble' up the towers by local fisherman at midnight. The idea was to climb to the top of the cone-shaped towers and grab as many of the lucky buns as possible. The tower buns were later distributed amongst the community, particularly the elderly, who hoped that their consumption would dispel bad fortune and the onset of disease. The bun scramble was banned in 1978 after a hundred people were injured when one of the bamboo towers bearing the small white buns collapsed under the weight of too many scramblers.

The Bun Festival has been touted as a tourist attraction by some guide books since the late 1970s (Clewlow, 1978). However, it was only in the 1990s that structured tourist activities began to occur in association with it. Even in 2004, only a few hundred international tourists attended. However, 23,000 visitors from other parts of Hong Kong went to the island to see the procession.[37] The numbers have been rising since then.

108 *Hilary du Cros et al.*

Nevertheless, tourism was given as one of the reasons that the government agreed to allow the resumption of the bun scramble associated with the festival. It had been lobbied by the Cheung Chau Bun Festival Organizing committee and local businesses wanting to increase the economic benefits of the festival to the island. The process through which this eventuated has implications for how Hong Kong cultural heritage managers and others view both intangible heritage *and* stakeholder consultation. However, it was not until 2005 that a uniquely Hong Kong compromise was made regarding safety, hygiene and traditional customs to revive the activity.

Most stakeholders initially appeared to be in favour of reviving the bun scramble tradition. However, it was called off in 2004 because of the festival organizers' inability to fulfil the safety requirements of the government's Leisure and Cultural Services Department (and not its Antiquities and Monuments Office, which has little official interest in intangible heritage). The requirements initially were for the towers to be made of steel and to be certified as 'structurally sound'. The Department also asked the committee to take out public liability insurance. The committee's chairman countered this, in the press, with statements such as 'bamboo scaffolding is a traditional Chinese art' and 'it looks strange when bun scramblers are dressed like mountaineers' (*SCMP*, 10 May 2004). However, the government held firm, and no bun scrambling proceeded that year. The committee did make good its threat to 'repackage' the festival in another way by ensuring that the lucky buns were available to visitors as well as locals. To ensure there were no food hygiene repercussions from this change, each bun was individually wrapped in plastic before being placed on the bun towers.[38]

The committee then invited key officials such as the Home Affairs Bureau Secretary (who is responsible for LCSD) and HKTB's chairwoman to attend. They both supported the plans for a climb in the year 2005, subject to a full compliance of the government's requirements. The Secretary of HAB was so inspired by the experience that he pledged that 'there will be a permanent bun tower which people can climb every day' (*SCMP*, 27 May 2004). At that point, in May 2004, only a few local and itinerant tourism academics thought that this sentiment was out of place.[39]

Three months before the 2005 festival was due to take place, however, problems emerged about reviving the bun scramble. The multicultural nature of the Cheung Chau community offered a diversity of opinions about the intrinsic values of the bun scramble, even before the commercial aspects are added. It is likely that the community consultation process conducted by the government was quite limited when it pushed ahead with the plans for reviving the tradition, regarding the support of the 2005 Organizing Committee as evidence of endorsement from the larger local population. Comments later recorded by the media on the commodification of the bun scramble for tourism indicate that many local residents, particularly those not benefiting directly from it economically, did not expect to see so many fundamental changes to the activity. The two key traditional bun tower builders were particularly disappointed in the way they and their skills were treated in the process.

Eventually, even the previous chairman of the festival committee (also the Executive Director of the Federation of Hong Kong Hotel Owners) became one of the project's deepest critics. Public criticism was also levelled at the government by the only opposing voice on the 2005 committee, who noted that he 'cannot see why it cannot be done [in bamboo], because even the scaffolding of the IFC was in bamboo'.[40] He also noted that in relation to international tourism, 'foreigners will come to see bamboo bun towers, not steel ones' (*SCMP*, 22 February 2005). This view was supported by more letters in the press, submitted by expatriates whose taste in heritage attractions is likely to be similar to that of international tourists whom the government appears to be targeting.

The issue about the alienation of the local population in the construction of the official climbing tower for the 2005 festival continued to be highlighted by the media. One of the traditional bun tower builders told a reporter that the new tower 'looks like a Long March No 1 [rocket]... it is definitely different from our bun towers'. He also felt confident that, with some strengthening, the original design was strong enough to safely maintain the tradition. Both the steel tower and the exercise in official training of a selected group of climbers were seen as distancing the tradition from the community (*SCMP*, 19 April 2005).

Special training exercises were held and used by the government to publicize the activity in advance of the festival, which portrayed it more like a sporting event that could be held anytime, like many of the other events managed by the Leisure and Cultural Services Department. After the publicity event, newspapers ran the headlines, such as 'Bun-snatching could become a regular sport' (*The Standard*, 10 May 2005), 'It's all Bun and Games' (*SCMP*, 13 May 2005) and 'Grab a Bun, have Fun after 27 Years' (*China Daily*, 13 May 2005). LCSD was now deeply involved, having committed $570,000 to the project and needed to have more to show for it than a short-duration festival tourist attraction of eight days, linked to a three-minute race for buns.

The Secretary for Home Affairs defended the LCSD's actions by stating that it had 'rescued a heritage in danger of losing its meaning, replacing the original tradition with a refined form of activity that preserves the spirit of the competition it was intended to satisfy. The best way to protect a heritage is to permit its evolution to accord with changing circumstance.'[41] However, this statement might also be interpreted in the context of Hong Kong's administrative tradition as letting market forces rule (in this case tourism needs). Indeed, the key redeeming feature of the event for many, when it was reported afterwards, was that a local resident won it (*SCMP*, 16 May 2005).

Was it worth it all, in terms of generating revenue from tourism and an enjoyable visitor experience? There is no doubt that stall-holders and shops benefited from the revenue that the festival generated by increasing domestic tourism, but not necessarily the heritage asset itself. One 2005 committee member promised the community that he would replace the steel tower with a bamboo one if he was elected as chairman for 2006 (he was not, and it has not been). He observed that 'the government had no right to stop us from reviving our own tradition the way it should be' and also that 'some elderly people say that this structure had adversely affected the island's Feng Shui by blocking the sea view of the Pak Tai Temple' (*SCMP*, 17 May 2005).[42]

The recent changes to the Cheung Chau traditions occurred just after the Yamato Declaration on Integrated Approaches for Safeguarding Tangible and Intangible Cultural Heritage in October 2004 (UNESCO, 2006). This is a special declaration designed to take into account Eastern attitudes to authenticity and integrity of tangible heritage in tradition. It was devised mainly by Asians with a strong Japanese influence because of the involvement of the Japanese Agency for Cultural Affairs. However, in Southern China, the Hong Kong government officials dealing with intangible heritage continue on, as if it and any other documents relating to the sensitive management of intangible heritage and living culture do not exist. Needless to say, local leaders on Cheung Chau and the LCSD do not appear to have implemented a rigorous process of stakeholder consultation, which has not aided the situation.

Finally, in 2006, the LSCD and HKTB combined to produce a classic example of staged authenticity – at the pier where people board the ferry to the island. The display was part of an eighteen-day festival of bits and pieces from a number of different contexts, synthesised by the Hong Kong Tourism Board at the cost of HK$9 million (see Plate 4.2). The festival was described by HKTB in the media as 'a temple fair, aimed at giving tourists a taste of the city's four most celebrated religious festivals, and to encourage them to travel to outlying islands to take part in the festivities' (HKTB in *SCMP*, 20 April 2006).

The implication of this case study for measuring how CHM leaders understand and manage intangible heritage, in a way that is sensitive to its intrinsic values, is evident. Hong Kong's intangible heritage assets are not managed sustainably in recognition of their intrinsic values in shaping cultural identity. They appear to be managed in the same way as those of tangible heritage, and that is to be completely subservient to extrinsic values, such as their value for revenue generation. This management style

Economic growth and cultural identity 111

Plate 4.2 This fake paper bun tower was part of a display for the 'Culture and Heritage Celebration' put on by the Hong Kong Tourism Board between 20 April and 7 May 2006 to promote the Cheung Chau Bun Festival – and a mishmash of other forms of intangible heritage in Hong Kong. (Hilary du Cros)

is guided by Hong Kong's unique administrative culture and unspoken practice of adhering to economic priorities rather than to international principles of CHM.

Implications for the preservation and conservation of cultural heritage assets

Amongst the three cities, there are clearly different attitudes to levels of government intervention in the conservation of cultural heritage. Guangzhou is still loath to allow too much self-determination or inclusiveness in its dealings with non-government stakeholders. Macau has pioneered some innovative public–private partnerships in at least one example of successful adaptive reuse, whereas Hong Kong has been attempting a number of different styles of consultation regarding policy at the macro- and micro-level. In all three cases, the level of government intervention varies depending on how administrations view their role regarding leadership and collaboration. In Hong Kong, it could be argued that leadership and collaboration patterns are more likely to favour powerful stakeholders in the private sector in order to fit with current land-revenue collection practices.

The influence of international factors on this scenario is difficult to ascertain. Local examples that follow best practice activities elsewhere are more common in recent years as a result of increased scrutiny done by local and international authorities (e.g., UNESCO Heritage Awards are proudly displayed and included in government publicity materials, such as those found in Hong Kong and Macau). However, all the cities have a long way to go to resolve problems within this phase of the model, in terms of balancing economic pressures with those of managing heritage assets in a way that enhances local cultural identity. There are also still problems with aspects of the early preservation framework (in the phases of inventory and legislation) that have not been updated successfully. The cultural reasons for this will be examined in the next chapter. If problems such as this one continue to haunt a local tradition of CHM from its earliest historical development, it is unlikely to reach a mature stage of practice easily.

The foremost of the economic pressures on CH is the tendency for all cities (to a greater or lesser extent) to allow market forces to rule with regard to urban planning policy, which in turn acts against the preservation of much of tangible heritage in the Pearl River Delta cities. The consequences of this attitude are serious for vulnerable heritage assets, such as certain types of intangible heritage and archaeological remains. At most risk, in terms of indigenous heritage, are street-level businesses and features that give the PRD cities their vitality and life. In Guangzhou, it seems that most did not notice that their lives were poorer for their loss, until many such features had disappeared and the lack of other landmarks, as a result of extensive redevelopment, were making districts blend together visually or become unrecognisable.[43] Archaeological remains in urban areas have been ignored as a class of heritage that requires special stakeholder relations, particularly to encourage developers to test for them before construction. The exception is those uncovered in Guangdong and occasional chance finds in Hong Kong, although the latter have not resulted in a clear or proactive policy for their investigation.

Overall, more still needs to be done to recognize the role that stakeholders, particularly those in the local community, can play in planning, managing and presenting heritage assets. The Hong Kong and Macau governments are starting to experiment with consultation processes for improving communication with stakeholders at least. The Chinese University of Hong Kong's initiative to provide a guide for practitioners of participatory projects (Lim, 2005) indicates that universities are also supporting the principles behind this sub-indicator by providing useful resources. Macau would benefit from more input on this score, but concerns about the conflicts of interest and lack of consensus tend to deter any strategic action to plan proactively for participation (outside that for adaptive reuse projects). Of the three case study cities, Macau tends to operate more informally in terms of consultation and urban planning and therefore the interests of the most powerful stakeholders do not always have to be stated in black and white to be acknowledged by the government. Guangzhou's practice is the most in opposition with the principles underlying this sub-indicator and it is unlikely to change its position unless it is required to do so by the central government through SACH, or unless local officials can see some other benefits associated with such activities (e.g. a UNESCO award or World Heritage inscription).

Notes

1 Interview with Guangzhou Cultural Bureau, 7 December 2004.
2 Interview with city planner Paulo Cheang, 2004.
3 Interview with Cultural Affairs Bureau officials, 2004.
4 Now known as the Hong Kong Tourism Board.
5 There has been a recent investigation into public museum management in Hong Kong. It found that it had a total of 209,046 unsold publications valued at HK$24.7 million going back to the transition period (*China Daily HK*, 27 April 2006). It is amazing that no one had thought to introduce a marketing approach similar to that used for the Heritage Year merchandise that would include producing more popular and attractive publications that would actually sell or had discovered this fact earlier.
6 The local Chinese liking for special occasions was evident in the display of memorabilia from the Gala Dinner as part of this exhibition. No doubt this has been carefully put away somewhere by AMO as a special heritage asset to commemorate both the Year and Hong Kong's CHM community's response to the uncertainties associated with the transition to Chinese control after the handover.
7 Interview with David Lung, 12 April 2004.
8 A similar case occurred, much to the embarrassment of SACH, in Beijing in 2002. CCTV and the archaeologists were all ready to open a tomb for what they thought would be the first time and do a live to air transmission of the dig. However, grave robbers had discovered it only a few days earlier and cleared it out.
9 Tung Chee Hwa, policy speech, 7 October 1998.
10 Public lecture, 'Cultural Policy and West Kowloon Development Project', 28 April 2005, University of Hong Kong.

114   *Hilary du Cros* et al.

11 Interview with David Lung, 12 April 2004.
12 The English and Chinese media regularly run articles concerning this issue. The *South China Morning Post* has a 'Talkback' section that is more informal than Letters to the Editor, as it allows short emails on questions that the paper poses. Every month or two in the last two years, it has posed a question on heritage preservation policy. The questions vary from 'should more money be set aside to preserve historic buildings?' for tangible heritage, to 'should the rules be revised so long-established *dai pai dong* (streetside restaurants) can survive?' regarding intangible heritage, such as Chinese street cuisine. Most letters have responded favourably towards preservation in both cases. A recent one was even exceptionally jaded in that it noted that the media regularly features heritage preservation debates over single buildings and was surprised that no overall policy had yet been generated after years of such case-by-case conservation battles (*SCMP*, 17 July 2006).
13 Note the emphasis on social cohesion and harmony, not that dissimilar to the mainland's view of cultural policy objectives. Overall, Chinese cultures are know to value consensus as important in decision-making, as will be discussed further in the next chapter.
14 Ada Wong's University of Hong Kong public lecture on Hong Kong Cultural Policy, April 2005.
15 In an interview with the *SCMP* (30 March 2004) about the review process, HAB Deputy Secretary Leo Kwan Wing-wah noted that the protracted nature of the consultation process was due to the slowness of response 'from the Departments of Housing, Planning and Lands to the feasibility of future proposals'. These are also the departments that work closely together regarding public land sales and premiums.
16 Respondents advocated a number of measures tried in other countries, but not mentioned in detail in the consultation booklet, as their ideal solutions to this question, such as transfer development rights, tax incentives, and a heritage trust (HAB, 9 November 2004). Some of these suggestions came from heritage professionals, but also a few from non-professionals with a concern about improving processes.
17 Some research needs to be conducted into how these villagers as a group view their responsibility to the larger community, given that increased visitation to heritage trails and assets under their control indicates that non-indigenous residents could also consider them to have social significance. It is possible that the situation is becoming close to that witnessed in Australia over Aboriginal heritage assets which have additional or competing claims of cultural significance emerging for more than one group (e.g. Uluru or Swan Brewery).
18 Exhumation of graves to smooth the path for development projects is not unusual in Hong Kong, given the high demand for land. Exhumation is not inconsistent with Section 13, Chapter 97 of the New Territories Ordinance (1992), which has been used from time to time by the government to deal with the customs and traditions of the indigenous villagers. From the point of view of the Lands and Planning Departments involved, they had offered compensation and gone through the motions. In this case, however, for them the ancillary issues of the police station's bad *feng shui* and the heritage trail's visitor impacts had complicated the issue. From the Tang's point of view, the graves and the trail were the last straw. They began to assert their indigenous cultural identity as the Territory was about to return to China. See AAB Committee Paper AAB(EP)/15/91: memo by AMO to AAB, October 1991.

19 Ibid.
20 A number of local Chinese academics have undertaken research into the history of resistance in the New Territories since the handover, which aims to use Chinese social and oral historical elements to interrogate previously accepted colonial historical accounts. Evidence of this postcolonial revisionism is best seen at a web forum on Hakka Diaspora that aims to collect information from Overseas Chinese who have indigenous Hakka villages in Hong Kong (Hakka Diaspora UK Research Forum: 2005).
21 The Planning Department has since developed an interest in *feng shui* as the administration is slowly Chinesifying.
22 The long-standing resentment about the police station was also added to the mix. A clan member told the English media that 'if the government can demolish the Ping Shan police station, we might consider allowing it to move the clan grave'. (*SCMP*, 3 March 2002).
23 AMO memo to AAB, May 1997.
24 There have, however, been some positive notes for Hong Kong's struggle with this phase. 'The Wanchai Experiment' by the University of Hong Kong's Centre for Urban Planning and Environmental Management (CUPEM) was the first of its kind to undertake inclusive community consultation on cultural identity and heritage management as part of urban planning. In 2001 it used workshops and exhibitions to generate suggestions from the community regarding improvements to their living environment. The project was initiated by Alison Cooke and Ng Mee Kam in an attempt to reverse the top-down approach by much of government to urban planning (Cook and Ng, 2001). More recently, the Chinese University of Hong Kong's Department of Architecture published a well-produced booklet on undertaking community consultation that has tried to remedy that approach (Lim, 2005). But, the planning tools, such as the EIA process, leave public consultation on a development proposal to near the end of the process, after designs have been drawn up and options reduced. However, this is still better than nothing at all. Reports are accessible online at a website administered by the government, but it is usually at the earlier stages of their development that stakeholder consultation is most urgently needed. In Hong Kong, EIAs can be carried out for developments in urban as well as rural settings. Hong Kong is, however, leading the region in the way it implements the EIA process in that many other administrations have little or only partial legislation and processes for assessment impacts on cultural heritage in development project planning, or for encouraging stakeholder participation.
25 After a number of years of study, with help from Guangzhou University's Institute of Architecture, there is no still no formal conservation plan, although the buildings have been fully documented. Some decisions have to go to the State Administration of Cultural Heritage because of the protection unit's status as a site of national significance.
26 Interviews with the secretary of the street committee and a representative of the Guangzhou University's Institute of Architecture, December 2004 and January 2005, respectively.
27 Interviews with the secretary of the street committee and a representative of the Liwan District Planning Bureau, December 2004 and December 2003, respectively.
28 Interview with Shamian street committee secretary, 8 December 2004.
29 In the interview, they even asked us to spread the word. The author du Cros did try this with a friend who is a consultant to a developer in Hong Kong and

Shanghai, but his opinion was that their mission may not succeed as the Hong Kong companies will want cheaper rates than they are willing to offer. However, some European and mainland Chinese companies have not found them too high, as they have already reused some buildings.
30 During an interview in December 2004 with the author du Cros.
31 Lan Kwai Fong is a successful bar and nightclub district on Hong Kong island.
32 Xintiandi is an upmarket Western-style shopping and restaurant complex established in a district of Shanghai with Western buildings similar to some of those in Shamian. It has been reasonably successful, although the refurbishment was very expensive and not always that respectful of the building's interiors.
33 The description of the street committee's current brand's meaning during an interview in December 2004.
34 Information sourced from several interviews in 2005 with Cultural Heritage Department representatives in Macau.
35 There are now very few indigenous villages, for instance, in the PRD near major urban centres that still retain aspects of their feng shui layouts, such as the forest in a U-shape that was maintained behind the village.
36 Cultural Institute homepage, 24 May 2004.
37 Dr Bob McKercher, personal communication, 2005. From a study of visitors to short-duration festivals in Hong Kong 2004, by the Hong Kong Polytechnic University.
38 One of the things that most expatriates and tourists always notice about Hong Kong is the obsession with packaging even before the SARS outbreak. It is likely that many visitors from other parts of Hong Kong to Cheung Chau would not think twice about the buns being in little plastic bags as they would buy everything from pastries to magazines like that daily in supermarkets. They would instead feel reassured about their safety for consumption rather than concerned about authenticity issues.
39 McKercher, ibid; members of the local community described some other members of the festival committee as 'loose cannons'.
40 This is the extremely tall International Finance Centre (IFC) building that graces the Hong Kong waterfront and which was used as a jumping platform for Angelina Jolie or her stunt woman in her second Tomb Raider film.
41 Patrick Ho has authored a series of small feature articles in the *South China Morning Post* on heritage and cultural topics. His comments are quoted from one titled, 'Cheung Chau Bun Festival: heritage worth fighting for'. It starts by stating that 'heritage is a precious legacy that can easily die unless it is kept alive in the context of an ever-changing world'. He has been, however, much more interested than previous HAB secretaries in heritage, but has his own unique way of showing it (once again, local factors are at play here).
42 If anything will prevent further intervention by the LCSD to make it a regular sporting event, it would probably be bad *feng shui*.
43 For instance, one of the CH official's comments that he felt lost in his own city.

5 The human factor and cultural affinity

Yok-shiu F. Lee and Hilary du Cros

Cultural heritage management does not operate in a void. A number of external social, cultural and human resource management issues, as outlined in earlier chapters, must be considered in order to better understand the impact of cultural affinities and differentiation on the development of CHM in Southern China. This chapter aims at explaining the nature of local conditions – which have shaped and are, in turn, shaped by cultural practices – in each of the case study cities, and how local conditions have helped to influence the way each of them approaches CHM. Such a discussion will help us understand what specific methods have been successfully cultivated locally and adopted, and what elements from among a plethora of global influences have been rejected, and why. To facilitate the discussion, it is necessary to identify, from a broad perspective, the major turning points in the development process of the Pearl River Delta region within the past fifty years. We will also re-visit some of the key themes already raised in earlier chapters and re-examine the underlying cultural dynamics that have brought about the ongoing activities that constitute the respective CHM frameworks, from the perspective of cultural affinity.

In order to help identify and delineate the essence of the cultural differences and similarities of the three CHM systems in the region, we will borrow a model developed by DiStefano and Maznevski (2003) for mapping cultural affinities. The model will be used primarily as an analytical tool to help invoke some debates about how the internal aspects of cultures can affect the actions of individuals as CH professionals. Through comments provided by the authors who have gathered insights on such issues through participant observation, we hope that this discussion will help explain why some local factors have become strongly featured in international best practices that are adopted by CH professionals in the region.

Cross-cultural influences on CHM: Britain, Portugal and China

There is no doubt that the three cities' historical and cultural antecedents have heavily influenced the development of their CHM frameworks. Both

Hong Kong and Macau were placed under the authority of European sovereign states until the late 1990s. Their respective cultural heritage management approaches have been shaped and modified by the three distinct phases of colonial, transitional and postcolonial administration. Guangzhou, on the other hand, has experienced numerous changes in its form of administration, but for different reasons. The demise of the imperial system, the collapse of the short-lived nationalist revolution, the rise of Communism, and the post-reform transition to market economy have all had an impact of how CHM has developed in Guangzhou (see Table 5.1 below).

In Macau, the most obvious impacts on CHM have come from the strong Portuguese influence during the colonial and transitional periods. Local influences, in terms of raising the importance of Chinese concerns in the CHM process, could only be integrated into a management system of cultural assets after the handover. Even then, some difficulties still remain (e.g. many historical materials only being in Portuguese). Other difficulties include the emphasis placed on protecting mainly historic buildings and gardens to the point that no new declarations are possible, including those that have come from the Chinese community as well as industrial heritage or newly discovered archaeological sites. Portuguese architects, such as the two previous heads of the then Cultural Institute, did work hard to leave a tangible legacy in the form of completed conservation projects and an intangible legacy in the form of communicating their passion for heritage to their younger Chinese CH colleagues.[1]

In Hong Kong, CHM stands out as a problematic issue that has been continuously constrained by economic factors and the biases of some of its British administrators, who preferred to document items away from urban redevelopment projects. Nevertheless, it also has been influenced by a stronger preference for documenting and excavating archaeological sites. Hong Kong has never considered 'closing' its list of declared monuments, although entry on to it seems painfully slow for some items, because of the way private property rights are negotiated. The legacy of the British in Hong Kong does not really have a strong tangible presence in terms of completed conservation projects on buildings, as found in Macau. As noted elsewhere (du Cros, 2004), the British colonial administration saw more glory in the construction of new buildings, such as one of the largest airports in the region. The ambivalence to its colonial past is only just being addressed now as the city's second Chief Executive is the first political leader to occupy the vacant historic building of Government House since the handover.[2]

In the case of Guangzhou, it is difficult to analyse the cultural roots of its CHM without some contemplation of its links with the rest of mainland China, particularly Beijing. As previously noted, it operates as a typical city on the periphery of the mainland administration system, despite

Table 5.1 Summary of CHM phases for the colonial, transition and postcolonial phases for Hong Kong and Macau, and for the historical events affecting Guangzhou

Case study	Inventory	Initial legislation	Increased professionalism	Stakeholder consultation	Review
Hong Kong Colonial	Initial work by amateurs. Initial difficulty in establishing museums and their collections	Only city in study that can not preserve group listings	Universities teach little local history or archaeology, but there are some anthropology and traditional architecture courses	Many historic buildings demolished in 1970s and early 1980s, despite protests	
Transition	Large inventory projects for archaeological sites and historic buildings by consultants for AMO	Review of legislation muted then abandoned	Professionals in AMO trained overseas, as little training available locally that is specific to CHM	Lord Wilson Heritage Trust established to fund community heritage projects, e.g. Heritage Year 1996–97	
Postcolonial	Struggling to achieve computerization of data collected earlier	Problems with inter-organizational relationships and zoning	Mainland Chinese archaeologists work on Hong Kong sites. AMO under ICAC scrutiny/reviews practices. More professionals and more local training available (e.g. HKU and CUHK). Tourism Commission instead of AMO leads reuse projects for historic police stations	AAB and Town Planning Board under pressure to open meetings. Consultation sought on built-heritage conservation policy. Guide for consultation processes published by CUHK	Some recognition of intangible heritage but no legislative protection and policy to manage it. AMO open New Resource Centre in late 2005 for greater public access to materials

Table 5.1 (cont'd)

Case study		Inventory	Initial legislation	Increased professionalism	Stakeholder consultation	Review
Macau	Colonial	Government-backed projects by non-professionals	Portuguese national legislation replaced by local ordinance. First Heritage Committee expected to collaborate with Tourism Centre	Officials in first museums and Committee mostly Portuguese and overseas trained. No local courses in heritage-related subjects	Some local stakeholders openly hostile to heritage protection, e.g. attacked Committee members	
	Transition	Emphasis on recording buildings by government, little local archaeology. List of declared historic sites does not have anything new added to it after 1984	Restructuring with more resources and control over conservation projects. Rationale for site preservation still related to utility in tourism development	Disappearance, then re-establishment of major public museums. Institute of European Studies of Macau established	Pre-handover heritage conferences invite some community groups. Heritage Fund established	
	Postcolonial	Increase in documentation of elements forming part of World Heritage nomination and some computerization. Some information available through the internet on World Heritage sites	Some integration of CHM with local planning decrees, e.g. there is a referral system for developments. No protection for undeclared heritage places outside buffer zones	Still very limited opportunity for local training in heritage-related professions. Masters programme in Public History at the Inter-University Institute of Macau. Schools teach local history only after 1999. Reliance on overseas expert's advice, not local	Some stakeholder consultation undertaken by ICM (CAB) for adaptive reuse projects, e.g. Tac Seng On. Some stakeholder consultation in relation to World Heritage nomination. No EIA or open planning decision-making process	Involvement of schools in conducting some historical research. Interest in protecting and conserving intangible heritage associated with food and language, but no legislation or policies. Community interest in broadening heritage definitions and making new declarations

Guangzhou Qing dynasty	'Four Haves' as explained in China Principles (2002), early excavations by scholars/amateurs	Four Haves	Most Chinese buildings rebuilt every once in a while to follow official pattern book by builders not architects	
			Some architects employed to generate policy and pattern books by government	
			Scholars have a side interest in collectables that relate to historical documents	
Nationalist War (1911–1949)	Some excavation and repository of artefacts in Guangzhou Museum by local archaeologists	Elementary legislation aimed at preventing further looting/sale overseas of movable cultural property – not well-enforced due to political upheaval and lack of resources	Training from Japan or elsewhere in China, possibly Beijing and Shanghai, in heritage professions. Some train overseas as well	
Communist takeover through to after the Cultural Revolution (1949–1978)	Inventory of some places in accordance with national law before the CR – mostly places of revolutionary importance and some archaeological sites	Several national acts at the time. Not enforced strictly and much destroyed during CR	National government training programmes for archaeology. A few universities run courses in architectural recording. Others have history departments etc.	
Open Door (1978+)	Inventory continues with more attention to gardens and archaeological sites than vernacular heritage	National Relics Protection Act 1982, amended 2003 strengthens penalties	Most professionals still trained internally. All employed in the public sector in some respect as there are no local private consultants allowed. Few architects in public office	Still not willing to consider stakeholder involvement beyond that of select heritage experts and local officials
				Recent acknowledgement of intangible heritage

its historical importance in the economic and cultural development of South China. It had maintained close links with Hong Kong historically and culturally, with some trading companies operating in both cities during its time as the treaty port of Canton. Alternatively, Macau's Cantonese residents have come from the south-western part of the Pearl River Delta, southwest of Guangzhou, and many still speak a version of Cantonese that has much in common with that spoken in that area.[3]

Although Guangdong has been culturally influential, in varying degrees, in both Hong Kong and Macau for an extended period of time because it is the origin of many of the most recent Chinese immigrants arriving in both cities, it has had limited influence on their CHM traditions until they became Special Administrative Regions. Likewise, CH managers in Hong Kong and Macau, up until the late transition period, have had limited contact with their counterparts in Guangzhou. What all three cities have in common, with regard to their CHM frameworks, is a concern that the use value of heritage assets has now been singled out and is being promoted to the public and other stakeholders to justify their conservation. The current focus on adaptive reuse of many historical buildings as tourism products or attractions follows from this policy bias, as does the increasingly close relationship between tourism development and CHM strategies in urban renewal projects.

If this is the case, is it then possible to discern any key differences in approaches among the three cities that would help illuminate their respective cultural backdrop to CHM decisions? The next section looks at how certain aspects of cultural identity and cultural development may have affected the nature of CHM in the case study cities. The opportunities and constraints that are associated with the sometimes contentious process of the formation of cultural identity, in relation to CHM practices, will be outlined. This understanding will then form the basis for further discussion, later in the book, regarding the question of how specific local aspects of CHM are linked to cultural attitudes.

Inter-ethnic and intra-regional influences in cultural identity

Cultural identity issues can help focus our attention on core stimuli that are responsible for past and potential changes in CHM. The issue of whose opinions (professional or otherwise) matter in relation to negotiating cultural identity is an issue for all three cities. In this connection, the issue of community involvement in heritage management decision-making processes is a key theme that requires further exploration to explain the results of the comparison. Hong Kong appears to encounter the greatest dilemma about its cultural identity, and it also faces the question of how to determine what kind of heritage assets should embody the largest social value. The background for this dilemma will be explored below.

Self-identification and cultural identity

There is a unique category of cultural identity within Hong Kong, probably not found elsewhere in China, of people who self-define as Hong Kong ethnic Chinese first and foremost. A government-sponsored survey conducted between October and December 2004 revealed that the proportion of ethnic Chinese who see themselves as Hong Kong Chinese only (twenty per cent) has not changed since 1997. These respondents, who do not have a great attachment to China in a nationalistic sense, can come from any age group. They are unified against proposed 'national education' as they fear it may be linked to an initiative by the central government to indoctrinate Hong Kong Chinese so that they become less critical of the governments in Hong Kong and in Beijing (RTHK, 2 June 2005).

What has not been explored in detail – and could be relevant to this study and the issue of cultural identity in Hong Kong and Macau – is the question of how recently these respondents have arrived in the two cities from mainland China, and why. In Hong Kong, some of the people interviewed in the above survey stated that the SAR was preferable to the mainland as their home because it was a freer society, with a more accountable and transparent administration. While there is a growing interest amongst Hong Kong ethnic Chinese to generate links with the mainland, particularly economic ties, there are still many who are wary about the lack of freedom there (RTHK, 2 June 2005). It is therefore not surprising that, at the time of writing, cultural identity in Hong Kong, in particular, has moved away from a type of nebulous idea of internationalism and sophistication towards a more specific concept of a free society under increasing pressure, within that of a totalitarian state. Accordingly, while 'Chineseness' for ethnic Chinese in Hong Kong is taken for granted, it is still a concept in need of some detailed examination in relation to the 'Motherland'.

At present, it is possible that the same debate is being enacted in Macau.[4] Radio talkback topics indicate that there is some concern with maintaining specific aspects of the city's local character, apart from the Casino and tourist development areas.[5] Both Hong Kong and Macau have seen an increase in debates about retaining unlisted, but locally cherished, landmarks. The need to retain local character within urban areas may trigger more debate about what it means to be a Chinese or a long-term non-Chinese resident in Hong Kong and Macau. In both cities, there are some small but significant non-Chinese ethnic groups who are long-term residents. However, they are not generally considered in the formulation of government public policies or CHM consultations. The classic case in point is the heritage conservation project for the Central Police Station Compound in Hong Kong, which has consistently ignored the role of the long-term Indian community – the employment of Sikh policemen in particular – in association with the site's history.

Comparisons between the case studies on inclusiveness of CHM approaches

Overall, there is always some kind of tension between local and global factors in relation to CHM in all the case study cities. This is particularly true with regard to the issue of stakeholder consultation, which is considered a part of the CHM toolbox being promoted internationally by UNESCO and ICOMOS. When these two international bodies attempted to introduce such tools through China's ICOMOS, however, amendments were made by the Chinese authorities, in order to accommodate the political and legal requirements of the central Chinese administration, so that much of this ideology in the conservation process was diluted and removed. The China Principles are 'Chinese' in character in the sense that the Beijing-based authorities have been selective about what was offered by international experts from the United States and Australia. Undertaking conservation work in the national interest and for rational economic reasons appear foremost in the document. Gaining consensus from non-experts as part of the planning process is not, however. In fact, local communities are often relocated, en masse, as part of urban renewal or conservation projects without giving much thought to how this might have weakened and dissolved the connectivity of the communities and their living culture.

Even though the China Principles are yet to have much of an impact on Guangzhou CHM, officials have appeared to avoid stakeholder consultation if it looks like it could become political and involve major criticism of government policy. The examples of stakeholder consultation processes that were discussed with the authors by officials in Guangzhou tended to involve heritage experts who had received special government approval. These experts, not the community or other stakeholders, were seen by the government as the arbiters of what was important for maintaining cultural identity. Significantly, not all of the experts are likely to follow the government line exactly, particularly if they have come from the older generation and feel that they have little left to lose, and have gained official respect to be heard due to their seniority.

There is also the possibility that not consulting members of the community closely on government policy is a practice that could be traced all the way back to dynastic times. At that time, mandarins (officials) had precedence over other segments of society. The officials, who were also scholars, were seen by many to wield authority over the 'uneducated' community members, regardless of whether the latter were tradition bearers or not. In this respect, mainland China may simply be re-visiting some of the Confucian values of earlier administrations and as such, avoid following international CHM practice.

One aspect of this practice that has been carried over – and has been found consistently in Hong Kong and Macau – is the concern with reaching a consensus amongst the community as a sign of public support for executive decisions, so much so that the governments are sometimes accused of subtly manipulating public opinion. Historically, in Hong Kong, such a practice has been a part of colonial policy in the interest of reducing public unrest. After the Second World War, some avenues for public consultation were created to allow the public to vent their opinion. However, both cities underwent some difficult times when the mainland was undergoing the Cultural Revolution. Not surprisingly, self-determination and democracy were not high on the list of public policy objectives at that time, when both colonial administrations were trying to quell riots in the late 1960s.

The rise of community organizations

The way the governments of the three cities conducted consultation at the community level on CH issues has a historical background. In Hong Kong, District Offices were part of the government apparatus and they were used as a liaison device to resolve difficulties with indigenous villages, clan members and others, particularly in the New Territories. In the late 1980s, District Councils were created throughout Hong Kong, and members of these Councils were elected, resembling some form of representative democracy. Some of the site examples observed in earlier chapters might include some appeals by stakeholders to their district councillors, with some follow-up actions taken by them. This would not commonly happen with the District Councils in Guangzhou, which do not need grass-roots support for their membership.

Mobilizing and getting grass-roots support for heritage conservation purposes is still a problem on the mainland. Many urban communities are mostly concerned about upgrading their living conditions in any way possible. Redevelopment and subsequent relocation of residents is accepted as the dominant paradigm by the public and by the District Councils and other planning organizations higher up in the administrative hierarchy. Even so, there are activists and government officials who are aware that cultural identity contained in urban neighbourhoods is being destroyed by such an approach to urban redevelopment.

Macau's early involvement of ethnic Chinese *kai fong* associations in civic programmes shows some concern for seeking grass-roots support and maintaining traditions. When they were first established in 1966, during the Cultural Revolution, these associations had close connections with workers' associations on the mainland.[6] Some of Macau's Chinese schools also had close connections across the border during this period, and their school teachers were dealt with very unsympathetically by the Portuguese government at the time.[7] It was not until the transition that such connections were smiled on again.

Whether World Heritage inscription for Macau's historic centre will have any impact on enlarging opportunities for stakeholder involvement is an interesting question. However, the increasingly critical tone in Chinese talkback radio sessions about mainland immigrants and visitors indicates that Macau society is suffering social impacts from increased visitation after the inscription and the de-monopolization of gambling over the last few years. Not least of the concerns is visitor congestion at popular temples, loss of local space and declining interest in visiting key attractions while they are congested with tourists.[8] A recent study of congestion at heritage icon attractions involved input from key stakeholders, including government, private and community groups (du Cros and Kong, 2006). Government organizations submitted feedback on the report but it was very difficult to get a response from the private sector and *kai fong* representatives who took part in the original research regarding their views on the study's findings. (It was probably the first time they had been formally asked about tourism impact concerns.) Macau still has a way to go regarding setting up regular channels of communications between all these groups on important issues that affect CH assets, such as over-use.

Overall, a number of cultural events have shaped the backdrop of CHM in this region. Chief amongst these – as far as cultural identity, self-determination and community inclusiveness are concerned – are the Cultural Revolution (on mainland China) and the return of Hong Kong and Macau to Chinese sovereignty. The Cultural Revolution (1966–1978) has had a major impact on the preservation and conservation of cultural heritage assets, the people associated with them and how their views are received by the mainland Chinese government. A whole book could be dedicated to chronicling and discussing the social-cultural impacts of this devastating socio-political event. At the moment, the long-term impacts are still not entirely clear, and the whole issue has yet to be addressed by the Chinese government. However, Guangdong is the first province where a private museum was established to outline the local impacts of the Cultural Revolution, even though it remains a taboo topic for public museums (*SCMP*, 15 May 2006). So far the most that has been said on the issue by the central government has come from the Ministry of Culture, which has admitted that much of China's cultural heritage was destroyed or trickled away overseas during this period (*SCMP*, 25 May 2006). It is still a topic that is dealt with sensitively in Hong Kong and Macau, although at the fortieth anniversary of the outbreak of the Cultural Revolution the English media carried a series of feature articles on the topic (*SCMP*, 15–19 May 2006). In any event, both Hong Kong and Macau have served as refuges for the victims of violence, havens for artefacts that were likely to be destroyed (even though most ended up in private collections or museums here and around the world), as well as a sanctuary for customs and expertise that were threatened with extinction (that have been changed or discontinued on the mainland as a result of the Cultural Revolution).

However, at the same time, in both Hong Kong and Macau, the Cultural Revolution caused both colonial administrations to clamp down on freedom of expression for a while. The opportunities for the two cities to regain and expand their freedom started to appear with the advent of the transition period. While the Chinese communities in Hong Kong and Macau have witnessed a greater continuity of cultural traditions and customs than their cousins on the mainland, sometimes the continued viability of that cultural heritage in the two cities is taken for granted.[9] A more strategic approach to maintaining the core values of intangible heritage, in particular, needs to be designed and applied in all three cities in conjunction with community stakeholders.

Bridging the gaps and creating new relationships

In this section, we will borrow a method, originally developed by DiStefano and Maznevski (2003) to explore the problem of how to make multicultural teams in businesses work together better, to examine the differences and similarities amongst the CHM approaches of the three case study cities. This model was premised on the argument that a better understanding, on the part of leaders of multicultural business teams, of the core cultural characteristics of their team members, would assist both groups to become more productive. Given that the DiStefano and Maznevski approach has a strong anthropological component, it could be adapted and used to help put any style of management practice into some kind of perspective. The model recognizes that personality, culture, professional experience, gender and other background characteristics have an impact on how people interact with the world around them. That is, how people notice things, make connections between them, and take action are all influenced by the different combination of characteristics and beliefs that individuals carry around with them. Cultural resource management developed in the United States often borrowed concepts such as this one from business management to examine its own strengths and limitations. Australian heritage management practitioners have also drawn on business management practices for similar purposes.[10]

The model is usually applied after collecting data through the use of special questionnaires to map differences across business cultures in order to improve the efficiency of multicultural business management. It was not possible for us to follow the exact same methodology with the use of questionnaires to collect relevant data. But the model is still useful in a general way to help explain the issue of how cultural characteristics have contributed to some of the similarities and differences of the CHM approaches adopted by CH professionals in the case study cities.

Assuming that culture means 'a system of values, beliefs, assumptions and norms that is shared among a group of people', the question that we would like to address is: 'Are there significant differences in terms of cultural orientation among the three case study cities in the Pearl River Delta region?' Data collected by DiStefano (2005) for a business culture survey found that only small differences had appeared statistically. However, it is still worth outlining the model in more detail and using it as a basis to gain some insights into the regional similarities and differences, from the point of view of the authors' of this book as participant observers.

The DiStefano and Maznevski model comprises the following dimensions for mapping cultural systems: relationship with the environment (nature), relationships amongst people, beliefs about the nature of humans, mode of activity, attitudes toward time, space and information (see Table 5.2).

The environment

The relationship to the environment can be subdivided into three categories: harmony, mastery and subjugation. It works like a triangle between what is seen to be totally controllable by humans who feel the need to put their stamp on their surroundings (mastery) opposed to those who think what happens out there is either God's will (subjugation) or requires special adjustments to their own behaviour to fit in (harmony). It is likely that all three cities with their underlying Confucian attitudes to the environment would tend towards mastery. The historic gardens in all three cities could be considered examples of highly modified and controlled landscapes, while the country parks and other urban spaces are principally zoned for recreational use and not necessarily for reasons of retaining biodiversity. Animals are still appreciated more for their use value as food, as a source of medicine or as pets before any other consideration, particularly in Guangzhou.

This tendency towards mastery has some implications for how professionalism has developed in these places. Experts or senior officials impress their views on the rest of the society. Some examples might include the

Table 5.2 Comparing cultural orientations for mapping exercises (based on DiStefano and Maznevski, 2003)

Orientation			
Relation to environment	**Harmony** See purpose in life to maintain a balance among elements of the environment, including people	**Mastery** See purpose and role to control nature and the environment	**Subjugation** See purpose and role to understand and submit to natural and supernatural forces that are part of a 'plan'
Relations among people	**Collectivism** Main responsibility is to/for a larger group of people	**Individualism** Main responsibility is to oneself and immediate family	**Hierarchy** Power and responsibility distributed unequally
Mode of engaging in activity	**Being** Doing everything in its own time – flexible	**Doing** Driven and continually engaged in accomplishing tangible tasks	**Thinking** Philosophical outlook that carefully considers all aspects before taking action
Nature of humans	**Bad** Sees humans as essentially bad, as good behaviour takes effort Closest monitoring needed	**Mixed or blank state** Sees behaviour as entirely determined by environment Monitor on case-by-case basis	**Good** Sees humans as essentially good Only loose monitoring needed
Time	**Monochronic** Time is linear and can be divided into equal units Attention to schedules, clocks, etc.		**Polychronic** Time is non-linear or parallel Flexible or soft attitude to deadlines
Time	**Past** Business and day-to-day decisions should be based on tradition and precedent	**Present** Business and day-to-day decisions should be based on immediate needs and factors	**Future** Business and day-to-day decisions should be based on long-term and future needs or factors
Ownership and division of space, and control of information	**Public** Space and associated information is open to everyone	**Public/Private** Space and associated information is open to everyone in theory, but is controlled by certain individuals and groups in practice	**Private** Space and associated information is owned by specific individuals or groups

way AMO in Hong Kong set up their first heritage trails and the way the Secretary of HAB in Hong Kong took a personal interest in modifications to the bun scramble festival on Cheung Chau. It might also be reflected in the way CAB (once the Cultural Institute) in Macau has been given control of contractors for conservation projects as a one-stop shop, or the way that Guangzhou's city authorities have designated whole streets to one theme. That is, all of these are attempts to centrally control or master urban heritage assets, communities and environments.

Where this view falls apart is when other aspects of urban heritage planning are taken into account, both historically and in the present, that indicate a lack of ability to make a mark by CH managers. For instance, the Hong Kong government is notorious for avoiding any urban planning policy that includes a sense of mission or policy, preferring to allow organic growth associated with the rule of market forces. Therefore it seems inevitable that as soon as the Wanchai Market was designated for demolition, the nearby outdoor market would be next in line for demolition as well, because the Central Business District is spreading eastward instead of across the harbour to Kowloon, as hoped for. This loss of the outdoor market is taking place despite the fact that, as shown in a number of community participation and planning workshops, people do care about street-level shopping and character.

Relations among people

The dimension about relationships among people focuses on the issue of loyalty. It describes whether they are centred on a group collectively or are arranged in other ways, e.g. hierarchical or individual. Inevitably, hierarchical arrangements in societies use some kind of principle, such as age, caste, gender or wealth to guarantee influence. Individualistic societies are generally seen as being responsible to their families, or individuals to themselves. An example of the latter is the 'American dream' where individuals are encouraged to outshine each other to reach the top. Collective cultures, in contrast, place more emphasis on the whole as a sum of many parts, working together for success.

It might be expected that all three PRD cities would have strong values for a mix of collectivism and hierarchy. Of the groups studied by DiStefano (2005), the business culture of Hong Kong is the furthest towards individualism and least collective or hierarchical. However, all three are still very close in scores. It is likely that a well-established business culture, such as that found in Hong Kong, would more likely be influenced by international business management notions on this point than CHM because financial success is the former's ultimate and clearly stated goal.

This dimension can also be further divided into attitudes that societies hold towards leadership and working in teams. This aspect has implications for this book's model, particularly in terms of how public administrations deal with planning processes and stakeholder participation. DiStefano (2005) did not provide sufficient detail on this, but it is likely that further survey work would uncover more similarities than differences between the cities in line with their general orientation towards a mix of collectivism and hierarchy.

The issue of leadership style is problematic culturally within the CHM context. The DiStefano and Maznevski model implies that the leader is required to be more commanding and responsible in a hierarchical organization than in a collectivist one, where responsibility is more evenly shared. In the former, there are rewards given to the leader when events go well, but dire consequences would follow if they go badly. This might explain the constant tension that many administrators have to deal with when they are trying to work in a mix of both systems, where the nature of a leader's role and responsibilities can become unclear. Such leaders may also be put under a great deal of pressure, as is the case throughout the civil service in Hong Kong, where a more Western model of transparency and inclusiveness has become the norm.[11]

Mode of activity

Mode of activity is an important dimension for understanding CHM in the Pearl River Delta. It looks at three key modes that comprise being, doing and thinking. A *being* culture will see more emphasis given to spontaneity and living for the moment, as in the case of many Latin societies, such as the Portuguese. A *doing* culture will be more goal-driven with a view to completing tasks as a way of affirming self-identity and existence. Some British and North American business cultures are very much in line with this mode. A culture with a strong *thinking* orientation will explore all the options first before leaping in, and will look for a rationally planned process when it does. The German, French and Confucian Chinese, with their history of philosophical discourse, could be considered in this category (DiStefano and Maznevski, 2003).

Evidence presented in DiStefano's study that showed distinct differences between and among the three case study cities on this particular score (DiStefano, 2005). Hong Kong comes out as having more of a *doing* business management culture, while mainland China has a *thinking* culture, and Macau a *being* one. It would be very convenient to link these distinctions back directly to their respective histories: Hong Kong (British and *doing*); Guangzhou (Chinese Confucian and *thinking*) and Macau

(Portuguese and *being*). Statistically the differences are not great, but they are there for the moment, nonetheless. It might be the case that a further integration of the PRD cities through CEPA and other programmes for economic cooperation could reduce the differences amongst the business communities in these three cities.

What does this mean in terms of CH professional communities and their leaders? Are they *doing, thinking* or *being* in terms of CHM practice? The following is only a preliminary view. It seems likely that Hong Kong is often under constraints, such as a lack of government support for the protection of heritage in its broadest sense, that make *doing* a difficult option. Recent changes introduced at the AMO have provided an approach that may be closer to *thinking*, while Cultural Heritage Impact Assessment (CHIA) consultants are more project-oriented and *doing*. Overall, the Hong Kong civil administration could be characterized as *doing*, mainly in response to market forces. Macau is a mix of *thinking* and *being* (as the Portuguese influence seems harder to shake). Guangzhou is likely to be *thinking* in orientation because the requirements of the administrative process are still not that dissimilar to those for business, despite market liberalization. More research is needed to help ascertain which approach is being used, particularly with regard to the questions of whether Guangzhou's orientation has overwhelmed its historical past, and whether Hong Kong's and Macau's approaches have prevailed over the historical influence of Britain and Portugal respectively.

Human nature

The way human nature is viewed in organizations is divided into three categories by DiStefano and Maznevski. Basically, authorities monitoring professional ethics and the behaviour of employees believe that people are inherently good, neither good nor bad, or inherently bad. The good view accords people with high trust and low monitoring or control, and the bad view brings forth the opposite. The mixed or 'blank' view means that monitoring and control is case- or task-related, e.g., security officers or bank tellers would have their backgrounds checked by their employers.

DiStefano's figures (2005) suggest that there is likely to be little difference among the three case studies on this issue because there is a shared view that tends towards seeing human nature as ultimately flawed. Currently, there is widespread corruption in local government on the mainland and both Macau and Hong Kong have anti-corruption authorities which closely monitor any conflict of interest situations for all government employees. Specific to CHM, the AMO in Hong Kong is still being monitored after the 2002 incident, although it is admittedly difficult for problems with professional ethics in private consulting practice to be picked up easily. Accordingly, mainland Chinese officials at the World Archaeology Congress conference in 2003 noted that SACH is loath to privatize archaeological impact assessment and salvage, as there are fears that important artefacts could disappear into the black market.[12]

Time

There are two key aspects to time and organizational orientations that have been presented by DiStefano and Maznevski (2003). One view holds that time is linear – moving from the past to the future – which requires that people pay attention to clocks and schedules (monochronic). An alternative view suggests that time is flexible, deadlines are less important, and there is flexibility in how stages of activities are commenced and completed (polychronic). Many industrialized cultures are obsessed with the former, while hunter-gatherer and some rural societies tend to be the latter. In addition to these categories are three sub-divisions that measure whether business cultures are past-, present- or future-oriented, in terms of their practices. A past orientation centres on making practice consistent with past activities, while a present orientation will highlight immediate concerns and promote urgency in dealing with threats and opportunities. A future orientation occurs where an organization will sacrifice current benefits in the hope of receiving a bigger pay-off in the future, and will incorporate long-term goals into current action and planning.

DiStefano's figures (2005) again show some consensus amongst the three cities, with a focus on a mix of past- and future-orientation, rather than present. This is not surprising in that most business operations involve, if they are driven to become successful, some long-term planning as well as the incorporation of past experiences. Those businesses that are too much focused on the present may not be economically sustainable, in the Asian view. However, the slight drop in values for present orientation may indicate a lack of flexibility that could lead to current opportunities being missed.

Transferring this understanding across to CHM is probably fraught, as much of the CHM practice is based in the public sector. It is difficult to see whether all three case study cities will have the same orientation in the PRD, although a *thinking* orientation is already in place. Accordingly, a mix of past and future fixations would be a complementary approach to thinking, for all three cities. It is also likely that all three cities are monochromic, being modern industrial and post-industrial societies, although the Portuguese influence might include a nuance of polychronic flexibility for Macau. People in the Portuguese enclave sometimes criticize each other for running on 'Macau time' when running late. Moreover, many development and conservation projects tend to have soft deadlines for completion.

Space

Space as a factor in organizational business practice is also of relevance here. The orientation evident regarding ownership and control has implications in CHM for what is designated as a heritage asset and what information is shared about its management with the public. A heavy public orientation to space suggests that the heritage asset in question and its associated information can be shared by everybody, while an intensely private orientation will see ownership accessible only by specific individuals. DiStefano and Maznevski (2003) note that public space orientations relate to open-plan office space, shared furniture and information sharing. Private orientations have closed-door separate offices and private furniture and facilities, with information requiring specific permission before being shared, if at all. How this might translate to the public sector is again a little problematic as financial considerations may motivate open-plan offices and shared facilities. Also, there has been a general move in many Western democratic societies towards greater transparency and sharing of information with the public by government.

Set against this backdrop, it would not be surprising that administrations that are most influenced by international trends, such as Hong Kong's, would have a more public-oriented CHM culture. However, it is Macau that is trying to put as much information about heritage assets online at present. All three cities are showing a perplexing mix of private and public space and information sharing at this present time, particularly as the mainland is moving towards new private space ownership arrangements for real estate that will inevitably affect some heritage assets. At present, Guangzhou heritage authorities barely have computer facilities, let alone the capacity and inclination, to put information about heritage assets and their management on the internet for public access.[13]

Macau authorities are concerned about the public use of heritage assets in relation to public versus private space issues. The increasing pressure of tourism has created a situation where Senardo Square (Largo do Senardo) – one of the elements of the World Heritage inscription – is valued more by the government as a tourist attraction than as a public space to put on community events. Such events could include outdoor modern award ceremonies, public information campaigns and sports ceremonies which might clash with its historic ambience.[14] Currently, the solution is to develop and upgrade facilities at another public square and move the activities there so that the tourists can better enjoy the traditional atmosphere of Senardo Square. However, the new location is also surrounded by historic buildings, and it is possible that the same complaint will also be made about it. The question would then become: 'At which point does tourist space end and local space begin?' Issues such as this one require an inclusive and integrated approach, as promoted in international best practice, but some sensitivity to local factors, such as the avoidance of uncertainty, is needed for a successful resolution to be crafted to the satisfaction of all the concerned stakeholders.

Conclusion

Overall, there are fewer gaps between and among the three case study cities (see Table 5.3) than one might imagine when reading about their recent historical and political development. The above discussion strongly suggest that they might be moving closer towards each other in terms of business management as well as CHM practices, as the SARs progress towards integration with the mainland, as envisaged in their legal constitutions. However, differences regarding financial and human resources, professional training and linkages to the heritage authorities operating outside the region may still play a role in shaping the future orientation of the CH professionals in Hong Kong and Macau. Moreover, there are still some strong local aspects associated with each of the three case study cities that set them apart from each other within the region; and these differences may become a source of pride for each of them as they start to integrate further. How these interactions between and among the three cities will

Table 5.3 Likely CHM orientations for Hong Kong, Macau, and Guangzhou

Type of cultural orientation	Hong Kong	Macau	Guangzhou
Relation to environment	Mastery	Mastery	Mastery
Relationship among people	Hierarchical and collective (slightly individualistic)	Hierarchical and collective	Hierarchical and collective
Mode of engaging in activity	Thinking and doing	Thinking and being	Thinking
Nature of humans	Bad	Bad	Bad
Attitude to time (response to enquiries/situations)	Monochronic	Monochronic/ polychronic	Monochronic
	Mix of past and future	Mix of past and future	Mix of past and future
Ownership and division of space (public/private)	Mix	Mix	Mix – mostly public, but real estate market is in transition
			No real information sharing

play out will closely influence the future of CHM in the region. This issue will be dealt with in greater detail in the next chapter.

For a change, it would be useful to end this chapter with an offbeat analogy to showcase the unique characteristics of the three cities. Imagine you are caught in the lift with three other people in the Pearl River Delta region. They are all Chinese. One is a businessman from Hong Kong, who pushes the close button for the lift doors with a couple of urgent pokes of his index finger. Even though he gets off at the first floor, he feels that it is quicker to take the lift than walking up the stairs. A fashionable young man from Macau wearing lots of bling (jewellery) is then standing closest to the button. He pushes it with a nonchalant flourish to make the doors close. When the lift gets to his floor, he pauses and then saunters out. The last person left in the lift with you is a middle-aged female official from Guangzhou. When the lift doors hesitate, she ignores the button briefly, then cannot help herself and gives it a resounding bang. All three will intervene in the action of the lift doors by pressing the button, but they will each do it in their own special way.

Notes

1 Stephan Chan, interviewed in February 2006.
2 The previous (and first) Chief Executive since the handover, Tung Chee Hwa, resigned for health reasons on 10 March 2005.
3 This observation was made by Y.S.F. Lee on a recent visit he made to Macau. He noticed that there were subtle differences in how Cantonese was spoken in Macau as against that spoken in Hong Kong, which were more likely to be related to the origin of the largest or most recent waves of immigrants from Guangdong to Macau.
4 Debate on the issue of cultural identity during the transition was limited to the academic community and CH professionals who attended several conferences on the same. However, the transition period saw the Portuguese policy trying to stamp some Portuguese or Western aspects on the cultural identity of Macau before it completely relinquished control. One clear example of this is the establishment of the Wine Museum – based around Portuguese wines, and the re-establishment of the city Museum, now known as the Museum of Macau. Even so, post-colonial cultural identity for the ethnic Chinese in Macau is not under as great a pressure in relation to the mainland at this stage as Hong Kong. Perhaps this is because Macau's executive-led government has been equivocal about its cultural policy since the handover, and there has been less concern about the introduction of democratic processes than in Hong Kong.
5 Institute For Tourism Studies public relations staff daily summarize talkback radio shows for staff. Since one of the authors moved to Macau in August 2005, it has been noticeable to them how public concern about heritage conservation has grown. This is possibly a result of WHS inscription in July 2005 and the increase in tourism impacts, as arrivals now exceed 20 million per year for this tiny city state. Concerns about the increasing 'Chinesification' of Macau are also raised by mostly non-Chinese residents in other contexts who want to

see certain Portuguese/Macanese languages and customs survive the greater exposure to the Chinese mainland contact.
6 Joe Luis de Sales Marques, interviewed in April 2005.
7 Stephan Chan, interviewed in February 2006.
8 Morning Talkback Show, TDM FM 100.7 Macau, January to March 2006.
9 As evident in the recent announcement by the councillor representing the Heung Lee Kuk (indigenous villagers land-rights association) in Hong Kong's Legislative Council. He would prefer to see the restricted border zone between Hong Kong and Shenzhen, which contains one of the last well-preserved examples of a village with a *feng shui* forest (a cultural landscape governed by Chinese geomantic principles) opened up for building factories to manufacture car parts (*SCMP*, 10 July 2006).
10 In fact, 1980s business negotiation practices (e.g. reaching win–win situations) were trialled by some CHM organizations openly, such as the New South Wales National Parks and Wildlife Service in consultations with Aboriginal communities and developers.
11 Hofsted (1991) has postulated that this kind of result may be explained by a strong need to avoid uncertainty by some societies. It is likely that the local factor of government avoiding a 'loss of face' from unexpected/unpredicted outcomes of community consultation makes them loath to undertake it. However, not only Asian governments are sensitive to this issue, so it is likely that uncertainty avoidance is more common internationally and a constant constraint that international best practice strives to overcome.
12 Another ethical problem is the endemic corruption associated with the tendering process for most projects. It is feared by many that private practice heritage projects could follow the example of certain construction projects where bribes and kickbacks allow certain players to succeed over others. The mainland lacks strong professional associations to peer-regulate accredited members or a free press to expose corrupt practice.
13 Very few of the people interviewed for this study worked in open-plan or shared offices, although some of their more junior staff did indicate something of the hierarchical nature of CHM and other types of activities in this part of the world.
14 A recent debate pertaining to a meeting entitled the 'Urban Redevelopment, Heritage and Cultural Identity Conference' was held in Macau in March 2006 by the International Studies Institute.

6 Conclusion

Yok-shiu F. Lee and Hilary du Cros

Key global and local factors revealed

Local factors have been dominant in the early evolution of cultural heritage management in Hong Kong, Macau and Guangzhou. These three cities have developed very different administrative systems as a result of their historical development: British-colonial-derived in Hong Kong; Portuguese-colonial-derived in Macau; and socialist-regime-in-transition-towards-market in Guangzhou. The stages of *inventory* and *initial legislation* as per the notional CHM model in Chapter 1 have been affected directly by these trajectories. It is worth revisiting briefly the differences in how the laws in these three cities have been developed in order to explore their respective impacts on CHM practices.

In Hong Kong, the beginning of the promulgation of its one and only heritage-protection act – the Antiquities and Monuments Ordinance – could be traced all the way back to 1957. It then took years of negotiation within the civil service before the bill was introduced into the Legislative Council in 1971 and a Provisional Antiquities Advisory Board (PAAB) established in 1972. The AAB's executive arm, the Antiquities and Monuments Office, was then set up in 1976. The ordinance was modelled on mid- rather than late-twentieth-century legislation brought in from overseas, and it has not been updated since its enactment. The lack of comprehensive revisions has rendered the ordinance largely ineffective in addressing contemporary CHM issues properly and has made it difficult, in particular, for CHM efforts to be articulated with the urban planning process in Hong Kong.

Early heritage protection legislation in Macau was directly linked to national laws promulgated in Portugal. A piece of heritage legislation enacted in Portugal in 1953 was extended to Macau because the latter was considered then to be an 'overseas province'. A local committee was then appointed by Macau's governor to study and identify the enclave's 'national heritage'. Consequently, the structures that were designated as national heritage were mostly military fortresses and government buildings. Buildings of Chinese architectural design were not designated until after 1976, but it was done without any particular input from the community.

On mainland China, one of the earliest ordinances on cultural property protection was passed by the failing imperial government in 1909. In terms of conserving the built environment, however, it was not until 1982 that a pertinent legislation was passed. The promulgation of the 1982 Law of the People's Republic of China on the Protection of Cultural Relics signified the central government's top-down approach to heritage conservation. Cities in China, including Guangzhou, had to formulate city-level laws that reflected aspects of the national law at the local level. Such legislation was also subject to provincial legislation, as part of a hierarchical response to China's centralized administration and legal system.

Efforts to improve local CHM practices so that they would come in line with internationally generated codes and charters for the phase of *increased professionalism* have been limited to a few postgraduate programmes and occasional seminars run by universities in the region. Part of the problem could be due to a lack of strong heritage NGOs advocating the relevant issues on behalf of the profession or the community. Mainland China, for instance, offers limited opportunities for CH managers to engage directly with their overseas counterparts in such international organizations as ICOMOS and ICOM, but even in events where such contacts were made possible, their activities are still centrally controlled by SACH. The recent ICOMOS general assembly, held in Xi'an in October 2005, was a case in point in that the Chinese papers selected required SACH's approval. This thus raises the question of whether, given current conditions in China, certain areas of international practice are applicable to, or likely to be implemented on, the mainland. As noted earlier, the China Principles have avoided much of what is considered common practice in other countries, such as stakeholder involvement in conservation planning. In this case, hence, local conditions have militated against global factors. Even though Hong Kong and Macau, unlike Guangzhou, are referring to and following international or overseas-developed charters in conservation practices in general terms, they are nevertheless still attempting to re-define approaches, in their own ways, to help initiate and strengthen stakeholder consultation activities on conservation projects.

As a result of recent inscription of the historic centre of Macau as World Heritage, CH professionals in Macau have maintained, in comparison to their counterparts in Hong Kong and Guangzhou, the closest links to and maximal reliance on UNESCO and other international heritage bodies. In considering certain conservation projects, the Macau government still prefers to seek advice from UNESCO-sanctioned regional experts than to engage PRD-based professionals. In some respects this indicates, on the part of the authority, a certain degree of lack of confidence in the technical proficiency or even some doubts about the ethics of local professionals. It is possible that the creation of stronger local branches of ICOMOS, ICOM and other international NGOs might assist in generating, on the part of the local governments, a greater level of confidence in local professionals and in mitigating any problems that might have arisen between the professionals and local heritage authorities.

In all three case study cities, the hierarchical nature of public administration is still quite opaque, and a top-down approach is the norm. This arrangement, coupled with the influences emanating from recent historical events of the last fifty years, is still working against the development of some sub-indicators associated with the stages of *stakeholder consultation* and *review* as per the notional model. Our earlier findings strongly suggest that the larger social conditions needed to allow the last two stages to be fully developed at the local level have been hampered by practices and policies that are rooted in major political events of the twentieth century, such as the advent of the Cultural Revolution in the case of Guangzhou and the dominance and demise of colonialism in the case of Hong Kong and Macau. Economic pressures associated with intense urban growth (Hong Kong and Macau) and reform (Guangzhou) have probably reinforced this situation in all three cases. Another possible reason is that many senior decision-makers in these three cities still prefer to avoid the uncertainty and change that greater inclusiveness and transparency, as advocated in international best practice, could bring into the process of heritage conservation.

The final phase of *review* – which could help pick up and amend CHM practice to deal with both older and emerging issues associated with earlier stages – has yet to develop fully in the PRD. For instance, none of the cities has revisited how they could better designate and list heritage assets with the cooperation of the community. Hong Kong is one of the few places in the world with its first piece of initial heritage legislation remaining almost untouched since it was first passed, while Macau is receiving calls for the first time from the local community to open up its list to community nominations/declarations. Meanwhile, Guangzhou (like the rest of the mainland) has almost all of its heritage management practice placed under the control of the government. None of these three cities has fully utilized or dealt with the relevant stakeholders to the level that might satisfy international best practice principles. This is one of the major stumbling blocks that any of the three cities would now need to overcome on its way to achieving a mature CHM framework as presented and argued in the notional model.

The future of CHM in the Pearl River Delta

It is unlikely that the hierarchical and centralized aspects of the three cities' administrations are likely to change in the immediate future. However, in order that the cities' officials would recognize the contributions that the community could make to conservation efforts through increased collaboration, the hierarchical aspects of the local governments need to be changed first. Economic and political factors that are preventing the generation of effective cultural and heritage management policies would also need to be addressed through action-research programmes. For instance, the tax system in Hong Kong, which has helped promote large-scale redevelopment projects and fuelled speculative activities, has made it very difficult to retain both tangible and intangible heritage assets, both of which are closely associated with the city's street life in established urban areas. It remains to be seen if the introduction of a goods and services tax (GST) would broaden the tax base in Hong Kong, and would be enough of a change to relieve this fiscal pressure, especially given that there is little political will to change the current policy and legislation to support the protection of group listings or areas and intangible heritage.

The strength of emphasis on heritage assets conservation requiring some kind of economic rationale for protection is most noticeable in Guangzhou. Only recently have officials considered conserving these assets for their intrinsic values, unless they are related to Communist historical events. A greater degree of integration between heritage conservation and urban planning may be possible for Guangzhou, if land speculation of the kind seen in Hong Kong can be regulated by the authorities. However, it is very likely that Hong Kong will remain a model for mainland urban governments in terms of urban planning approaches in their hope of repeating the SAR's economic success. This is a prospect that would spell disaster for many types of heritage assets that are not well preserved in mainland cities, should the rest of China copy Hong Kong's approach to urban development too closely.

Some authorities have floated the idea of setting up a wealthy heritage trust to dispense money to help resolve the many difficulties associated with funding the retention of historic buildings, gardens and settings. However, such initiatives to establish heritage trust-like bodies might fail, because the basic conditions to support them are mostly lacking in the region. The fulfilment of these conditions requires answers to be provided to such questions as: 'How will the interests of local stakeholders be served in the most equitable manner?' 'What is the best strategy to attract philanthropic donations on a large scale?' 'What should be the terms of reference that will allow heritage assets to be preserved in a way that would satisfy the needs of present and future generations?' In any event, in all of the cities concerned, trust bodies of various kinds are needed to supplement government efforts.

Professional development is still an unresolved issue for all the case study cities, and the future of CHM will be greatly influenced by the shape that it will adopt in the coming years. Agreement on standard terms and principles would help forge closer links and collaboration on heritage-conservation projects among professionals operating in the region. A substantial amount of work, however, would need to be done to reach an agreement among all the concerned parties on how to establish a regional association of heritage professionals that will assist the development and promotion of regional standards and cross-city collaboration. International bodies based elsewhere, such as the UNESCO network, the Asian Academy of Heritage Management, will need to continue to play a role in training local professionals and in inspiring practitioners to upgrade their skills. In the past, exemplar projects with overseas consultants have played an important role in improving local practices in some cities, but more needs to be done to encourage local CH managers and their counterparts in other sectors to aim for the creation of local examples of best practice as well. There appears to be a 'chicken and egg' situation with regard to the establishment of more full-time local private professional heritage practice in the case study cities, primarily because there is a lack of projects that require local private expertise, but also because of the perceived lack of such expertise in these cities.

In summary, it is worth returning to the modes of activity outlined in Chapter 5 for each city, to see how the above issues might be brought into play for CHM in this region in the future. Hong Kong needs more *thinking* (which is proactive) and less *doing* (which is reactive) with regard to its work on policy. Macau lacks a transparent and inclusive system to allow it to go beyond *being*. Guangzhou and other mainland Chinese cities need to undertake *thinking* in a way that will include more than just government decision-makers and selected individuals, with a view to *doing* more to conserve heritage assets that are not designated as World Heritage or of national status, but are nonetheless significant.

Further research agenda for CHM in the other parts of China

This book is a preliminary attempt to come to terms with the question of how three different jurisdictions in Southern China have conducted CHM in the face of rapid political, social and economic changes. Given that the process used in Guangzhou differs somewhat from those followed in the two post-colonial cities, it is difficult to envisage how integration among the three cities with regard to CHM could be achieved. Research into the questions of how this integration might take place and how the PRD might influence practices elsewhere was beyond the scope of the book because of limited resources and incomplete research materials. This book's analysis of CHM in Southern China is, however, a useful counterpoint to studies that have been undertaken on the Silk Road and other World Heritage sites by the Getty Conservation Institute as well as other international and mainland researchers. As already stated, we need to take into account not just World Heritage but other categories of heritage assets as well to conduct a thorough and complete appraisal of the evolution of CHM in the region. Detailed information about the latter is not currently available, however, except on a limited case-by-case basis. In the course of undertaking the research for this book, it was found that self-reflexive studies of overall practice were limited to specific disciplines (e.g. archaeology) and did not include the administration or the care of cultural heritage as a whole. It is likely that this is a problem not specific to studying CHM in China because many other countries have yet to analyse their CHM frameworks in some fashion. Particularly difficult in Guangzhou's case, however, is a lack of in-depth research that examines the historical development of legislation and policy on CHM across China since the establishment of the Communist state. Research into this specific topic is urgently needed, and should be accorded a higher priority than that of digitally recording historic buildings (a popular topic currently), for instance.

Understanding how CHM works in China at the ground level needs to include a detailed local-level investigation because the tension between the central government and the local authorities would reveal much about what is really occurring at the city-level as against the glossed-over versions provided in conference papers and government reports. In order to understand how well the China Principles and other initiatives have been applied by local officials, we need to develop a clear understanding of how this central–local administrative tension has been resolved, as well as a good knowledge of how professionalisms have been and could be diffused and strengthened across the spectrum.

In China, issues about stakeholder involvement are becoming topics of interest to researchers, who are concerned with preserving intangible heritage as they begin to recognize the importance of local residents and tradition bearers. At present, there is probably an appreciation of their importance primarily in an economic sense because their withdrawal could mean that some tourist attractions involving them would be less appealing. Their withdrawal may also sometimes lead to some social unrest. China has always been sensitive to the issue of CH and to the issue of what it terms 'ethnic minorities', such as the Tibetans or Uighurs, who might use heritage assets for economic and/or political purposes. Research into this issue is sorely needed but it will not be a straightforward topic to study, especially if the authorities consider it politically awkward.

Implications and lessons for Western-derived frameworks

Local cultural, historic and economic factors have heavily influenced the way CHM practices have developed in the Pearl River Delta cities. The way the three cities have developed their respective CHM approaches has indicated much about the lack of power of CH authorities in the face of massive changes and large-scale urban redevelopment projects. Neither legislation nor community/media pressure has been able to persuade high-ranking government officials and developers to recognize and care for a broader category of heritage than monuments and antiquities. These other categories – such as intangible, industrial and even urban archaeological heritage – have received little or no legislative or policy protection in the PRD region. Curiously, the lack of recognition of the importance of intangible heritage in particular is not an Asia-specific problem, as both Japan and Korea have seen a strong concern about intangible heritage built into their local CHM frameworks and are working to encourage living culture and community connectivity in association with tangible heritage.

The PRD region is not the only place that needs to revisit outdated legislations and policies or review current practices. In fact, this is an issue that would probably attract attention from many cultural heritage managers from around the world who are concerned about developing a mature and proactive CHM framework. Although cultural heritage management is still developing with different degrees of sophistication in many places, the authors believe that it is never too early or too late for CH managers to reflect on their own local practices, perhaps using the notional framework proposed in this book as a general reference point. An improved understanding about how changes in attitudes and in practices have been associated with various factors (both global and local) to allow the CHM framework to evolve into a mature methodology could assist CH managers in identifying the best possible ways to anticipate, prevent or ameliorate current problems in heritage conservation. It could also give them a cushion of moral support when dealing with the more reactionary or 'unharmonious' elements found in their policy-enabling environment. Knowledge of how a CHM approach might have been and could be developed would prove to be crucial to heritage professionals coming from all kinds of disciplines. Developing a more proactive, integrated and strategic system for managing cultural heritage assets should be the ultimate aim for such individuals, whether they are working in the West or elsewhere. Ultimately, such knowledge should give everyone concerned about heritage the focus needed to ensure that the best care is made available for heritage assets of all kinds.

Glossary of common heritage terms

Authenticity Non-distortion of evidence, being true in substance to the core cultural values of a culture. Western practice places greatest value on tangible heritage being genuine, while many Asian cultures, such as Japan, emphasise intangible heritage (*see below*).

Best practice The best the world has to offer. Most practitioners use the various charters of principles or codes of ethics produced by ICOM or ICOMOS as a guide.

Carrying capacity The maximum number of visitors a single site can accommodate before damage to heritage assets, the environment, and/or the visitor experience takes place. The maximum number is quoted as the 'visitor ceiling'.

Codes of practice A set of rules governing proper visitor behaviour within a site, or a set of rules governing the way in which sites are planned, developed, and managed.

Conservation/Preservation Warning: these terms are almost synonymous to Americans and Australians. To Americans, the retention and care of heritage assets are rolled together as one action. For Australians (and most British) 'preservation' is the act of maintaining the fabric of a place in its existing state and retarding deterioration. For the British 'conservation' is the process of looking after a place so as to retain its cultural significance (Kerr, 2000). That is to mean the practice of caring for heritage assets for the enjoyment of present and future generations. In recent years, Americans now seem to prefer to use the term 'stewardship' instead of either preservation or conservation (see *CRM: Journal of Heritage Stewardship* published by the National Park Service).

Conservation of materials Chemical preservation or special works carried out by specialised practitioners such as conservators (for objects) or conservation architects (for buildings).

Conservation plan A document that is produced to outline what is significant about a tangible heritage asset (*see below*) to enable that significance to be retained in its future use and development.

Cultural heritage The record of a people, manifest in the tangible (cultural relics, handicrafts, monuments, historic towns and villages) and intangible (literature, theatre, music, folk customs) heritage of their culture.

Cultural heritage assets Assets that attract tourists, or are used by a destination to attract tourists, because of their links with the cultural heritage. Hopefully these assets have received some commodification to cope with the tourists they attract and provide a satisfactory tourism experience for them.

Cultural heritage management The systematic practice of implementing elements of established codes and charters of conservation principles, to preserve cultural heritage assets for present and future generations.

Cultural identity A sense of shared cultural identity eventuates when each individual, community or nationality shares some core cultural values with others that can provide a basis for their social behaviour in a wider context.

Cultural landscape A landscape that has tangible and/or intangible heritage assets that require to be seen as a sum of individual parts. *The China Principles* (Agnew and Demas, 2002) describes cultural landscape as a 'humanistic landscape or setting'.

Cultural tourism Travel concerned with experiencing cultural environments, including landscapes, the visual or performing arts, archaeological remains, buildings, particular lifestyles, values, traditions and events (*see* cultural heritage and cultural heritage assets).

Cultural values The value (in terms of importance) of cultural assets to an area in terms of their intrinsic significance of historical, aesthetic, social, scientific or spiritual value evident in a tangible or intangible form.

Environmental Impact Assessment (EIA) A formal study of the impact a specific development will have on its surrounding natural, socio-cultural, and economic environment. When only dealing with the cultural heritage of an area, it is known as a CHIA.

Globalization Process whereby aspects of one particular culture are adopted worldwide.

Host community The community which attracts or works around and accommodates tourists within it at a particular destination.

Intangible heritage Heritage assets that are a culture's non-physical legacy. Special or local kinds of 'soft' culture, such as stories, customs, knowledge and expertise needed to make handicrafts, visual and performing arts (*see also* tangible heritage).

Interpretation strategy How to communicate the importance and significance of a heritage asset to the visitor in a highly interesting, stimulating, and engaging way.

Limits of acceptable change A broader concept than that of 'carrying capacity' for sites. It concerns all cultural and heritage assets, and deals with managing the absorption of new influences by them and impacts of tourism on them.

Stakeholders Those people who have a specific interest in or are likely to be affected by any changes to a heritage asset (tangible or intangible).

Socio-cultural impacts Positive and/or negative impacts or changes that the introduction of tourism and other factors from outside have upon a society and its culture.

Tangible heritage Physical manifestations of culture which include buildings, archaeological sites, cultural landscapes, gardens and all categories of movable cultural property considered to be of cultural significance (*see also* intangible heritage).

Tourist precinct *or* **Tourist area** Areas that attract large volumes of tourists (and locals) both during the day and night-time. These areas, or precincts, incorporate attractions, food and beverage outlets, entertainment, and historic buildings converted into merchandising centres.

Visitor interpretation An explanation of the cultural values and importance of a heritage asset to the history and culture of a region. This should *not* include trivial facts and statistics, for instance.

World Heritage inscription The act of putting a tangible heritage asset of outstanding universal value, as per the World Heritage Convention criteria, on the World Heritage List.

References

Agnew, N. and Demas, M. (eds) (2002) *Principles for the Conservation of Heritage Sites in China*. The Getty Conservation Institute, Los Angeles (English Language version).

Agnew, N., Demas, M., Sullivan, S. and Altenburg, K. (2005) 'The begetting of charters: genesis of the China Principles', *Historic Environment* 18(1): 40–46.

AMO (1997) Antiquities and Monuments Office, *Heritage Hong Kong* 1: 17–18.

Ancient Monuments Society (2005) 'About the AMS', available at website: http://www.ancientmonumentsociety.org.uk

Arnstein, S. (1969) 'A ladder of citizen participation', *Journal of the American Institute of Planners* 35(4): 216–224.

Ashworth, B. (2001) *Post-colonial Futures*. Continuum, London.

Ashworth, G.J. and Howard, P. (1999) *European Heritage Planning and Management*. Intellect Ltd, Exeter.

Ashworth, G.J. and Tunbridge, J.E. (2000) *The Tourist-Historic City: Retrospect and Prospect of Managing the Heritage City*. Pergamon/Elsevier Science, Oxford.

Asian Academy for Heritage Management (2003) 'Asian Academy for Heritage Management. Networking for capacity building in heritage conservation and management in Asia and Pacific'. Unpublished report by Asian Academy for Heritage Management c/o UNESCO, Bangkok.

Askew, M.R. and Logan, W.S. (eds) (1994) *Cultural Identity and Urban Change in Southeast Asia: Interpretative Essays*, Deakin University Press, Geelong.

Au, K.F. (2004) 'Heritage preservation: everybody's concern: The Hong Kong Archaeological Society: pioneer in heritage preservation'. In Ng, L. (ed.) *Conference Papers on International Conference: Heritage and Education, 1997*. Antiquities and Monuments Office, Hong Kong: 15–18 (partly in English).

AusAnthrop (2006) 'Repatriation and Cultural Property', available at website: http://www.ausanthrop.net/research/repatriation.php

Australian Heritage Commission (1998) *Protecting Local Heritage Places: A Guide for Communities*. Australian Heritage Commission, Canberra.

Australian Heritage Commission and the Collaborative Research Centre for Sustainable Tourism (2001) *Successful Tourism at Heritage Places: A Guide for Tourism Operators, Heritage Managers and Communities*. Australian Heritage Commission and the Collaborative Research Centre for Sustainable Tourism, Canberra.

Baker, D. (1999) 'Introduction: contexts for collaboration and conflict'. In Chitty, G. and Baker, D. (eds) *Managing Historic Sites and Buildings: Reconciling Preservation and Presentation*. Routledge, London: 1–22.

Ballantyne, R. (1998) 'Interpreting "visions": addressing environmental education goals through interpretation'. In Uzzell, D. and Ballantyne, R. (eds) *Contemporary Issues in Heritage and Environmental Interpretation*. The Stationery Office, London: 77–97.

Bard, S. (1988) *In Search of the Past: A Guide to the Antiquities of Hong Kong*. The Urban Council, Hong Kong.

Bard, S. (1999) 'Preserving Hong Kong's heritage: the first steps'. Proceedings of the International Conference on Heritage and Tourism, December 1999. Antiquities and Monuments Office, Hong Kong: Paper no. 5.

Barker, C. (2000) *Cultural Studies Theory and Practice*. Sage Publications, London.

Bell, D. (1997) *The Historic Scotland Guide to International Conservation Charters*. The Stationery Office, Edinburgh.

Binghamton University (2004) 'Public Archaeology Facility', available at website: http://paf.binghamton.edu.

Boniface, P. and Fowler, P. (1993) *Heritage and Tourism in the 'Global Village'*. Routledge, London.

Bramwell, W.M. and Lane, B. (1993) 'Sustainable tourism: an evolving global approach', *Journal of Sustainable Tourism* 1(1): 1–5.

Breeze, D.J. (1997) 'Ancient monuments legislation'. In Hunter, J. and Ralston, I. (eds) *Archaeological Resource Management in the United Kingdom: An Introduction*. Sutton Publishing, Gloucestershire: 44–55.

Butler, R. (1980) 'The concept of the tourism area cycle of evolution: the implications for managers of resources', *The Canadian Geographer* 24: 5–12.

Byrne, D. (1991) 'Western hegemony in archaeological heritage management', *History and Archaeology* 5: 269–276.

Campanella, T.J., Zhong, M., Lee, T. and Sze, N.D. (2002) 'The Pearl River Delta: an evolving region'. In Yeh, A.G., Lee, Y.F., Lee, T. and Sze, N.D. (eds) *Building a Competitive Pearl River Delta Region: Cooperation, Coordination and Planning*. Hong Kong University Press, Hong Kong: 9–26.

Centre for Asian Studies (2004) *Annual Report 2003–4*. Centre for Asian Studies, University of Hong Kong, Hong Kong.

Chan, L.K. and Cunich, P. (2002) *An Impossible Dream*. Oxford University Press, Hong Kong.

Chapman, W.R. (1985) 'Arranging ethnology: A.H.L. Pitt Rivers and the typological tradition. In Stocking, G.W. (ed.) *Objects and Others: Essays on Museums and Material Culture, A History of Anthropology, Volume 3*: 15–48.

Cheung, S.H. (1999) 'The meanings of a heritage trail in Hong Kong', *Annals of Tourism Research* 26(3): 570–588.

Cheung, S.W. (2004) 'Heritage in historical and cultural context: the role of the South China Research Circle in heritage education'. In Leisure and Cultural Services Department (ed.) *Conference papers on International Conference: Heritage and Education, 1997*. Leisure and Cultural Services Department, Hong Kong: 51–55.

Chiao, C. (1993) 'Development of anthropology in China and Hong Kong: a personal and casual review', *The Hong Kong Anthropologist* 7: 20–25.

Chippendale, C. (1983) 'The making of the first Ancient Monuments Protection Act', *Journal of the British Archaeological Association* 153: 1–55.

Chiu, F.Y.L. (1997) 'Politics and the body social'. In Barlow, T.E. (ed.) *Formations of Colonial Modernity in East Asia*. Duke University, USA: 295–322.

Chiu, S.T. (2004) 'The launching of the Year of Heritage: some observations and inspirations'. In Leisure and Cultural Services Department (ed.) *Conference papers on International Conference: Heritage and Education, 1997*. Leisure and Cultural Services Department, Hong Kong: 57–60.

Chu Hai College (2006) 'History', available at website: http://www.chuhai.edu.hk/en/content/about/overview/.

Chu, C. and Ubergang, K. (2002) 'Saving Hong Kong's cultural heritage'. In Civic Exchange (ed.), *Conservation in Hong Kong*. Civic Exchange, Hong Kong: 51–104.

Chui, J. (2001) 'Macau heritage preservation from an urban planning perspective: modern Asian architecture network', available at website: http://www.m-aan.org/macao-conference02.html.

Clark, M. (1982) 'Opening address'. *The Proceedings of the First Australian Symposium on the Mahogany Ship*. The Mahogany Ship Committee, Warrnambool.

Clayton, H.C. (2003) 'City of museums: reflections on exhibiting Macao', *Review of Culture (International Edition)* 5: 98–125.

Cleere, H. (1997) 'British archaeology in a wider context'. In Hunter, J. and Ralston, I. (eds) *Archaeological Resource Management in the United Kingdom: An Introduction*. Sutton Publishing, Gloucestershire: 115–124.

Clewlow, C. (1978) *Hong Kong, Macau and Canton*. Lonely Planet Guides, Melbourne.

Collins, R. (1991) *A Disorderly Excursion: Notes of a Conservationist in the Asia-Pacific Region*. Pepper Publications, Singapore.

Cook, A. and Ng, M.K. (2001) *Building Sustainable Communities: The Wanchai Experiment*. The Centre for Urban Planning and Environment Management, University of Hong Kong, Hong Kong.

Cotter, M., Boyd, B. and Gardiner, J. (eds) (2001) *Heritage Landscapes: Understanding Place and Communities*. Southern Cross University Press, Lismore.

Council for British Archaeology (2004) 'Stakeholder participation in strategic land-use planning for the historic environment: report by the Council for British Archaeology', available at website: http://www.britarch.ac.uk/conserve/planning/stakeholder.html.

Cultural Affairs Bureau (2005) 'Administrative structure', available at website: http://www.icm.gov.mo/icm/feicm.asp.

Culture and Heritage Commission (2002) 'Statement of vision for HK', from defunct website.

Davison, G. (1991) 'Paradigms of public history'. In Richard, J. and Spearritt, P. (eds) *Packaging the Past? Public Histories*. Melbourne University Press, Melbourne: 4–15.

DiStefano, J. (2005) Hong Kong, Macau and China: Cultural Perspectives Project, unpublished preliminary results.

DiStefano, J. and Maznevski, M. (2003) 'Culture in International Management: Mapping the Impact', *IMD Perspectives for Managers* 105: 1–4.

du Cros, H. (1983) 'Skeletons in the closet: a history of the prehistoric archaeology of New South Wales (*c.*1890–1940)'. BA. Hons thesis, University of Sydney.

du Cros, H. (1996) 'Committing Archaeology in Australia'. Unpublished Ph.D. thesis submitted to the National Centre for Australian Studies, Monash University, Melbourne.

du Cros, H. (2000) 'Planning for sustainable cultural heritage tourism in Hong Kong SAR: report to the Lord Wilson Heritage Trust, Hong Kong', available at website: http://www.lordwilson-heritagetrust.org.hk/project/index.php.

du Cros, H. (2002a) 'Conflicting perspectives on marketing Hong Kong's cultural heritage tourism attractions'. In Spanish National Committee of the International Council on Monuments and Sites (ed.) *Strategies for the World's Cultural Heritage Preservation in a Globalised World: Principles, Practices and Perspectives.* ICOMOS XIIIth General Assembly, Madrid: 319–321.

du Cros, H. (2002b) *Much More than Stones and Bones: Australian Archaeology in the Late Twentieth Century.* Melbourne University Press, Melbourne.

du Cros, H. (2004) 'Postcolonial conflict inherent in the involvement of cultural tourism in creating new national myths in Hong Kong'. In Hall, C.M. and Tucker, H. (eds) *Tourism and Postcolonialism: Contested Discourses, Identities and Representations.* Routledge, London: 153–168.

du Cros, H. (2006) 'The "Romantic European Culture Island" with a turbulent history: the intrinsic and extrinsic values of Shamian Island, Guangzhou', *China Tourism Research* (Chinese and English) 1(2&3): 193–220.

du Cros, H. and Kong, F. (2006) 'A preliminary study of factors influencing congestion at popular World Heritage tourist attractions in Macao'. Unpublished report to the Office of the Secretary for Social Affairs and Culture, Macao.

du Cros, H. and McKercher, B. (2000) 'World Heritage listing and "best intentions": a case study from Australia'. In Robinson, M., Evens, N., Long, P., Sharpley, R. and Swarbrooke, J., *Tourism and Heritage Relationships: Global, National and Local Perspectives. Reflections on International Tourism.* University of Northumbria, Newcastle and the Centre for Tourism, Sheffield Hallam University, UK: 147–158.

du Cros, H., Fryxell, G., Bauer, T. and Song, R. (2005) 'Market liberalisation and the sustainable use of heritage assets in China: case studies of the Hutongs and the Huanghua section of the Great Wall', *Journal of Sustainable Tourism* 13(3), available at website: http//:www.channelviewpublications.net.

Durão, L.A., Chan, K.S. and Parreira, M.J. (2004) 'Asserting an identity: cultural heritage policy in Macao'. In Leisure and Cultural Services Department (ed.) *Conference Papers on International Conference: Heritage and Education, 1997.* Leisure and Cultural Services Department, Hong Kong: 91–93.

Dwivedi, O.P. (2003) 'Challenges of culture and governance in Asian public administration'. In Peters, B.G. and Pierre, J. (eds) *Handbook of Public Administration,* Sage, London: 514–522.

Endacott, G.B. (1964) *A History of Hong Kong (Second Edition).* Oxford University Press, Oxford and Hong Kong.

Engelhardt, R. (2004) 'The UNESCO World Heritage Education Project'. In Leisure and Cultural Services Department (ed.) *Conference Papers on International Conference: Heritage and Education, 1997.* Leisure and Cultural Services Department, Hong Kong: 95–104.

English Heritage (2005) 'Who are we?', available at website: http://www.english-heritage.org.uk/default.asp?wci=mainframe&URL1=default.asp%3FWCI%3DNode%26WCE%3D83.

Fabian, J. (2001) *Anthropology with an Attitude: Critical Essays.* Stanford, California: Stanford University Press, 2001.

Fforde, C. (1992) 'The Royal College of Surgeons of England: a brief history of its collections and a catalogue of some current holdings', *World Archaeology Bulletin* 6: 22–31.

Fowler, P.J. (1981) 'Archaeology, the public and the sense of the past'. In Lowenthal, D. and Binney, M. (eds) *Our Past Before Us: Why do we Save it?* Temple Smith, London: 56–69.

Freidson, E. (1994) *Professionalism Reborn: Theory, Prophecy and Policy.* Polity Press, Cambridge.

Fringe Club Memory Capsule Project (2006) available at website: http://www.23hq.com/Memory_capsule/album/list.

Garrett, V. (2002) *Heaven is High, the Emperor Far Away: Merchants and Mandarins in Old Canton.* Oxford University Press, Oxford.

HAB (2001) 'Cultural consultation paper received public support'. Press release, 9 September 2001, by the HAB.

HAB (2003) 'Government response to Culture and Heritage Commission policy recommendations'. Unpublished report to the Hong Kong Legislative Council by the Culture and Heritage Commission.

HAB (2004) 'Extract of the paper on review of built heritage conservation policy'. HAB, Hong Kong.

Hakka Diaspora UK Research Forum (2005) 'Martyrs, mystery and memory behind the colonial shift', available at website: http://hakkadiaspora.proboards29.com/index.cgi?board=general&action=display&threat.

Hall, M. and McArthur, S. (1998) *Integrated Heritage Management.* The Stationery Office, London.

Hall, P. (2002) *Urban and Regional Planning (Fourth Edition).* Routledge, London.

Harris, R. (2003) *Sustainable Tourism: A Global Perspective (Second edn).* Butterworth–Heinemann, London.

Harvey, D.C. (2001) 'Heritage pasts and heritage presents: temporality, meaning and the scope of heritage studies', *International Journal of Heritage Studies* 7(4): 319–338.

Hase, P. (2001) 'The District Office'. In Sinn, E. (ed.) *Hong Kong British Crown Colony Revisited.* Centre for Asian Studies, University of Hong Kong, Hong Kong: 123–146.

Hillier, B. (1981) 'Why do we collect antiques?'. In Lowenthal, D. and Binney, M. (eds) *Our Past Before Us: Why do we Save it?* Temple Smith, London: 70–82.

Hitchens, C. (ed.) (1988) *The Elgin Marbles: Should they be Returned to Greece?* Chatto and Windus, London.

Ho, P.Y. (2004) *The Administrative History of the Hong Kong Government Agencies 1841–2002.* Hong Kong University Press, Hong Kong.

Hofsted, G. (1991) *Culture and Organisations: Software of the Mind.* McGraw-Hill, London.

Hong Kong Government Logistics Department (2004) *Showcasing the Achievements of the Hong Kong Civil Service*. Government Logistics Department, Hong Kong.

Hong Kong Tourism Board (2006) Banner on website, available at: http://www.discoverhongkong.com/eng/heritage/monuments/index.jhtml.

Hopkinson, L. and Lei, M.L.M. (2003) *Rethinking the Small House Policy*. Civic Exchange, Hong Kong.

Hou, J. (2004) 'A survey of propaganda and education for cultural heritage in China'. In Leisure and Cultural Services Department (ed.) *Conference Papers on International Conference: Heritage and Education, 1997*. Leisure and Cultural Services Department, Hong Kong: 165–168.

Huang, M.H. (2004) 'The importance of publicity about heritage preservation with reference to the theft of the ancient tombs at Hengzhigang in Guangzhou'. In Leisure and Cultural Services Department (ed.) *Conference Papers on International Conference: Heritage and Education, 1997*. Leisure and Cultural Services Department, Hong Kong: 169–172.

ICOMOS (2004) *Heritage@Risk Report 2003–2004*, available at website: http//:www.icomos.org.

ICOMOS (2005) 'Charters', available at website: http//:www.icomos.org.

ICOMOS (2006) 'Venice Charter dossier', available at website: http://www.international.icomos.org/venicecharter2004/index.html.

IFT (2006) Institute for Tourism Studies, 'General information', available at website: http://www.ift.edu.mo/eng/about/about.htm.

Imon, S.S. (2006) 'Sustainable urban conservation: the role of public participation in the conservation of urban heritage in Old Dhaka'. Unpublished Ph.D. thesis, Department of Architecture, University of Hong Kong.

Indonesia ICOMOS (2006) 'Indonesian Charter for heritage conservation'. Summary available at website: http://www.icomosindonesia.org/index.php?name=News&file=article&sid=15.

Jafari, J. (1996) 'Tourism and culture: an inquiry into paradoxes'. Proceedings of the round table debate on culture, tourism, development: crucial issues for the 21st century. UNESCO, Paris: 43–47.

Johnston, C. (1994) *What is Social Value? A Discussion Paper*. Australian Government Publishing Service, Canberra.

Johnston, C. (2005) 'Communities and heritage'. Presentation at a public seminar on CHM and stakeholders. Institute For Tourism Studies, Macau, November.

Jokilehto, J. (1995) 'Authenticity: a general framework for the concept'. In Larsen, K. (ed.) *Proceedings of the Nara Conference on Authenticity in Relation to the World Heritage Convention*. UNESCO World Heritage Centre (France), Agency for Cultural Affairs (Japan), ICCROM (Italy) and ICOMOS (France): 17–36.

Kass, T. and Liston, C. (1991) 'The Professional Historians Association'. In Richard, J. and Spearritt, P. (eds) *Packaging the Past? Public Histories*. Melbourne University Press, Melbourne: 215–221.

Kerr, J. (2000) *Conservation Plan* (Fifth edn). National Trust (Australia).

Kirkpatrick, C. and Lee, N. (1997) 'Market liberalisation and environmental assessment'. In Wilson, F.A. (ed.) *Towards Sustainable Project Development*, Cheltenham, Edward Elgar: 56–57.

Klosek-Kowzlowska, D. (2002) The protection of urban heritage: the social evaluation of the space in historic towns – local intangible values in a globalised world. In Spanish National Committee of ICOMOS (ed.) *International Council on Monuments and Sites, 13th General Assembly Proceedings*, ICOMOS, Spain 2002: 87–89.
Koo, K.F. (2004) 'Television and heritage education in Hong Kong' In Leisure and Cultural Services Department (ed.) *Conference Papers on International Conference: Heritage and Education, 1997*. Leisure and Cultural Services Department, Hong Kong: 191–196.
Koshar, R. (1998) *Germany's Transient Pasts: Preservation and National Memory in the Twentieth Century*. University of North Carolina Press/Chapel Hill, London.
Lai, G., Demas, M. and Agnew, N. (2004) Valuing the Past in China: The Seminal Influence of Liang Sicheng on Heritage Conservation. *Orientations* 35(2): 82–89.
Lai, L. (1997) *Town Planning in Hong Kong: A Critical Review (The Hong Kong Economic Policy Study Series)*. City University of Hong Kong Press, Hong Kong.
Langford, R. (1983) 'Our Heritage – Your Playground'. *Australian Archaeology* 16:1–8.
Larkham, P. (1996) *Conservation and the City*. London: Routledge.
Larsen, K. (ed.) (1995) *Proceedings of the Nara Conference on Authenticity in Relation to the World Heritage Convention*. UNESCO World Heritage Centre (France), Agency for Cultural Affairs (Japan), ICCROM (Italy) and ICOMOS (France).
Lau, C.K. (1997) *Hong Kong's Colonial Legacy: A Hong Kong Chinese's View of the British Heritage*. Chinese University Press, Hong Kong.
Layton, R. (1989) *Conflict in the Archaeology of Living Traditions (One World Archaeology Series No. 8)*, Unwin Hyman, London.
Lee, Yok-shiu F. and So, Alvin Y. (eds) (1999) *Asia's Environmental Movements: Comparative Perspectives*. M.E. Sharpe, Armonk, NY: 285–306.
Lilley, I. (ed.) (2000) *Native Title and the Transformation of Archaeology in the Postcolonial World (Oceania Monograph No. 50)*, Oceania Publications, Sydney.
Lim, B.V. (ed.) (2005) *Practitioners' Guide to Design and Implementation of Participatory Projects*. The Chinese University of Hong Kong, Hong Kong (bilingual).
Logan, W. (ed.) (2002) *The Disappearing 'Asian' City: Protecting Asia's Urban Heritage in a Globalising World*. Oxford: Oxford University Press: xii–xxi.
Lord Wilson Heritage Trust (2005) 'Introduction', available at website: http://www.lordwilson-heritagetrust.org.hk/intro/index.htm.
Lowenthal, D. (1985) *The Past is a Foreign Country*. Cambridge University Press, Cambridge.
Lowenthal, D. (1988) 'Classical antiquities as national and global heritage', *Antiquity* 62: 726–735.
Lowenthal, D. (1992) 'Authenticity? The dogma of self-delusion'. In Jones, M. (ed.) *Why Fakes Matter: Essays on the Problems of Authenticity*. British Museum Press, London: 184–192.
Lowenthal, D. (2003) 'Epilogue'. In Mitchell, N., Hudson, L.J. and Jones, D. (eds) *Speaking of the Future: A Dialogue on Conservation (Conservation and Stewardship Publication No. 4)*. Conservation Study Institute, Vermont: 42–43.

Lu, L. (2002) The Transformation of Academic Culture in Mainland Chinese Archaeology, *Asian Anthropology* 1: 117–152.

Lugard, F.D. (1910) *Hong Kong University: Objects, History, Present Position and Prospects*. Pamphlet in Public Records Office, Hong Kong.

Lung, D. (1999) 'In search for soul, memory and identity: heritage in Hong Kong's urban development', *Planning and Development* 15(1): 2–8.

Ma, S.Y. and Chan, W.Y. (2004) 'Heritage preservation and sustainability of China's development', *Sustainable Development* 12(1): 15–31.

Macau Heritage Net (2005) *The History of Heritage Conservation in Macau*. Available at website: http//: www.macauheritage.net/Education/CycloDE.asp?id=69.

Macintosh, B. (1999) 'The National Park Service and cultural resources', *CRM: The Journal of Heritage Stewardship* 4: 41–43.

Mai, Y.H. (2004) 'Enlightenment gained from the discovery of the palace remnants of the Southern Yue Kingdom of the Western Han Dynasty in Guangzhou'. In Leisure and Cultural Services Department (ed.) *Conference Papers on International Conference: Heritage and Education, 1997*. Leisure and Cultural Services Department, Hong Kong: 237–242.

Mallam, M. (1989) 'Can Heritage Charities be Profitable?' In Uzzell, D.L. (ed.) *The Visitor Experience Vol. 2*. Belhaven Press/Pinter Publishers, London: 44–50.

Marrie, A. (1989) 'Museums and Aborigines: a case study in internal colonialism', *Australian and Canadian Studies* 7(1–2): 63–80.

Mason, R. and Avrami, E. (2000) 'Heritage Values and Challenges of Conservation Planning'. In Teutonico, J.M. and Palumbo, G. (eds) *Management Planning of Archaeological Sites*. The Getty Conservation Institute, Los Angeles: 13–26.

McBryde, I. (ed.) (1985) *Who Owns the Past?* Oxford University Press, Oxford: 1–10.

McKercher, B. and du Cros, H. (2002) *Cultural Tourism: The Partnership between Tourism and Cultural Heritage Management*. The Haworth Press, Bingamton, New York.

McKercher, B., Bauer, T., du Cros, H., Young, L. and Ho, P. (2003) 'The Northern New Territories tourism development plan'. Unpublished report to the Hong Kong Tourism Commission, Hong Kong.

McKercher, B., Ho, S.Y. and du Cros, H. (2004) 'The relationship between tourism and cultural heritage: evidence from Hong Kong', *Tourism Management* 26: 539–548.

McKinlay, J.R. and Jones, K.L. (eds) (1979) *Archaeological Resource Management in Australia and Oceania*. New Zealand Historic Places Trust, Wellington.

Miners, N. (1998) *The Government and Politics in Hong Kong*. Oxford University Press, Hong Kong.

Mintz, S. (2001) *Guangzhou Museum* (English version of pamphlet). Guangzhou Museum, Guangzhou.

Mok, K.H. (2000) *Social and Political Development in Post-Reform China*. Macmillan, Basingstoke.

Moore, A.C. (1998) *The Powers of Preservation: New Life for Urban Historic Places*. McGraw-Hill, New York.

Mowforth, M. and Munt, I. (1998) *Tourism and Sustainability: New Tourism in the Third World*. Routledge, London.

Mulvaney, J. (1991) 'Past regained, future lost: the Kow Swamp Pleistocene burials', *Antiquity* 65: 12–21.

Murtagh, W.L. (1997) *Keeping Time: The History and Theory of Preservation in America*. John Wiley & Sons, New York.

Nadeau, B. (2006) 'Vanishing acts'. Article in *Newsweek*, available at World Monuments Fund website: http://www.msnbc.msn.com/id/12113285/site/newsweek//print/1/displaymode/1098/.

National Park Service (2006) 'Cultural resources of the National Park Service staff directory: National Center for Cultural Resources (under the Associate Director for Cultural Resource Management)', available at website: http://www.cr.nps.gov/staff.htm.

National Trust for Historic Preservation (2006) 'Community partners', available at website: http://www.nationaltrust.org/community_partners/index.html.

New Mexico State University (2004) 'Public history program', available at website: http://web.nmsu.edu/~publhist.

Newman, A. and McLean, F. (2004) 'Editorial', *International Journal of Heritage Studies* 10(1): 5–10.

Olsen, R. (1985) 'Organizational structure of the National Park Service: 1917 to 1985: administrative history', available at National Park Service website: http://www.cr.nps.gov/history/online books/olsen/adhi.htm.

Pacific Area Travel Association (PATA) (1980) *Macau: A Study of Tourism Development*. PATA, Bangkok.

Pacific Area Travel Association (PATA) (1994) *Macau: Tourism in Transition*. PATA, Bangkok.

Page, S.J. and Hall, M. (2003) *Managing Urban Tourism*. Prentice Hall, London.

Palmer, N. (1989) 'Museums and cultural property'. In Vergo, P. (ed.) *The New Museology*. Reaktion Books, London: 172–204.

Pardoe, C. (1991) 'Competing paradigms and ancient human remains: the state of the discipline', *Archaeology in Oceania* 26(2): 79–85.

Pearson, M. and Sullivan, S. (1999) *Looking after Heritage Places*. Melbourne University Press, Melbourne.

Poon, A. and Wong, W.Y. (2005) *Equity vs Excellence: A Preliminary Exploration of Hong Kong's Education Reform*. Centre for Asian Pacific Studies, Lingnan University, Hong Kong.

Ricketts, S. (1992) ' "Raising the dead": reconstruction within the Canadian Parks Service'. In Environment Canada Parks Service (ed.) *Proceedings of the Canadian Parks Service Reconstruction Workshop*. Environment Canada Parks Service, Hull, Quebec: 21–29.

Royal Asiatic Society (1980) *Hong Kong Going and Gone: Western Victoria. Photographic Series No. 1*. Royal Asiatic Society of Hong Kong, Hong Kong.

Ryan, T.F. (1958) *Archaeological Finds on Lamma Island, near Hong Kong*. Ricci Publications, Ricci Hall, University of Hong Kong, Hong Kong.

Rykwert, J. (2000) *The Seduction of Place: The History and Future of the City*. Vintage Books, New York.

Sauvegrain, A. (2001) ' "Traditioning": a dialectical form of architectural preservation: a case study: Hanoi, Vietnam'. M.Sc. (Architecture) thesis, University of California, Berkeley.

Schiffer, M.B. and Gumerman, G.J. (eds) (1977) *Conservation Archaeology: A Guide for Cultural Resource Management Studies*. Academic Press, New York.

School of Chinese (2006) University of Hong Kong, 'History', available at website: http://www.hku.hk/chinese/.

Sofield, T. and Lee, S. (1998) 'Tourism development and cultural policies in China', *Annals of Tourism Research* 25(2): 362–392.

Spearritt, P. (1991) 'Money, taste and industrial heritage'. In Richard, J. and Spearritt, P. (eds) *Packaging the Past? Public Histories*. Melbourne University Press, Melbourne: 33–45.

Stone, J. (1992) 'The ownership of culture: reconciling our common and separate heritages', *Archaeology in Oceania* 27(3): 161–167.

Sullivan, S. (2001) 'A well baked charter', *Historic Environment* 15(3): 11–19.

Sun Yat Sen University (2005) 'History of the university', available at website: http://www.gzsums.edu.cn/english/msgshow.php?bk=english&newsid=1fea3d718dba0d139971b44e05d1111c.

Taylor, K. (2004) 'Cultural heritage management: a possible role for charters and principles in Asia', *International Journal of Heritage Studies* 10(5): 417–433.

Throsby, D. (2000) 'Conceptualising heritage as cultural capital'. In Australian Heritage Commission (ed.) *Heritage Economics: Challenges for Heritage Conservation and Sustainable Development in the 21st Century Conference Proceedings*. Australian National University, Canberra: 6–13.

Town Planning Board Bulletin (2005–2006) Available at website: http://search.info.gov.hk/cgibin/se.cgi?lmode=1&gr_1=+&pq=&pg=&qu=%22Town+Planning+Board+meetings%22&fu=-www.legco.gov.hk+-%2Fgia%2F+-www0.info.gov.hk&pn=0&qm=0&la=1&de=0&so=0&ma=100&nu=10&ca=0&ta=all&ft_1=alltype&temp_qu=Town+Planning+Board+meetings&submit=+Go+&mode=1.

Townsend, J. (1999) 'The Department of Everything Else, Including Historic Preservation', *CRM: The Journal of Heritage Stewardship* 4: 5–10.

Trigger, B. (1989) *A History of Archaeological Thought*. Cambridge University Press, Cambridge.

Tunbridge, J.E. and Ashworth, G.J. (1996) *Dissonant Heritage: The Management of the Past as a Resource in Conflict*. Wiley, London.

UMAG (2006) University Museum and Art Gallery, the University of Hong Kong. 'About us', available at website: http://www.hku.hk/hkumag/about_us.html.

UNESCO (2006) 'The Convention for the safeguarding of the intangible cultural heritage', available at website: http://www.unesco.org/culture/ich_convention/index.php.

UNESCO (2006a) 'World Heritage Convention', available at website: http://whc.unesco.org/en/convention/.

UNESCO (2006b) 'Asia-Pacific strategic pillar 5: engendering a paradigm shift in tourism in favour of culture and nature conservation', available at website: http://www.unescobkk.org/index.php?id=1077.

UNESCO (2004) *UNESCO-ICCROM Asian Academy of Heritage Management Press Kit* February 2004.

UNESCO and Nordic World Heritage Office (2000) *Sustainable Tourism and Cultural Heritage: A Review of Development Assistance and Its Potential to Promote Sustainability*. UNESCO and Nordic World Heritage Office, Norway.

University of Macau (2005) 'History of the university', available at website: http://www.umac.mo/fi.

Urban Renewal Authority (2004) Public response to Wanchai District Council's position paper for the Hong Kong Legislation Council panel on Home Affairs, 9 November 2004.

Wang, G. (1985) 'Loving the ancient in China'. In McBryde, I. (ed.) *Who Owns the Past?* Oxford University Press, Oxford: 175–195.

Wang, J.H. (1998) 'Introductory remarks'. In UNESCO (ed.) *International Conference for Mayors of Historic Cities in China and the European Union*. UNESCO, Paris: 11–12.

Wilson, D. (1985) 'Return and restitution: a museum perspective'. In McBryde, I. (ed.) *Who Owns the Past?* Oxford University Press, Oxford: 99–106.

World Tourism Organization and ICOMOS International Committee for Cultural Tourism (2005) *Site Congestion Management for Natural and Cultural Sites*. World Tourism Organization, Madrid.

Zheng, W. (1996) 'An agenda for the archaeological work in Macau'. In Macau SAR Government, *Macau Yearbook* (in Chinese).

Index

Aberdeen, in Hong Kong, 27
Agriculture, Fisheries and Conservation Department, in Hong Kong, 32
Ancient Monuments and Archaeological Areas Act, in the UK, 44
A-Ma Temple, in Macau, 29
Antiquities Advisory Board (AAB), in Hong Kong, 38, 56, 64–65, 67, 76–77, 87, 90, 94–95
Provisional Antiquities Advisory Board (PAAB), 37, 44, 139
Antiquities and Monuments Office (AMO), in Hong Kong, 27, 30, 37, 42–43, 55, 59, 60, 62, 64–65, 67, 70–71, 76, 88, 90, 95, 97–99, 100, 106, 108, 130, 132, 139
Antiquities and Monuments Ordinance, in Hong Kong, 27, 37, 89–90, 139
Ap Lei Chau, in Hong Kong, 27
Architects Association of Macau (AAM), 61–62
Architectural Services Department, in Hong Kong, 62, 65
Asian Academy for Heritage Management, 58, 143
Au, Ka-fat, 29, 58
Australia, 3, 7, 32, 44, 65–66, 79, 124
Australian Labor Party, 3
Australian Heritage Commission, 65
Australian Museum, The, 44
Authenticity, 2, 16, 110, 147
Nara Declaration on Authenticity, 16

Bard, Solomon, 27, 44, 55
Beijing, 25, 36, 55, 58, 66, 69, 79, 90, 101, 118, 123

Beijing University, 55
Bender, Barbara, 49
Big Buddha, in Hong Kong, 28
Bowring, John, 31
Britain, 25, 35, 37, 44, 64, 117, 132
Built Environment Conservation Policy Review, in Hong Kong, 95–96
Burra Charter, 16, 65–66, 79

Cambridge University, 55
Canada, 3
Canton International Trade Fair, 39
Center for Research in History and Languages within the Central Research Institute, in Guangzhou, 26
Central Business District (CBD), 74, 94, 99, 130
Central Police Station Compound, in Hong Kong, 67, 94, *100*, 124
Chan, Stephen, 66
Chan, W.K., 59
Charters of conservation principles, the use of, 65 (*See also* Burra Charter, China Principles, Venice Charter)
Chen Clan's Ancestral Hall, in Guangzhou, 39, 75
Cheng, Jian-jun, 54
Cheng, Kung-chu, 27
Cheung Chau, in Hong Kong, 28
Cheung Chau Bun Festival, 107–108, 130
Cheung Chau Bun Festival Organizing Committee, 108
China, 24
China Principles, 65, 66, 78, 87, 124, 140, 144, 148 (*See also* Principles for the Conservation of Heritage Sites in China)
Chinese Charter, 16

Chinese Communist Party, 45, 51
Chinese University of Hong Kong (CUHK), 55, 57, 59, 64, 113
Chiu, Ling-yeong, 56
City Hall Museum, in Hong Kong, 31
Civic Exchange, in Hong Kong, 95
Clayton, Cathryn Hope, 33, 57
Clock Tower, in Hong Kong, *100*
Comemorações Henriques, 34
Committee for Culture, in Macau, 92
Communist Revolution, in China, 25
Conserve, 3, 8, 12, 31, 69, 79, 143
Conservation, 6, 12–13, 17, 20, 30, 34, 38, 41, 44, 52–57, 59–62, 65–66, 68–69, 71–72, 74, 76–79, 85–90, 92, 95–97, 101–105, 111, 118, 122, 124, 126, 130, 133, 140–145, 147
Cotai Casino Strip, in Macau, 29
Cultural Affairs Bureau (CAB), in Macau, 42, 59, 62, 66, 71, 76, 89, 103, 130
Cultural affinity, 117
  DiStefano and Maznevski model, 117, 127–135
Cultural Heritage Department, in Macau, 61, 72, 103
  Committee for the Defence of the Architectural, Environmental and Cultural Heritage (Comissão de Defesa do Património Arquitectónico, Paisagístico e Cultural), 61
  Committee for the Defence of Macao's Urbanistic, Natural and Cultural Heritage, 61
  Decree Law no. 56/84/M, 61, 74
  Decree no. 83/92/M, 61, 103
Cultural heritage management (CHM), commodity and educational resource, 5
  community organizations, 17, 125–127
  cross-cultural influences on, 117–118, 122
  cultural policies, 92–95
  culture, 127–136
  defined, 1, 148
  government intervention in CH conservation, 111–113
  internal administrative restructuring in, 53, 60–64
  international best practices in, 8, 17, 52, 56, 78, 87, 117, 135, 141
  linkage between urban planning, land use and, 72–76, 79
  power and, 2–3
  quality of life and, 3–4
  specialist and community care and, 4–5
  stakeholders and, 85–86
  sustainable development and, 1, 4, 6
  tourism and, 4, 16, 20, 38–39, 50, 53, 55, 58, 65, 69, 71, 79, 85–86, 89, 92–93, 101–103, 106, 108–110, 122, 126, 134
  urban renewal and, 77, 122
Cultural heritage management (CHM) framework, 6–14, 141, 144–145
  increased professionalism, 3rd phase of, 12, 49–84, 105, 140
  influence of global and local factors, 14–16
  initial legislation, 2nd phase of, 13, 23, 36–42, 95
  inventory, 1st phase of, 14, 23, 26–36
  review, 5th phase of, 8, 13, 95, 105, 141
  stakeholder consultation and participation, 4th phase of, 8, 51, 87–90, 99, 101, 103–105, 108, 124, 140–141
Cultural heritage (CH) managers, 2, 5, 7, 17, 23, 49, 52–53, 58–60, 62, 66, 78–79, 105–112, 122, 128–130, 140, 143, 145
  background and career paths of, 58–60
  in Guangzhou, 58–60, 122
  in Hong Kong, 59–60, 107, 122
  in Macau, 59–62, 122, 140
  in Pearl River Delta, 23, 49, 79, 105–112
Cultural identity, 49–51, 85–116, 122–123, 148
  defined, 50, 148
  economic growth and, 85–116
  in Guangzhou, 91
  in Hong Kong, 89, 92–94, 110–112, 122–123
  in Macau, 89, 123
  in Pearl River Delta, 105
  inter-ethnic and intra-regional influences in, 122–127
  self-identification and, 123–124
Cultural Institute, in Macau, 34, 59–62, 89, 106, 118, 130

Cultural Property Bureau, in Macau, 61
Cultural relic conservation, 79
Cultural relics, 26, 91
Cultural resources management, 7, 127
Cultural Revolution, 25, 30, 36, 51, 55, 68, 101, 125–127, 141
Culture and Heritage Commission, in Hong Kong, 93–95

Danwei, 68
Deng, Xiao-ping, 51
Department of Education, in Hong Kong, 88, 90
DiStefano and Maznevski model, 127–135
  environment and, 128
  human nature, 132
  mode of activity, 128, 131
  relations among people, 128, 130
  space, 134–135
  time, 133
du Cros, Hilary, 55

Education and Manpower Bureau, in Hong Kong, 94
Engelhardt, Richard, 49
English Heritage (Historic Buildings and Monuments Commission for England), 44
Environmental Assessment Ordinance, in Hong Kong, 76
Environmental Impact Assessment (EIA), in Hong Kong, 68, 76, 99
Environmental Impact Studies (EIS), 7
Environmental Protection Agency, in Hong Kong, 76
Esparteiro, Marques, 31
Everhardt, Gary, 7

Fangcun Baie Tan Romantic Feeling Bar Street, in Guangzhou, 75
Fangcun District, in Guangzhou, 75
Fanling, in Hong Kong, 28
Federation of Hong Kong Hotel Owners, 109
Feng, Yong-qu, 74
Finn, Daniel, 27, 55
Flagstaff Museum of Tea Culture, in Hong Kong, 36
France, 44
Free Independent Travellers (FIT) scheme, 89

Fung Ping Shan Museum of Chinese Art of Archaeology, in Hong Kong, 32

Geographic Information Systems (GIS), 69, 71
Getty Conservation Institute, 65, 144
Globalization, 2, 4, 148
Government House, in Hong Kong, 91, 118
Government-organized non-governmental organizations (GONGOs), 86
Guangdong, 23, 25, 54, 112, 126
Guangdong Art Museum, 75
Guangdong Museum of Folk Arts and Handicrafts, 39, 40, 75
Guangdong University, 54 (*See also* Zhongshan University)
Guangzhou, 17, 23, 27, 30, 31, 32, 33, 34, 35, 36, 39, 41–43, 45, 46, 50, 54–58, 65, 68–69, 72, 74, 78–80, 85, 87, 91, 97, 99, 103, 111, 112–113, 118, 122, 124–125, 128, 132, 134, 136, 139–144
Guangzhou, CHM in,
  cross-cultural influences on, 118, 122
  cultural heritage managers, 58–59, 122
  cultural identity, 91
  District Councils, 125
  early inventory efforts, 26, 29, 30
  early legislation efforts, 37, 39–42
  government intervention in CH conservation, 111–112
  intangible heritage assets, 112
  linkage between urban planning, land use and, 72–76, 79
  public-private relationships and professional ethics, 66–69
  review, 141
  stakeholder consultation, 99, 124
  trainings available for heritage professionals, 54–55
Guangzhou Cultural Bureau (GCB), 74
Guangzhou Institute of Cultural Relics and Archaeology, 74
Guangzhou Municipal Cultural Relics Bureau, 30
Guangzhou Museum, 27, 32, *33*, 35, 59, 68, 75

Guangzhou Museum of Art, 59, 68
Guia Fortress, in Macau, 38
Gumerman, George, 7

Hac Sa Beach, in Macau, *30*
Han Tomb Museum, in Guangzhou, 75
Heritage assets, 1–8, 12, 14, 17–20, 24, 26, 30, 31, 35, 37, 39, 40, 41, 42, 43, 44, 51–53, 68–69, 71, 79, 86–87, 89, 91–92, 94, 95, 105, 107–111, 112–113, 123, 126, 134, 142, 144, 148–149
   intangible, 40, 69, 87, 105–106, 108, 110, 112, 118, 127, 142, 143–144, 148, 149
   tangible, 1, 3, 24, 26, 35, 36, 54, 71, 74, 78–79, 94, 105–106, 110, 112, 118, 142, 144, 149
Heritage conservation, 1, 17, 20, 59–60, 71, 76, 78–79, 87–89, 91, 97, 99, 103, 124, 126, 140–142, 145
Historic Centre of Macau, 62
Ho, Peng-yoke, 56
Home Affairs Bureau (HAB), in Hong Kong, 93, 95, 106–107, 108
Hong Kong, 17, 23–25, 27, 28, 30–38, 40–44, 46, 47, 49–52, 55–62, 63–69, 76–80, 85–99, 101, 102, 106–113, 118, 122–127, 130–134, 136, 139–142
   executive-led government and, 42
   goods and services tax (GST), 94, 142
   Heritage Year 1996–1997, 89–90
Hong Kong, CHM in,
   community organizations, 125
   cross-cultural influences on, 117–118, 122
   cultural heritage managers, 58–60, 108, 122
   cultural identity, 89, 92–93, 110, 122–123
   cultural policies, 92–94
   District Councils, 125
   early inventory efforts, 26, 29, 30
   early legislation efforts, 37, 39–42
   government intervention in CH conservation, 111–112
   intangible heritage assets, 106, 108, 110
   internal administrative restructuring, 64–65
   linkage between urban planning, land use and, 76
   membership in international organizations and use of charters, 65–66
   public-private relationships and professional ethics, 66–67
   review, 95, 141
   stakeholder consultation, 87–91, 99, 108
   tangible heritage assets, 110
   trainings available for heritage professionals, 55–56
   urban renewal and, 76–77
Hong Kong Archaeological Society, 27, 30
Hong Kong Club, 31
Hong Kong Conservancy Association, 59
Hong Kong General Chamber of Commerce, 59
Hong Kong International Airport, *28*, 76
Hong Kong Jockey Club, 99
Hong Kong Tourism Association, 90, 92
   Heritage Tourism Taskforce, 92
Hong Kong Tourism Board (HKTB), 108, 110
Hopewell Centre, in Hong Kong, 99, *100*
Housing, Planning and Lands Bureau, in Hong Kong, 94
Hu, Zhao-chun, 27
Huanan University of Education, 59
Huang Hua Archaeological Institute, in Guangzhou, 27

Increased professionalism, 52–80, 140
   ethics and, 53, 66–68, 78, 132
   indicators for, 69–77 (*See also* inventory)
   membership in international organization and the use of charters, 65–66
   public-private sector relationships and, 66
   rise of professionalism and, 49–84
   trainings available for heritage professionals, 54–58
Independent Commission Against Corruption (ICAC), in Hong Kong, 67

India, 55
Indonesian Charter, 16
Initial legislation, 8, 23, 39, 40, 41, 95
  early efforts in Guangzhou, 37, 39–42
  early efforts in Hong Kong, 36–38, 40, 41
  early efforts in Macau, 36–38, 40, 41
  impacts of global/colonial factors on, 43–44
Institute For Tourism Studies (IFT), in Macau, 58
Intangible heritage assets, 40, 69, 87, 105–108, 110, 112, 118, 127, 142, 144, 145, 149
  defined, 148
  in Guangzhou, 112
  in Hong Kong, 106, 107–108, 110
  in Macau, 106
  in Southern China, 105–106
Integrate, 8, 12
Intergovernmental Organization (IGO), 8, 53, 86
International best practices, 8, 17, 52, 87, 117, 141
International Centre for the Study of the Preservation and Restoration of Cultural Properties (ICCROM), 2, 53
International Council of Museums (ICOM), 53, 69, 140
International Council on Monuments and Sites (ICOMOS), 1, 2, 8, 14, 16, 53, 66–67, 69, 124, 140
Inventory,
  archaeological sites and, 26–30
  historic buildings survey and, 30, 31
  in Guangzhou, 36, 30, 33, 34
  in Hong Kong, 27–32, 34
  in Macau, 30, 33–34
  museums and museum collections, 31–34
  refinement of, 69–72, 79
Israel, 44

Jaoi, Tsung-i, 27
Japan, 145
Japanese Agency for Cultural Affairs, 110
Johnston Street Shop Houses, in Hong Kong, *100*
Journal of Archaeology, 27

Kai fong, 88–89, 126
Kam Tin, in Hong Kong, *28*
Koo, Kai-fai, 88
Korea, 145
Kun Iam Temple, in Macau, *29*

Lamma Island, in Hong Kong, 27
Land Development Corporation (LDC), in Hong Kong, 77
Lantau Island, in Hong Kong, 27
Law of the People's Republic of China on the Protection of Cultural Relics, 39–40, 45, 140
Leal Senado Square, in Macau, 88
Lee Tung Street, in Hong Kong, *100*
Legislative Council, in Hong Kong, 37, 87, 139
Leisure and Cultural Services Department (LSCD), in Hong Kong, 106, 108–110
Liang, Si-cheng, 36, 39
Liwan District, in Guangzhou, 75
Liwan District Museum, in Guangzhou, 75
Lo, Hsiang-lin, 27, 56
London, 60
Lord Wilson Heritage Trust (LWHT), 65, 78, 88, 90, 99
Lou Lim Leoc Garden, in Macau, 38
Lowenthal, David, 4, 35
Lu, Yuan-ding, 54
Lung, David, 56, 66

Ma, Meng, 56
Macanese, 50
Macao Museum of Art, 58
Macau, 17, 23–25, 30–31, 33, 34, 38, 40–47, 50–51, 56–66, 68, 71–72, 74, 78–80, 86, 88–89, 92, 97, 103–104, 106, 109–113, 118, 122–127, 128, 131–137, 139–141, 143
Macau, CHM in,
  Committee for Culture, 92
  community organizations, 125–126
  cultural heritage managers, 59–62, 122
  cultural identity, 89, 123
  cultural policies, 91
  Decree no. 31/89/M, 92
  early inventory efforts, 26, 30, 31
  early legislation efforts, 37, 34–42
  government intervention in CH conservation, 111–112

intangible heritage assets in, 106
linkage between urban planning, land use and, 72–76
Macau's Historic Centre and, 29, 42, 126
material and immaterial cultural heritage, 106
membership in international organization and use of charters, 65–66
review, 141
stakeholders and private-public partnerships, 103–105, 110, 112
tourism, 79
trainings available for heritage professionals, 57–58
urban renewal and, 77
Mai, Ying-hao, 58
Marine Police Headquarters Compound, in Hong Kong, 67, 94
Market liberalization, 43, 51, 132
Marques, Jaime Silverio, 38
Mausoleum of the 72 Martyrs, in Guangzhou, 75
Ministry of Culture, in China, 126
Ministry of Foreign Trade, in China, 39
Ministry of Internal Affairs, in China, 36
Mok, Ka-ho, 68
Moore, Arthur Cotton, 4
Municipal Services Branch of Urban Services, in Hong Kong, 63
Museu Luis de Camões, 34, 62
Museum of Art, in Hong Kong, 32
Museum of History, in Hong Kong, 32, 57, 59
Museum of Macau, 63

Nanyue Kings Tomb Museum, in Guangzhou, 69
Nanyue Palace, in Guangzhou, 72
Nanyue Palace Site, in Guangzhou, 72, 75
National Cultural Relics Protection Act, in China, 91
National Heritage Act, in the UK, 44
New York, 60
New Zealand, 7
Ng, Louis, 59
Ngong Ping, in Hong Kong, 28

Non-governmental organizations (NGOs), 8, 16, 41, 51–53, 66–67, 85–87, 140
in Guangzhou, 87
in Hong Kong, 87
North America, 32
Northcote, Geoffrey, 32

Ohel Leah, in Hong Kong, 65
'One-country, two systems', 25
Open Door policy, 51
Oregon University, 56

Pacific Asia Tourism Association (PATA), 39
Palestine, 44
Paris, 33, 41
Pearl River Delta (PRD), CHM in, 6, 17–20, 23, 26, 34, 35, 49, 53, 66, 69, 79, 85–86, 105, 112, 117, 119, 131, 134, 136, 141, 143–145
Performance-based Administrative System,
Hong Kong and, 43–44
Macau and, 44
Ping Shan, in Hong Kong, 28
Ping Shan Heritage Trail, in Hong Kong, 97–98, 99
Pitt Rivers Museum, in Oxford, 32
Portugal, 33, 38, 42, 44, 58–59, 117, 132, 139
National Monuments and, 42
Preserve, 8, 12, 35, 38, 40, 43, 44, 91, 109, 142
Preservation, 2, 6–8, 24, 35, 37–38, 42, 44, 57, 63, 87, 91, 95, 111, 112, 126, 147
Preservationist, 7, 35, 36
Principles for the Conservation of Heritage Sites in China, 65 (*See also* China Principles)
Provisional Antiquities Advisory Board (PAAB), 37, 44, 139

Radio Television Hong Kong (RTHK), 88
Archaeology and Antiquities, 88
Hong Kong Yesterday, Today and Tomorrow, 88
This Home of Ours, 88
Red Guards, 39
Relics Protection Act, in China, 66
Revenue Tower, in Hong Kong, 100

Review,
  5th phase of CHM framework,
    12–13, 96, 105, 141
  in Pearl River Delta, 105
  increased professionalism and,
    105
  legislation and, 105
  stakeholder partnerships and, 105
Ricci Island West Limited, 57
Royal Asiatic Society (RAS), 27, 30,
  31

Schiffer, Michael, 7
Second World War, 23, 27, 36,
  54–55, 125
Senardo Square (Largo do Senardo),
  in Macau, 134–135
Shamian Island, in Guangzhou, 52, 75,
  99–103
  Lan Kwai Fong model, 102
  National Heritage Protection Unit
    designation, 101
  Romantic European Culture Island,
    103
  White Swan Hotel, 102–103
  Working Committee of the Chinese
    Community Party of Guangzhou
    Liwan District Shamian Street,
    101–102
  Xintiandi (Shanghai) model, 102
Shellshear, 27
South China University of Technology,
  in Guangdong Province, 54
Southwest Tasmanian World Heritage
  Area, 3
Special Administrative Regions (SARs),
  17, 25, 66, 87, 94, 122–123, 135,
  142
St Paul's Ruins, in Macau, 29
Stakeholder consultation, 8, 85,
  87–90, 99, 103, 105, 108, 124,
  140–141
Stakeholder participation, 8, 52, 131
Stakeholders, 2, 8, 13, 20, 43, 85,
  88–89, 90, 92–94, 95, 97, 99,
  103, 105, 108, 112–113, 122,
  124–127, 135, 140–142, 149
  types of, 85–86
State Administration for Cultural
  Heritage (SACH), 39, 45, 58, 65,
  79, 91, 101, 113, 133, 140
Sun, Yat-sen (Sun Zhongshan), 54
Sun Yat Sen Memorial Hall, in
  Guangzhou, 75

Sun Yat Sen University, in Guangzhou,
  54 (*See also* Zhongshan
  University)
Sustainable development, 1, 4, 6
Sydney, 44, 60

Taipa House Museum, in Macau, *29*
Tak Seng On Pawn Shop, in Macau,
  104
  Cultural Heritage Department and,
    103
  Decree Order 83/92M, 103
  UNESCO Pacific Heritage Awards in
    2002, 105
  Yinghe Development Ltd, 104
Tangible heritage assets, 1, 3, 24, 26,
  35, 36, 54, 61, 71, 74, 78–79,
  94, 105–106, 110–113, 118, 142,
  145, 149
Target Management Responsibility
  System, 43
Ting, Joseph, 59
Tourism, 4, 16, 20, 38, 50, 53, 55,
  58, 65, 69, 71, 79, 85–86, 89,
  92–93, 101–103, 106, 108–110,
  122, 126, 134
Tourism Commission, in Hong Kong,
  67, 94
Tourist precinct, 87
Town Planning Board, in Hong Kong,
  77, 94
Tradition bearers, 16, 49, 87

UNESCO Heritage Awards, 65,
  112–113
UNESCO Pacific Heritage Awards, 105
UNESCO World Heritage Convention,
  1, 38
United Nations Educational, Scientific
  and Cultural Organization
  (UNESCO), 2, 8, 46, 53, 58, 65,
  69, 72, 86, 124, 140, 143
United States, 4, 7, 79, 124, 127
United States National Park Service
  (NPS), 7
University Museum and Art Gallery,
  in Hong Kong, 32, 36, *100*
University of East Asia (UEA), 57
  (*See also* University of Macau)
University of Hong Kong (HKU), 7,
  27, 32, 55, 59, 64, *100*
  School of Professional and
    Continuing Education (SPACE),
    57

University of Macau, (*See also* University of East Asia) 57
University of Sydney, 57
Urban Renewal Authority (URA), in Hong Kong, 77, 94

Venice Charter, 1, 16, 65, 78

Wanchai, in Hong Kong, 99
Wanchai Market, in Hong Kong, *100*, 130
Ward, Barbara, 55
West Kowloon, in Hong Kong, 93–94, *100*
West Rail, in Hong Kong, 98
Western Market, in Hong Kong, 77
World Archaeology Congress conference, 133
World Heritage Committee, 41
World Heritage inscription, 41, 113, 126, 134, 149

World Heritage List, 62, 149
World Trade Organization (WTO), 51

Xie, Ying-bo, 26

Yamato Declaration on Integrated Approaches for Safeguarding Tangible and Intangible Cultural Heritage, 110
Yuexiu District, in Guangzhou, 75
Yuexiu Mountain, in Guangzhou, 32

Zeman, Allan, 102
Zheng, Wei-ming, 58
Zhenhai Tower, in Guangzhou, 32
Zhongshan University, in Guangzhou, 54 (*See also* Guangdong University, Sun Yat Sen University)